Soviet-Born

Soviet-Born

The Afterlives of Migration in Jewish American Fiction

KAROLINA KRASUSKA

Rutgers University Press
New Brunswick, Camden, and Newark, New Jersey
London and Oxford

Rutgers University Press is a department of Rutgers, The State University of New Jersey, one of the leading public research universities in the nation. By publishing worldwide, it furthers the University's mission of dedication to excellence in teaching, scholarship, research, and clinical care.

Library of Congress Cataloging-in-Publication Data
Names: Krasuska, Karolina, author.
Title: Soviet-born : the afterlives of migration in Jewish American fiction
   / Karolina Krasuska.
Description: New Brunswick : Rutgers University Press, 2024. | Includes
   bibliographical references and index.
Identifiers: LCCN 2023047880 | ISBN 9781978832763 (paperback) | ISBN
   9781978832770 (hardcover) | ISBN 9781978832787 (epub) | ISBN
   9781978832794 (mobi) | ISBN 9781978832800 (pdf)
Subjects: LCSH: American fiction—Jewish authors—History and criticism. |
   American fiction—21st century—History and criticism. |
   Immigrants—United States. | Soviets (People)—United States. |
   Emigration and immigration in literature. | Women in literature. | Group
   identity in literature. | BISAC: LITERARY CRITICISM / Jewish | LITERARY
   CRITICISM / Comics & Graphic Novels | LCGFT: Literary criticism.
Classification: LCC PS153.J4 K73 2024 | DDC 813/.609352924047—dc23/eng/20240301
LC record available at https://lccn.loc.gov/2023047880

A British Cataloging-in-Publication record for this book is available from the British Library.

Copyright © 2024 by Karolina Krasuska
All rights reserved.
No part of this book may be reproduced or utilized in any form or by any means, electronic or mechanical, or by any information storage and retrieval system, without written permission from the publisher. Please contact Rutgers University Press, 106 Somerset Street, New Brunswick, NJ 08901. The only exception to this prohibition is "fair use" as defined by U.S. copyright law.

Open access edition funded by the University of Warsaw.

Cover art: Zoya Cherkassky, *Red Tulips*, 2019, tempera on paper. Courtesy of the artist and the Rosenfeld Gallery, Tel Aviv.

References to internet websites (URLs) were accurate at the time of writing. Neither the author nor Rutgers University Press is responsible for URLs that may have expired or changed since the manuscript was prepared.

♾ The paper used in this publication meets the requirements of the American National Standard for Information Sciences—Permanence of Paper for Printed Library Materials, ANSI Z39.48-1992.

rutgersuniversitypress.org

Contents

	Preface	vii
	Introduction: Soviet-Born Writing	1
1	Diasporic Spaces	15
2	Redefining Survival	35
3	Afterlives of Communism	61
4	Soviet Intimacy	80
5	Keyword: Migration	100
	Conclusion: Jewish American Literature as a Site of Critique	121
	Notes	127
	Bibliography	165
	Index	183

Preface

I taught Soviet-born writing for the first time in 2013 to graduate students in Warsaw, after it had already become a known quantity on bookstore shelves, familiar to both critics and readers. While discussing one of the stories—David Bezmozgis's "Natasha," from his first collection, *Natasha and Other Stories* (2004)—the class became exceptionally dynamic. Students would usually come alive when we discussed contemporary texts. This time, however, it felt different: was it because of the tangible connection of this text with post–state socialist Eastern Europe? The late Cold War years (when this Toronto story takes place) were not yet too far back, nor were the transformations of 1989 and 1991—still within the reach of students' family memory. The works of Bezmozgis and other immigrants from the former Soviet Union *felt*, therefore, closer to the class than other American literary texts we had discussed. And thanks to that, our conversations about race, ethnicity, and migration in North America took on an extra dimension.

Importantly, it was also an entry point to talking about Jewishness in Poland, its growing presence in the social and cultural life of the city we lived in, and the existence of latent antisemitism. At that particular juncture—in a Warsaw that was much less culturally, ethnically, and racially diverse than in 2024, and in an all-white class—this seemed a particularly important political imperative. And, with the rise of the Right in Poland, where antisemitism, racism, and anti-immigration sentiment coalesce in political discourse, it still does. In addition, in the past years historians' critical research on the Holocaust within Nazi-occupied Polish territories and local communities has often been weaponized to serve nationalist causes, smeared by select politicians in power, and explicitly threatened with defunding at public research institutions. So teaching Jewish studies—as well as the much-demonized gender theory—from these perspectives is just as important in the current moment as it was a decade ago.

That great class incentivized me to include other, similar works on syllabi. Because of my interest in transnationalism—a remnant of the research for my first book (in Polish, *Płeć i naród: Trans/lokacje* [Gender and nation: trans/locations], 2011)—I soon began to write about the literature of Soviet-born immigrants to North America. The current book is the result of my fascination with these texts, and an attempt to read them as a non-Jewish person schooled in American cultural theory and dedicated to a critical approach to the region, and to read them through a decolonial queer feminist lens. I also wrote this book while living in Eastern Europe, and as someone who caught the tail end of state socialism, having been part of the last class of students to receive mandatory Russian language instruction from fifth grade onward. If I believed in discrete generations, I would say this marks the end of the Polish Generation X.

These initial publications on Soviet-born writing would not have existed without a number of people who encouraged me along the way. Barbara Krawcowicz sent me the call for papers for a special issue of *Eastern European Jewish Affairs* titled "The New Wave of Russian Jewish American Culture," guest edited by Anna Katsnelson, which resulted in an article published in 2016. I would also like to thank the coeditor of the journal at the time, David Shneer, who passed away prematurely in 2020, for his encouragement and faith in this project. Thanks to this article, I was invited in March 2017 to the Festival of Russian-Jewish-American Culture at the Center for Jewish History in New York, where I met not only others writing on similar topics, including Maggie Levantovskaya, and generous colleagues, such as Nick Underwood, but also various other writers and artists like Ellen Litman and Anya Ulinich. This, in turn, served as an impulse to organize or co-organize panels at the conferences of the Association for Jewish Studies (AJS). My reading of these texts benefited from presentations and ensuing discussions at these AJS conferences in 2017, 2019, 2020, and 2022, as well as panels at the Memory Studies Association conference in 2021, the Association for Slavic, East European, and Eurasian Studies conference in 2021, and the Modern Language Association convention in 2022. Thank you to everyone who participated in these sessions, and above all Miriam Finkelstein, Kathryn Hellerstein, Alex Moshkin, Sharon Oster, Gabriella Safran, David Shneer, Jonathan Skolnik, and Natasha Zaretsky.

Sometimes it may seem that while conferences and talks take place palpably within the academic community, writing itself is quite a lonely affair. This was not the case here. I am very grateful for the opportunity to take part in the first Summer Writing Group for women, trans, and non-binary scholars that the AJS organized in 2020. Laura Leibman was an incredible leader of this event, and my small subgroup provided wonderful, detailed feedback: thank you to Laura, as well as Samantha Freedman and Abigail Lewis. While this group provided me with support in writing the first chapter and the book proposal, a subsequent summer workshop headed by Sarah Abrevaya Stein in 2022 led me through writing the introduction. Thank you to Alexis Lerner and Daniela Weiner for being so patient with my many revisions and for being such good readers. Importantly, that first writing group in 2020 was also the start of an unforgettable shared adventure for three of us, who continued to workshop our monographs together for a full two years. Together with Jessica Roda and Ronnie Olesker, I formed a writing group that met regularly online until the spring of 2022, reading each other's work as it came together. Thank you, friends, for this time spent together and all the inspiration—it is thanks to you that I was able to sustain writing over the long months of the pandemic, then find support when I was *not* writing during the first weeks of the full-scale Russian invasion of Ukraine.

Many people have read and commented on the whole monograph or its parts. My special thanks go to Sarah Casteel, Laura Levitt, Allison Schachter, and Werner Sollors (as well as the reviewers at Rutgers University Press), who read the whole manuscript. I cannot thank you enough for making me believe that all of this made sense. Josh Lambert has generously helped me shape the initial chapters of the book and has supported the project all along. The first chapter also benefited from the comments of the guest editors of the special issue "Regionalism in American Jewish Literature" in *Studies in American Jewish Literature*; while the issue has never materialized, their feedback survives in this book. Chapter 2, on the memory of the Holocaust, benefited greatly from the meticulous editorial process of Victoria Aarons and Phyllis Lassner, the coeditors of the *Palgrave Handbook of Holocaust Literature and Culture*, where a part of this chapter was published. Another part of that chapter was expanded following Natalia Aleksiun's invitation to contribute to the Polish journal *Autobiografia*. Big thanks are due to Yelena Furman and Melissa Weininger for reading select chapters with their sharp, gender-sensitive eyes. And to Sasha Senderovitch for his knowledgeable and perceptive comments on the introduction. Several portions of the manuscript were also feverishly discussed within the Gender/Sexuality Research Group at the American Studies Center by Ludmiła Janion, Aleksandra Kamińska, Agnieszka Kotwasińska, Anna Kurowicka, Natalia Pamuła, and Marta Usiekniewicz. Sometime in 2020 I joined Twitter, now X, as @karolinakrasusk, which I used in the final months of editing the manuscript as an accountability tool; so thank you, #AcademicTwitter.

I have just reread the above and it is wonderful to see how many people have been a part of this endeavor. I often say that everyone moving to Zoom meetings in 2020 was the best thing that happened to me academically while I was completing this manuscript—the communities I outline above existed

x • Preface

largely online. But going places and meeting people in real life mattered too, and this (and much more!) was possible though a large three-year grant that I received in 2019: research grant no. 2018/31/D/HS2/02124, funded by the National Science Centre of Poland. I would like to express my deepest gratitude to two reviewers for that grant, who believed in my initial project and relayed that belief to the granting agency. Other travel for this project was made possible through the University of Warsaw Excellence Initiative Microgrants, as well as an AJS travel grant. Excellence Initiative Microgrants also helped fund language editing, which additionally received financial support from the American Studies Center, University of Warsaw. I would like to thank Grzegorz Kość, the director of the American Studies Center, for his continuous support (including course relief) and encouragement when completing this project. Open Access cost was generously covered by the University of Warsaw Excellence Initiative. After finishing the book I was fortunate enough to receive the 2023 Cashmere Subvention Grant from the Gender Justice Caucus of the AJS.

This book would not be the same without a number of people who contributed to its final shape. Special thanks to the authors Yelena Akhtiorskaya, David Bezmozgis, Boris Fishman, Nadia Kalman, Sana Krasikov, Ellen Litman, Anya Ulinich, and Lara Vapnyar for taking the time to grant me interviews and for agreeing to the use of excerpts from them in this publication. I would like to thank the artists of the illustrations in these works and the publishing houses for granting me permission to reprint them in my book. Still more special thanks go to Zoya Cherkassky-Nnadi and the Rosenfeld Gallery for allowing me to use her work as a cover image. Manuscript editor Jonathan Farr, with his incredible feel for my idiosyncratic English, made sure it reads so much better. Thank you, Katie Van Heest, for giving me ideas on how to develop this monograph, Mert Alçınkaya, for transcribing the interviews, and Filip Boratyn, for helping me with the technicalities of the manuscript. I have also been very fortunate to meet editors at Rutgers University Press who have been enthusiastic and encouraging. Working with Elisabeth Maselli, who acquired the book, Christopher Rios-Sueverkruebbe, who shepherded it along the way, and Carah Naseem, who guided me at the end of the process with much insight, was not only an extremely professional experience but also simply nice. I am grateful to copy editor Julia Kurtz for being so wonderfully meticulous with my manuscript and my production editor Cheryl Hirsch for her professionalism and flexibility. Indexer and proofreader Rachel Lyon has been the best person to wrap up the work on this book with. Thank you all for helping make this book happen!

I wrote this book largely in the midst of a pandemic, when everything was in a state of emergency. Without the support and understanding of those closest to me—my mother Elżbieta and those I share my every day with, Matthew

Chambers, Sofia, and Bela—I would not have been able to stay away for long hours in front of the computer. In the meantime, Matt published his own book (on top of reading every single line I have written and then rewritten), and even our daughters started producing their own because this is apparently what one does: Bela crafted dozens of illustrated booklets, and Sofia has begun writing fan fiction. We are a very bookish bunch.

Warszawa and Pomiechówek, 2024

Soviet-Born

Introduction

Soviet-Born Writing

A tweet-length popular origin story of the ascent of Jewish American literature might go like this: "The postwar mainstreaming of Jewish American writing mirrored the midcentury sociological development of 'Jews becoming white.' In order to join the mainstream, prewar proletarian immigrant writing had to overcome its marginalized and parochial status."[1] In this rendition, migration serves as an origin story, a natural scene of arrival, something to be transcended, in terms of class, race, and gender hierarchies. Yet, that narrative having calcified within so-called Jewish American literature, a robust metacritical impulse has emerged to interrogate the canon and the criticism. Self-critically examining their practice and objects of study, scholars have expanded the literary archives and multiplied genealogies. Amid divergent methodological approaches and, often, conflicting outcomes, this interrogation has collectively created a space and vocabulary for thinking about another locus that might challenge the hegemonic practice of Jewish American literary criticism: "Soviet-born writing."[2]

In 2010, the *New Yorker* published a list of twenty writers under the age of forty who were supposedly "key to their generation." The list included five Jewish-identified writers, two of whom—American Gary Shteyngart and Canadian David Bezmozgis—were Soviet-born.[3] This publicity came after nearly a decade of literary output by Soviet-born writers in North America. Since the turn of the century, Shteyngart, Bezmozgis, Lara Vapnyar, and a few dozen other Soviet-born authors have published in English, becoming known to the public through their pieces in mainstream magazines, their participation in popular events, and the various awards they have received. Moreover, Soviet-born authors who co-initiated this wave in the early to mid-2000s are numerous: Ellen Litman, Anya Ulinich, Keith Gessen, Sana Krasikov, Irina Reyn, Michael Idov, and Nadia Kalman, for instance.[4] Others followed in their steps a few years later or published their first novels only in 2014 (Yelena Akhtiorskaya, Boris Fishman) or in the late 2010s (Yelena Moskovich, Julia Alekseyeva, Maria Kuznetsova, Olga Zilberbourg). New voices keep proliferating.[5]

The speed with which twenty-first-century Jewish Soviet-born writing in English gained popularity may have paradoxically hinged on the mainstream framing of Jewish American literature—namely, as a variation on the hegemonic Ashkenazi tradition, or what is often called Ashkenormativity.[6] For critics, expanding the archives of Jewish American literature also means looking critically at the tacit historical, national, and sociological assumptions behind the label "Jewish American." For literary scholar Dalia Kandiyoti, "U.S. Jewishness is an American invention that has no prior existence and bears all the manifestations of an identity invented to conform to predominant U.S. social ideologies, based on competing and mutually exclusive identities."[7] It is therefore projected as both externally recognizable and internally coherent: this is the sedimentation of "American Jewish," still very much in use in 1970s literary histories, into "Jewish American."[8] Such legibility, however, comes at a cost: embracing a historical normativity and narrowness.[9] In their introduction to a special issue of *MELUS*, Lori Harrison-Kahan and Josh Lambert attempted to expand the category of American Jewishness while at the same time drawing attention to the ossified canon: "While contemporary writers are altering the landscape of Jewish American fiction today, their work—in its deep and wide-ranging engagement with various national, transnational, literary, linguistic, and liturgical traditions—also demands a rethinking of the canon of Jewish American literature as it has been constructed in the past."[10] No one represents that canon, nor the postwar "Jewish American renaissance," more convincingly than Philip Roth.

Some Soviet-born narratives confront Roth rather directly. In Anya Ulinich's graphic novel *Lena Finkle's Magic Barrel*, the protagonist, Lena, napping on a Greyhound bus, dreams that the man seated next to her is precisely Philip Roth (figures 1 and 2). The autobiographical Soviet-born Lena is a writer and a divorced mother of two school-age girls, making ends meet and trying to date. In her dream, Lena enthusiastically explains to Roth, "Listen, I love your books! You and I are so much alike!" and continues to eagerly list the commonalities between herself and Roth's protagonists, and between herself and Roth as a writer.[11] As someone formatively shaped by anxieties around gender and sexuality, she sees Roth's characters as individuals she can identify with. The shared affinities appear so great that, to her mind, they become biological bonds. But

FIGURES 1 (LEFT) AND 2 (RIGHT) Anya Ulinich, *Lena Finkle's Magic Barrel* (New York: Penguin, 2014), 182–183.

it is not a vertical genealogy descending from Roth, with all the anxieties of influence and their painful negotiations. Instead, to Lena, Roth is more of a peer, and she anachronistically likens him to a sibling: "It's like we had the same parents!"

The dreamt-up Roth interrupts Lena coldly. Rendered in bold font, he vehemently protests, "Oh, stop that! You're nothing like me!" and methodically explains, "First, you're a woman, and not even a pretty one! Second, you're an immigrant!"[12] After a bit more bickering, Roth discourages Lena from reading his oeuvre and recommends instead Bernard Malamud's "The Magic Barrel"—a short story in the collection that the man actually sitting next to Lena has in his hands.[13] In the graphic novel, this scene is one of the few moments that can be read as explicitly Jewish. A Jewish theme appears not through explicit religious, social, or historical references, which remain scarce throughout the text, but instead intertextually, by playing with the established positions of Roth and Malamud in the Jewish American literary canon.[14] While such intertextual play locates Ulinich within the orbit of Jewish American writing, at the same time it gestures at the distance of Lena's character—and, more generally, of Soviet-born writers and their writing—from the established narrative of Jewish American literature.

When Ulinich's Roth condescendingly tags Lena as an immigrant or foreign-born, we can suspect that he deduces it from Lena's accent. Her Russian accent and her interest in Jewish themes bring to mind the well-publicized Cold War social movement to free Soviet Jews (known as the Soviet Jewry movement) and lead him to the unspoken conclusion that she is Soviet-born and Jewish. That assumption may be understandable. As a whole, the Soviet-born diasporic literary wave is a far-reaching effect of evolving Cold War geopolitics and the subsequent changes to immigration law that this evolution entailed.[15] The fictional Lena, as well as Ulinich herself, belongs to the most recent sizable wave of Soviet-born Jewish migrants, who entered the United States beginning in the late 1980s. Over 300,000 Jewish immigrants from the (former) Soviet Union arrived in the United States between 1989 and 2009. Next to Israel and Germany after reunification, the United States was the most frequently chosen immigration destination.[16] An earlier, smaller influx of a little over 100,000 post-Soviet Jews had arrived between 1970 and the dissolution of the USSR.[17] Immigrants from the former Soviet Union and their children make up 10 percent of American Jews, with up to a quarter of this population living on the East Coast.[18] Soviet-born Jewish writers arrived either as children brought by their immigrant parents or as young people themselves from the USSR or the former USSR in the last three decades of the twentieth century.

Taking a cue from Ulinich's staged exchange about the Jewish American literary mainstream, I consider Soviet-born writing a challenge to that tradition's gendered and nativist modes. The "Jewish American renaissance" narrative casts Roth's generation of writers—most of whom were men—as the fathers of Jewish American literature, enshrining a patriarchal genealogy.[19] For Ulinich, despite Roth's critical stance toward the category of "Jews," gender remains his blind spot, manifesting here in a sexist remark about Lena's looks.[20] Lena, as an immigrant and a woman, cannot claim relation or affinity with Roth according to this vision of Jewish American literary lineage because it is both patriarchal and *post*-migrational. As Ulinich diagnoses, masculinity—tacitly assumed to be straight and cis—forms a part of this normative complex.[21] Using texts by Soviet-born authors, this book illuminates how their standpoint, determined by the legacy of Soviet regulations concerning gender and sexuality as well as by their "new immigrant whiteness," demonstrates the limits of the literary label "Jewish American" and allows for the critique and expansion of this category.[22]

This book's entry point into the critique of "Jewish American" is literary fiction—novels, short stories, and graphic novels—by Soviet-born Jewish writers published in English in the first two decades of the twenty-first century. It discusses, with varying detail, literary works published between 2002 and 2022 and especially engages with the work of the following authors: Anya Ulinich (*Petropolis*), Yelena Akhtiorskaya (*Panic in the Suitcase*), David Bezmozgis (*The Free World, Natasha and Other Stories, Immigrant City and Other Stories*), Boris Fishman (*A Replacement Life*), Julia Alekseyeva (*Soviet Daughter*), Sana

Krasikov (*The Patriots*), Keith Gessen (*A Terrible Country*), Ellen Litman (*Mannequin Girl*), Lara Vapnyar (*The Scent of Pine*, *There Are Jews in My House*), Nadia Kalman (*The Cosmopolitans*), and last but not least Gary Shteyngart (*Lake Success*).[23] Because on the surface this literature is a variation on Ashkenormativity, it could relatively seamlessly enter the Jewish American literary complex and thereby be domesticated—that is, cast using its well-known vocabulary.[24] But its relation to nonimmigrant Ashkenazi American writing—like the relation of Ulinich to Roth—may be that of an "evil twin"[25]: very close *but not identical* in provenance, and because of this affinity able to expose critical differences, which is the aim of this book.

Entering an immigrant, Soviet-born standpoint creates an alternative and sometimes complementary pattern of how the East Central European past and present is narrated in Jewish American writing. The texts considered here often create different emplotments of their key themes, including cultural geography, memory of World War II and the Holocaust, gender and sexual order, communism, and, finally, migration.[26] While Jewish *American* emplotments have sedimented over the course of the Cold War, these narratives here shift the logic from the "Cold War" to the "Soviet experience," then to the post-Soviet experience.[27] With this shift, these Soviet-inflected texts are able to add or renew layers of meaning.[28]

Because a large number of these Soviet-born writers are women producing gender-critical narratives, the study provides a critique of gendered assumptions across the thematic spectrum. This critique is even more thorough because it comes from a position that anthropologist Kristen Ghodsee has succinctly summarized as "second world, second sex": it not only questions masculinist assumptions of Jewish American literature and criticism but also sheds new light on how patriarchy functions, de-universalizing its norms though Soviet-inflected, equality-driven reconsiderations of gender norms.[29] Such a perspective informed by gender and sexuality critique transforms how we might think about narrative literary historical terms with currency beyond Jewish American literary study; for instance, "generation" appears as deeply derived patterns that are based on reproduction and the normative nuclear family.

Focusing on migration along with gender intervenes in the very structure of our thinking about the Jewish American literary complex. The book attempts to make Jewish American writing—with its emphasis on state apparatuses, their complex mechanisms of control, and the possibilities of resistance—usable for the study of American writing more generally.[30] It advocates for what I call comparative literacy: reading in broader cultural and social contexts in which memory flows multidirectionally and requires examining one's own position and de-universalizing identity assumptions.[31] Thus understood, readings accentuating memory and postmemory are a way of shaping comparative literacy. Comparative readings, for instance with other literatures of migration, does

6 • Soviet-Born

not occur below, but it is implicit in how they are approached and made sense of. With an increasingly multiethnic and globalized literary market, academy, and classroom, it is vital that comparative literacy not remain theoretical but rather become a broadly taught core competency.

The Challenge to "Jewish American Literature"

This book participates in the recent critique of Jewish American literary criticism and its search for more expansive formulas in terms of both the literary texts that fall within its purview and the critical perspectives that form its core. "Immigrant" and "woman" do not fit smoothly into the established narrative of postwar Jewish American literature.

Soviet-born Jewishness—immigrant, often secular—may seem un-American. One author has described it as "DIY forms of Jewish identification" or, in other words, as not fitting smoothly into the myriad of established Jewish American patterns.[32] Accordingly, critics have read it as "American-Jewish-Russian," emphasizing "overlapping identities, embedded in each other like a matryoshka,"[33] or as "Russian-American" in the context of the transnational Russian diaspora.[34] What is more, precisely because of these multiple possible identity coordinates, the texts have also been approached independently from Jewishness, whether under the rubric of Russianness (with their authors styled "Russian hybrid writers"), as a part of "global Russian cultures," or as post-Soviet and postsocialist cultural manifestations in the United States.[35] Yet because of immigration patterns, including special provisions for Soviet Jews, and because literary institutions have welcomed and promoted Jewish American literature, much of this literature—such as Ulinich's text described above—lends itself to readings that place it within the context of Jewishness in the United States, and especially its textual presences. Reading these texts "Jewishly"—against the grain, so to speak, seeing as Jewishness appears sometimes to have only a perfunctory presence in them—expands the notion of Jewishness to better encompass its current plurality.

This book may not have "gender" or "queer" in its title because *thematically* the categories "Soviet-born" and "migrant" serve as better signposts and constitute the key contribution I hope to offer to the field, but there is a reason it opens with a vignette by a woman author cheekily taking on a veritable giant of Jewish American fiction. My approach to literature and its culturally transformative potential is based in feminist and queer theory. This may manifest itself most literally in chapter 4, "Soviet Intimacy," but also emerges in how I read various elements—plot (especially in chapter 5), setting (especially in chapter 1), and protagonists—as inflected by gender and sexuality norms. Gender does not mean only women, and thus I provide a critical reading of masculinities, especially in chapters 2 and 5. Queer presences appear in chapters 4 and 5, and a queer perspective on genealogy fundamentally shapes how I read Nadia Kalman's *The Cosmopolitans*. Feminist sensibilities also determine what texts are included and where—whose voices we hear: there is no "male chapter," and indeed a few chapters include only women authors. Generally, women's voices have grown stronger and more numerous in Jewish American fiction, but as literary scholar Allison Schachter eloquently argues, the mid-twentieth century "saw the rise of a new male canon of Jewish American writers."[36] As Schachter notes, Alfred Kazin might have been content that these authors "transcended the immigrant world of Jewish writing," but what was transcended was "a generation that included significant women writers such as Mary Antin and Anzia Yezierska."[37] We must read critically through gender and sexuality in order to identify and challenge unspoken norms of the Jewish literary complex.

The authors whose texts I engage certainly do not constitute an accurate ethnographic representation of Soviet-born migrants in the United States. Sociologically, Jews from the former Soviet Union are on average more conservative than American-born Jews, but the narratives employed in this literary production are generally culturally critical and progressive.[38] As such, the works serve as a litmus test of the existing cultural discourse that these writers question but that many other Soviet-born immigrants likely embrace. But they do not attempt a representativeness of the cultural attitudes of a national-ethnic group, nor do they seek to diagnose changing cultural attitudes (though this may in fact be the case, as it is across the broader Jewish American spectrum).[39] Rather, these texts show narrative possibilities that sometimes directly conflict with what is expected. They therefore do not demonstrate so much a mechanism of social regulation, but instead promise what, following Walter Benjamin, can be called a "redemptive" potential of cultural production.[40]

The complicated legibility of Jewishness here hinges greatly on its being "Soviet-born." This modifier often appears when referring to migrants from the former Soviet Union in popular discourse in the media, and occasionally in literary criticism.[41] Contrary to other, parallel modifiers denoting migration, however, it does more than merely indicate a state or citizenship at birth (like "French-born," for example) or even provide a clear temporal point of reference and "date" an individual (as in "Ottoman-born"). "Soviet-born" also explicitly links the person to a particular political system—communism, with its imposed secularism—and locates them within a Cold War orbit. It seems a universally useful keyword, at one and the same time stating a single, undeniable fact of political geographical origin *and* opening a whole domain of meanings that go well beyond this matter-of-fact categorization. As I demonstrate in the chapters that follow, often in popular discourse place of birth and ostensibly inborn, essential, natural, and unreformable political communist proclivities become one.

Approached critically, however, the popular entanglements within the adjective "Soviet-born" provide a chance to look at phenomena—in this case, literary production—in categories not pertaining to identity, unlike "Russian Jewish American." The conditions of one's birth are not determinative of who one is; they merely provide a starting block. "Soviet-born" is a gesture toward a place of "origin" that may matter and become a marker of identity for some, but not for others. However provocative it may seem with its essentialist connotations, it can perhaps participate in a different critical work than the descriptive identity-based modifiers used earlier to circumscribe these literary works. It is also more expansive or inclusive than "Russian" and opens up the possibility of different locations of this fiction—not only Moscow and Leningrad but also Riga, Minsk, and Odessa, as well as the Caucasus and Siberia. But even this list fails to represent the full range of Jewish places and spaces in the former Soviet Union, which are much more diverse than what "Russian" might suggest. "Soviet-born writing" suggests an authorship by writers who emigrated from the USSR or the former USSR and, at the same time, emphasizes that these texts themselves produce the field of meaning for "Soviet-born," intervening in its popular connotations and genealogies.

"Soviet-born" also locates one radically in the past, as part of a nonextant political entity, the end of which has initiated a whole new vocabulary both regionally and globally. The compound stands in a complementary position to post-Soviet, post-socialist, and post-communist, straddling the 1989/1991 "transformation" often imagined as fundamentally dividing two eras.[42] Yet the emphasis of the "Soviet-born" is different: with its backward perspective, it does not determine the present, which has recently been the critique of a continuous reliance (for over thirty years now) on "postness" in relation to the region and its people.[43] Additionally, in 2022 this assumed "postness" too has met with crisis, triggered by the full-scale Russian invasion of Ukraine and diagnoses of the "new Cold War."[44] Political transformation of the Global East is key for the development of this literature, most notably because the dissolution of the Soviet Union sparked post-Soviet migration generally. However, because of the exceptional status of Jewish immigrants in earlier decades, it is only partly responsible for the immigration of the authors considered here.[45] The timing of their immigration varies, as do their ages at the time of migration. They are not a generation in the sociological meaning of the word: many of them were born in the 1970s and arrived as children or young people during the Cold War, but others were born in the last years of the Soviet Union and immigrated only in the 1990s.[46] They hail from diverse former Soviet republics and cities, which make appearances in their writing. Formally, the writers are not a unified school, even if sometimes they participate in events together and their writing sometimes appears in specific magazines or ends up under the same rubric in mainstream bookstores.[47] The permutations are many, and the minimalist descriptor "Soviet-born"—palpable, everyday, and indeterminate—hopes to encompass this multiplicity.

Cold War Afterlives

Soviet-born writing narrates Cold War afterlives as a Soviet-born experience, which grounds the underlying rationale of how it approaches Americanness and American Jewishness.[48] As such these narratives are not more authentic or universal—they are as "made" as any other. They uncover a different, Soviet-born point of view or—to use another, more theoretical register—subject position. Rather than reinvigorate the mainstream Jewish American literary complex, these works unsettle many of its preconceptions, formed as it was in the spirit of Cold War liberalism, with an emphasis on the language of rights coupled with anti-communism.[49] The Cold War coinage "Jewish *American*," which has replaced "American Jewish" in discussions of literature, marks a willing and often enthusiastic participation in the fight for the "free world" on the part of critics and canonized writers.[50] From this point of view—and to return to the author as something of a benchmark—Philip Roth's advocacy for dissident writers in Eastern Europe is a symptom of the mainstreaming of the Jewish American literary complex that at the same time mutes women and immigrants.[51] The often perceived insularity of Jewish American literary criticism may derive from its reliance on these modes of thought, which scholars in other fields of literary study have exposed and critically reapproached: it is not the insularity of Jewishness in the United States, which thrives in its rich and striking multiplicity, but literary critical practice that relies on the unexamined premises of Cold War–tinted Americanness, premises that do not resonate with current critical and theoretical practice in the literary field in general.

Jewish American literary criticism is only just beginning to reckon with "Cold War afterlives," or, to put it more thoroughly, with how Cold War geopolitics continues to shape understandings of Jewish American literary history. Recently, Benjamin Schreier briefly used the Cold War timeline to map out this literature's intellectual formation, pointing to the ascent of Yiddish as "part of the professional signaling apparatus of Jewish American identity"; he also noted that "the field of Jewish American literary study developed relatively hermetically in the Cold War academy."[52] Schreier merely signals these entanglements, engaging in a mode of thought akin to certain critiques of American studies and U.S. comparative literature, but which in the context of specific literary fields deserves further elucidation and elaboration—especially how foregrounding Cold War Jewish studies genealogies might connect that field's internal logic to that of other fields and thereby make it less insular.

More specific case studies have also appeared, including both on the immediate context of the Soviet Jewry movement—to date the most visible intersection of Jewish American textual production and the geopolitical context of the Cold War—and in the form of broader explorations of the Jewish American literary canon through a Cold War lens.[53] Sasha Senderovich has persuasively argued how the peculiar figure that became known in the Cold War era as the "Soviet Jew" was a discursive construct, "the creation of an American Jewish discourse that marks Jews in the USSR as beneficiaries of a civilizing mission that can be accomplished through emigration."[54] The figure represents an Orientalizing, othering trope known in many historical contexts involving encounters between Jews marked as coming from different regions. The hierarchical power dynamic between American-born Jews and Soviet-born immigrant Jews bears markers of other imperially tinged encounters. As a result, the Soviet Jew served to define the self through the other: it said more about the authors who participated in its making than the actual people it supposedly referred to—a claim that resonates in sociologist Shaul Kelner's argument about how the Soviet Jewry movement remade American Jewry.[55] This book does not contribute further to Cold War genealogies of the Jewish American literary field per se, but rearranges and revalues some of these genealogies, excavates their current manifestations, and explores their afterlives in the negotiation of Soviet-born fiction's place relative to that field.

When read through the prism of literature by Soviet-born English-language writers, Cold War afterlives go beyond geopolitical conditioning, "casting lingering shadows over US and global politics that continue to shape global challenges to liberal democracy," as historian Penny Von Eschen has put it.[56] Similarly, they also exceed the tacit structural coordinates of literary and cultural study or dominant discursive narrative patterns.

Afterlives exist also as speaking subjects, producing texts both literary and nonliterary—voices of the people who *are* the afterlife of the Cold War.[57] Indeed, one could argue that *we all* are this afterlife, and especially—because of hierarchized divisions of power—those who lived through communism and its "fall." For these are Cold War afterlives, but also afterlives of communism, and post-Soviet Russian literature has struggled (and continues to struggle) with the spectral presence of its past.[58] Recent narratives from East Central Europe negotiate their "post-dependence" condition,[59] while post-socialist American literatures, to use Claudia Sadowski-Smith and Ioana Luca's term, explore contemporary writing by immigrants from the same region.[60] Soviet-born Jewish migrants in North America are in a particular position to narrate and fictionalize these lives, lives unsettled by changing political circumstances and disparate expectations, which is only made more conspicuous by divergent notions of Jewishness in North America and in the Soviet Union and by the sometimes exceptional immigration routes taken by Soviet and post-Soviet Jewish refugees. In other words, moments of Jewishness in these texts often serve as points of focus for these afterlives.

These afterlives relate also to the inherited memory of communism—the way received memory, especially family memory, informs narratives.[61] Marianne Hirsch's notion of "postmemory" encapsulates the "uneasy oscillation between continuity and rupture," between memories of one's own and memories inherited.[62] In Hirsch's formulation, postmemory relates to traumatic events: "the relationship that the 'generation after' bears to the personal, collective, and cultural trauma of those who came before—to experiences they 'remember' only by means of the stories, images, and behaviors among which they grew up."[63] Fiction by Soviet-born writers textualizes "communist postmemory," or postmemory concerning traumatic Stalinist state violence. Communist postmemory also includes World War II and the Holocaust as filtered through communist modes of remembering and forgetting. The tacit and often taken-for-granted Cold War–generated frames of thinking about World War II and leftism in a Jewish American context resurface in this fiction.

Yet the field of inherited memory of communism, and state socialism, is broader, going beyond the traumatic to help articulate "hopeful memories," too.[64] These memories constitute a past that might inspire and help build bridges to, for example, current progressive or feminist activism. This includes the memory of state socialist social politics as equality-driven gender and family regulations or unionizing.

"Afterlives" also point to the autobiographical conditioning of this fiction: textualized migrant lives that become legible only after the act of writing and visible only after publication of this writing. In order to emphasize the relation of this fiction to the situatedness of the author, both generally and on the literary market, this book uses author interviews, some conducted specially for this study, to better illuminate how their literary production fits—or does not fit—into the Jewish American literary complex. By no means do these interviews function here as a source of interpretative authority. On the other hand, interviews—even with their performative aspect—can easily reveal the social, cultural, and political entanglements of literature as a business. This is especially the case since, in the age of social media, the literary market is to a large extent personality driven. The interviews serve, then, as a testimony to how the literary market and institutional literary complex made (or failed to make?) this writing into Jewish American literature. When writing about contemporary literary texts, for which archival research is barely an option, curated author interviews attempt to complement published materials.

Toward New Coordinates

Soviet-born writing encourages us to rethink several categories of Jewish American literature that have become ossified as such during the Cold War and continue to tacitly inform Jewish American cultural and literary criticism, including that focused on popular texts. Post–Cold War understandings shape cultural discourse around major themes of literary study that rely on and employ the category of "Jewish American," including the notion of "Eastern European" and post-Soviet space, the Holocaust, leftism, gender and intimacy, as well as relation with other migrant groups. In each of its chapters, this book approaches one of these themes while zooming in on two or three novels, short stories, or a graphic memoir, with a host of other texts also making brief appearances; it shows how the gendered lens of migration from the former Soviet Union changes the logic of many dominant narratives that has become natural to the Jewish American literary complex, and it introduces new themes that rewrite the legacy of the Cold War from the perspective of migration and the Soviet experience.

Chapter 1, "Diasporic Spaces," begins the investigation into constitutive themes of Jewish American writing by asking how fiction by Soviet-born authors imagines Eastern Europe. The texts discussed here, with an eye on post–Cold War transnationalism, reconceptualize received notions of space and place, countering monolithic and often myopic understandings of "Eastern Europe" and the (former) Soviet Union. While Holocaust-themed literature often imagines Eastern Europe as an empty, lifeless place or an Orientalized space beyond time, some Soviet-born writing also renegotiates the spatial divide between the United States and the former Soviet Union in a way that disrupts this memory logic of Holocaust literature as well as the prominent absence of the former "Second World" on the map of American transnationalism. Examples include Anya Ulinich's *Petropolis* (2007) and Yelena Akhtiorskaya's *Panic in a Suitcase* (2014).[65] Their settings encompass or straddle both American and post-Soviet spaces (also in Asia) through migration and post-migration tourism narratives that construct and reinforce diasporic networks. These texts enable such a renegotiation by forging links between post-Soviet and migrant U.S. settings through characters' interactions in and with those settings. The movement of characters through these spaces dramatizes affinities and connectivities both spatial and conceptual. These texts therefore call into question the otherness of the so-called "Second World"—by zeroing in on geographical units smaller than "worlds" and staging connections between them. The received meanings of the former Soviet space are only amplified by the gendered vulnerability of the protagonists: two young women whose intersections with their respective families start throwing light on aspects of the Soviet-inherited gender order.

While chapter 1 contrasts the spacial logic of this fiction with literary tropes related to Holocaust memory, chapter 2, "Redefining Survival," goes one step further and asks about the ways in which the Holocaust is represented in this fiction. In David Bezmozgis's *The Free World* (2011), Boris Fishman's *A Replacement Life* (2014), and Julia Alekseyeva's graphic novel *Soviet Daughter* (2017), aspects of Sovietness related to the war, the Holocaust, and memory help us rethink two key themes in the American literary Holocaust imaginary: the survivor and the relationship between the war and the Holocaust. These novels, all of which revolve partly around Jewish Red Army veterans, offer further evidence of a close link between narrating the war and the Holocaust, which was characteristic of Jewish American writing in the late 1940s, centered on the figure of the Jewish American soldier. Narrating evacuations into the Soviet interior and the experiences of indirect survivors, they explore yet another facet of Jewish survival. These texts contribute to what I call post-Soviet migrant memory of the Holocaust. This literature stages converging histories of the same events on a global scale by adding a story determined by the Cold War and by the Soviet strategy of curbing movement and migration—a story that now enters migrant writing in English. All the texts considered in this chapter are written by the grandchildren of Holocaust survivors and nominally belong to, and share the characteristics of, American third-generation Holocaust literature. These stories of survival are deeply embedded in a migration narrative, which decidedly, however, influences how these narratives develop and what kind of stories they tell. Soviet and post-Soviet masculinities and femininities also inflect these narratives, with Alekseyeva's text explicitly staging Soviet-born women's transgenerational memory.

Chapter 3, "Afterlives of Communism," takes us to the post-Soviet Russia of the 2000s to explore communist postmemory as well as larger issues of leftism. The novels discussed in this chapter, Sana Krasikov's *The Patriots* (2017) and Keith Gessen's *A Terrible Country* (2018), point toward the once lost and now rediscovered ways of narrating emancipation from state socialism/communism in the United States that do not lead to its demonization and the adoption of a conservative stance. They locate American leftism, both prewar and current, in the context of state socialism/communism and Russian post-Sovietness, respectively. In these narratives, American progressivism, past and present, becomes intimately bound to Soviet and post-Soviet Russia—bound both ideologically and through the romantic and gendered family bonds of Soviet-born American Jews who travel to Russia in the 2000s. Simultaneously, the afterlife of communism appears as stories unearthed by immigrant offspring in Soviet police secret files or as narratives about post-Soviet new left social movements. Soviet-born Jewish American protagonists come to these stories through their personal family attachments, generating affective bonds that challenge the possibility of simple demonizations.

Chapter 4, "Soviet Intimacy," specifically explores fiction that focuses on late Soviet and perestroika gender order narrated from the perspective of young women and girls. Ellen Litman's *Mannequin Girl* (2014), Lara Vapnyar's *The Scent of Pine* (2014), and her short story "Lydia's Grove" (2003) revolve around body and gender normativity, abortion, same-sex desire, and sex education.

These are the only texts from this literary wave to centrally address the 1980s and filter this decade through the lens of intimacy. However differently intimacies are regulated in Soviet and U.S. contexts, as a leading theme in these works they make this otherwise often demonized late Cold War period relatable for the American reading public. In general, this chapter also performs a bit of background work for other gender-centered arguments in the book, illustrating the limits of late Soviet intimate citizenship, how it functioned, and how it was perceived by girls and young women. It also serves as a narrative mnemonic prequel to many of the other narratives analyzed in this book. Importantly, the gender and sexuality focus of the fiction discussed in this chapter rather displaces Jewishness, which appears only marginally or implicitly. In fact, this constitutes a kind of lesson in Soviet Jewishness, namely how it has often been socially erased and made invisible except when discriminated against.

While previous chapters used Soviet and post-Soviet migration as an unchallenged variable to reveal differences with the well-sedimented narratives of nonimmigrant American Jewishness, chapter 5, "Keyword: Migration," focuses on migration and migrants, both Jewish and non-Jewish, to probe what I call "comparative literacy." "Soviet-born" is put into dialogue with "foreign-born" to explore both inter-Jewish and (what I call) *intermigrant* solidarities, and their limits to offer yet another reflection on how to think about Soviet-born writing beyond post–Cold War bipolarity. Intermigrant solidarities help explore how this fiction locates itself within literature of migration. The historical, geographical, and ethnic landscape this covers is vast but only hints at the larger comparative contexts in which Soviet-born writing can participate. Nadia Kalman's *The Cosmopolitans* (2010), Davis Bezmozgis's "Immigrant City" (2019), set in Toronto, and Gary Shteyngart's *Lake Success* (2018) illuminate the boundaries of Soviet Jewish affinities with literary characters from earlier Jewish texts, with recent refugees, or with immigrants with no Soviet Jewish background. In my readings, these affinities are delimited by gender and/or sexuality, and this chapter most fully illustrates the stakes of reading migration and gender together, as mutually articulating and as constitutive of a less insular Jewishness.

1

Diasporic Spaces

Writer Anya Ulinich's dialogue with nonimmigrant Jewish American male writers includes not only Philip Roth, discussed in the introduction, but also her peers, who are considered Roth's literary heirs.[1] Her 2008 short story "The Nurse and the Novelist" stages an encounter in New York City between the titular characters: a Soviet-born nurse and an author who is a thinly veiled Jonathan Safran Foer. The text features an immigrant nurse, ever "a family provider" and now a single working mother, alongside a successful writer, with a partner and young twins, who moves upstate after being mobbed in the city.[2] In four short, titled sections, Ulinich presents a synopsis of the Holocaust postmemory novel *The Butterfly* by the titular novelist, a Soviet Jewish war story about the nurse's grandparents, an encounter between the two protagonists as condominium neighbors, and a self-reflective paragraph in the novelist's voice. The contrasts sketched by Ulinich encompass several social axes, including gender, class, and immigrant status, as well as literary aesthetic, which—as the short story suggests—is directly conditioned by the former elements. Together, these various points of contrast lead to Ulinich's critique of Eastern Europe's mode of representation, which, as in *The Butterfly*, characterizes early twenty-first-century Jewish American writing that, as the literary scholar Michael Hoberman claims, used the shtetl to establish its ethnic credentials.[3]

For Ulinich, this mode of representation relies on two factors: a projection of the U.S. memory culture of the early 2000s onto post-Soviet Eastern Europe, paired with the removal, via magical realism, of the post-Soviet Eastern European reality as an actual contemporary geopolitical space. For the immigrant nurse from the former Soviet Union in Ulinich's short story, the fictional novel

The Butterfly—set in former USSR territory, just like Foer's *Everything Is Illuminated*—relies on an assumed transnational and even transatlantic continuity of memorialization. Contrary to that, Ulinich denounces the novel's projection of U.S. memory culture onto Minsk and its Belarusian characters. Talking to the titular novelist, Ulinich's nurse suggests, "Where no one remembers the Jews, no one remembers the Jews."[4] This dissonant tautology echoes the partly institutionalized forgetting of anti-Jewish atrocities in the former Soviet Union. A categorical and provocative argument emerges: that "where no one remembers the Jews," or where, to put it differently, there is no politics of memory centered on Jewishness and the Holocaust, in fact "no one remembers the Jews." In other words, her statement may be read more broadly as radically juxtaposing the early twenty-first-century spatiotemporal political reality to the fictional reality of the novel. Indeed, Belarus, for example, remains one of the Eastern European countries with the least record of institutionalized Holocaust memory building.[5] This space differs from Jewish American spaces, but only in terms of post-Soviet legacies and current political situations, not magic.

Ulinich underscores this disconnect when the story addresses the novel's titular golden butterfly charm, a material witness with a distinct aura and a prompt for the memorial journey that de-actualizes the Belarusian setting. We hear the nurse say, "Let me tell you a few things. . . . Jewelry gets lost very easily. I mean, these are tiny things."[6] Further, the nurse's climactic bon mot in the short story follows the classic Saidian anti-Orientalist logic exposing the constitution of the self through the other: "In your novels, past calamities are nothing but milestones of self-discovery."[7] "Past calamities" are here historical events that are appropriated for individual identity construction and molded accordingly. This, in turn, leads to the flattening of their local characteristics and contextualization, placing them outside of historical change, frozen in the time of the Holocaust, or rather, in a dominant, and at times similarly frozen, narrative of the Holocaust.[8]

Just as Ulinich's short story—with its impersonal, universalizing title—functions as an exemplum, its imaginary novel *The Butterfly* stands in for the whole framework of representation that follows established patterns of assigning meaning to geographical entities, or metageography, to use the term of geographer Martin Lewis and historian Kären Wigen.[9] Eastern Europe (or in this case, Belarus) emerges as a decontextualized space impervious to historical change—in short, as Oriental. Similar to *The Butterfly*, generalized Eastern European space appears within the conventions of magical realism, beyond the rules of sociocultural logic, or as multimediated text of memory.[10] In Nicole Krauss's highly celebrated *The History of Love* (2005), for example, Eastern Europe is mostly recreated only within survivors' memories of a long-lost world. The only trace of its actual political existence comes in an aside about the failed relationship of the adolescent protagonist with an immigrant Soviet-born Jew.[11]

A similar dynamic prevails in Jonathan Safran Foer's Holocaust postmemory text *Everything Is Illuminated*, which Michael Hoberman reads as "bypass[ing] the town's actual story": "what he [the novel's main protagonist] sees in the land of his ancestors exercises little influence over his descriptions of the place."[12] In contrast to these works that simply recreate a generalized "Eastern Europe" in Jewish American literature, Soviet-born writing makes the "actual story" of this place and space paramount.[13] For example, Ulinich's nurse's story of her grandparents is not set in a former shtetl, where "magical realism kicks in," but in Leningrad, among university graduates, some of whom survive the war in the East, on the front or in Leningrad's siege. Post-Soviet space here is not the far-removed or distantly remembered "land of [one's] ancestors" but a palpable, fully realized place from which the characters themselves migrate. As a result, Soviet-born authors shift from the historical and cultural construct of "Eastern Europe" to the historical and political entity of the (former) Soviet Union.

As such, this body of writing provides yet another example of filling up the "spatial 'blind spot'" of Jewish American literary histories.[14] Attempting to rehabilitate a spatial perspective—and, in particular, the landscape—as a significant key in how to approach Jewish American writing, Sarah Phillips Casteel draws attention to how an "urban orientation" has hindered Jewish studies and, as a result, produced "its lack of attention to space more generally."[15] If "space" is assumed to be self-evident, it does not seem to be a useful category of analysis, which has contributed to the primacy of historicity and the temporal axis. From this perspective, it is not surprising that "Eastern Europe" exists mostly on a temporal axis: it is not a differentiated *space* (with a specific topography as well as a peculiar spatial logic influenced by geopolitics), but *a point in time*, one that serves as a point of reference for American Ashkenormative genealogies.

If the "hemispheric reframing of the field" that Casteel calls for leads to the adjective "American" more capaciously including Canada and the Caribbean, taking "space" seriously means also rethinking the functioning of other locales that are taken for granted within Jewish U.S.-American fiction.[16] And this certainly includes Eastern Europe, especially following Irving Howe's notorious 1977 introduction to *Jewish American Stories*, which made immigration from Eastern Europe and alienation in the United States both the "bogeyman and [the] raison d'être" of Jewish American literary study.[17] A certain version of Eastern Europe—a past left behind—underpins the dominant literary narrative. A plethora of academic books on the representation of the shtetl testifies to the prevalence of this theme.[18] To be sure, this is not a call to be more attentive to particular places, but rather an attempt to try to reframe their space as actually belonging to "global crossroads."[19] Diasporic positioning makes these texts especially responsive to how spaces function more broadly in relation to migration and ethnicity, and not only within Jewish contexts.

With its attention to "global crossroads," this body of writing not only recasts Eastern European as Soviet and post-Soviet, but also, with its many Euro-Asian settings in (post-) Soviet space, calls into question the unity of "Soviet" and, consequently, "post-Soviet." An emphasis on diversity and, as cultural critic Madina Tlostanova puts it, on imagining the "ex-second world as a diverse, contradictory, non-homogenous semi-alterity with its unique intersectionality" is central to reading diasporic Soviet-born literary production.[20] This formulation stresses that what has been stabilized by the Iron Curtain as the East should not be homogenized by a simple application of postcolonial theory to the "ex-second world," with imperial Russia or the Soviet Union simply stepping into the shoes of a Western imperial power.[21] Tlostanova imagines the "ex-second world" empire as characterized by multiple power asymmetries: "In the case of Russia/the Soviet Union and its colonies, in my view, it will be a narrative of a Janus-faced empire which always felt itself like a colony in the presence of the West, as the imperial difference generated Russia's secondary status in European eyes and, consequently, as open or hidden orientalization."[22] The multiple axes of difference that Tlostanova emphasizes parallel the fragmentation and multiplicity of locations in Soviet-born writing, post-Soviet locations that the writers know and draw on when inventing their biographically informed narratives in English. The spatiotemporal adjective "post-Soviet" serves as a strategically essentialist term that I employ to question the metageography inherent in a good deal of contemporary mainstream Jewish American fiction, but which itself invites deconstruction as a misleadingly homogenizing category.[23] In addition, by emphasizing local and global colonial entanglements, such broader thinking about space allows for potentially putting this writing in a dialogue with other diasporic texts.

The frozenness of Eastern Europe/Soviet space owes a great deal not only to the centrality of Holocaust writing, teleologically overshadowing the interwar years, but also to Cold War discourse and the disremembering of alternative discursive strands. As Jewish studies scholar Susan Glenn notes, "the Cold War between the United States and the Soviet Union had both global and domestic manifestations that disrupted the internal politics of American Jewish life."[24] What Glenn terms the Jewish Cold War meant, among other things, "the censure and isolation of Jewish Communists," and in turn produced a marginalization of interwar Jewish writers of the Left, whose narratives centered on the new Soviet Union.[25] This included numerous travelogues from "secular pilgrimages" to the recently formed socialist state.[26] The old and new worlds stood in a peculiar, nonobvious relation to each other. In historian Daniel Soyer's words, the "visit to the 'old home' was simultaneously a journey into a new social order considered by many to be more representative of the future than of the past."[27] These older narratives seem to rely on transnationalism and a critical perception of spatial relations that is echoed in contemporary Soviet-born writing.[28]

Although Soviet-born fiction has the potential to nuance our understanding of dominant metageography and expand spatialized notions of American Jewishness, the function of post-Soviet space and its relation to American settings varies across texts. In the wider landscape of this fiction, some texts are set exclusively in the United States and only marginally attempt to rethink the hegemonic spatial divide sketched above, although they may endeavor to do more for the *social* map. Good examples of this are David Bezmozgis's *Natasha and Other Stories* (2004) and Nadia Kalman's *The Cosmopolitans* (2010), discussed in chapter 5, as well as Boris Fishman's *A Replacement Life* (2014), discussed in chapter 2. Their settings are most often the urban East Coast of the United States (with the exception of Bezmozgis's Toronto), which reflects the actual geographic prevalence of Soviet-born Jewish migrants and the classic locale of Jewish American fiction.[29]

Another group of texts is set exclusively in the (former) Soviet Union; these include Ellen Litman's *Mannequin Girl* (2014), some of Lara Vapnyar's short stories, David Bezmozgis's *The Betrayers* (2014), and the short story "Repatriates" in Sana Krasikov's *One More Year* (2008). These novels and short stories, some of which are the subject of chapter 3, focus directly on particular places and could have addressed, and attempted to rewrite, the metageography of post-Soviet space by exposing its diversity and its inherent regional power relations—and specifically, how these things conditioned localized versions of Jewishness. Yet these texts, with the exception of Krasikov's stories, focus on the emblematic location of Moscow, and so instead they mirror the hegemonic geographic horizon of expectations. This body of work is still relatively small, but one can expect a larger variety of locations interrogated in future texts, a part of the post-2022 push to decolonize Russian studies.[30]

Finally, one group of novels directly renegotiates the spatial divide between the United States and the former Soviet Union in a way that disrupts the imagined radical distinctiveness between Soviet/post-Soviet space and the United States. Examples of these "global crossroads" and diasporic spaces include Anya Ulinich's *Petropolis* (2007) and Yelena Akhtiorskaya's *Panic in a Suitcase* (2014), discussed in this chapter, as well as other more recent instances, some of which I turn to in chapters 3 and 4.[31] Their settings encompass or straddle both spaces through narratives of migration and (post-migration) tourism that construct and reinforce diasporic networks. These texts enable such a renegotiation by forging links between post-Soviet and migrant U.S. settings through characters' interactions in and with those settings.[32] The movement of characters through these spaces dramatizes affinities and connectivities both spatial and conceptual. These texts therefore call into question the otherness of the so-called "Second World"—by zeroing in on geographical units smaller than "worlds" and staging connections between them.

Ulinich's *Petropolis* connects U.S. and Soviet imperial frontiers. Ulinich pairs the borderlands of Siberia and the U.S. Southwest (more specifically, Arizona) only to later return to the more traditional settings, for Jewish American fiction, of Chicago and New York City. Akhtiorskaya's *Panic in a Suitcase* is divided between, and propelled by the relationship between, Brooklyn's Brighton Beach and post-Soviet Odessa, weaving connections between coastal settings.[33] In addition, Akhtiorskaya's attention to the littoral opens another, alternative framework of connectedness: the ocean itself. Indeed, this pairing gains an extra dimension read post-2022 when this connectedness has been broken down again through the ongoing war as well as bombing of Odessa. Through their focus on smaller geographical units and their migrant point of view, these novels apply spatial tropes known from other diasporic writing. As such they challenge the post–Cold War notion of separate "worlds" and suggest alternative metageographies that rely on diasporic connectedness.

Borderland Affinities: Anya Ulinich's *Petropolis*

Anya Ulinich's *Petropolis* is the American immigration tale of a nominally Jewish, Afro-Russian teenager, Sasha Goldberg, born and raised in a small industrial town in Soviet and post-Soviet Siberia, which she flees, leaving behind her mother and her infant daughter. Ulinich's depiction of Sasha's hometown, Asbestos 2, is somber, a space of forced exile and a forsaken promise of national economic progress. Using various American and, more generally, Western clichés about Russia and Russians, Ulinich sets a part of the novel in the Russian Northeast and thus "taps into the Western fascination with the quintessentially Russian 'heart of darkness.'"[34] Yet *Petropolis* goes beyond this restaging of a surface fascination with the stereotypical Other and attempts to reconfigure this exoticizing gaze by pairing the Russian borderland location with the American Southwest, where Sasha first arrives after emigrating.[35] Ulinich's rewriting of geographical meanings manifests here precisely as this pairing of the two borderlands within "postfrontier horizons," to use literary scholar Stephen Tatum's phrase.[36] Through her narrative, Ulinich crafts parallels between these two settings. *Petropolis* thus shows transregional affinities between specific borderland places—Asbestos 2 and Phoenix, Arizona—that might otherwise be thought of as belonging to different worlds. Sasha's multiple-subject position (Black, Jewish, and Russian) probes assumptions about the former Soviet Union; at the same time, this easy-to-misread combination of identities reveals an underlying ethnic framing in the Southwest.

Readers first encounter Sasha Goldberg in Asbestos 2, the novel's initial setting. Later, after Sasha has moved to the United States, Ulinich revisits the town through its representation in television and print media, as well as when Sasha takes a few trips back to Siberia. This traveling back and forth goes against the "self-protective" measures that many immigrants embark on, which include refusing to visit their "childhood country" despite economic and technological possibilities.[37] Throughout the novel, Asbestos 2 thus remains a recurrent point of reference, a dynamic geopolitical location defined by familial ties and determined by historical contingencies. In an interview, Ulinich explains the narrative construction of Asbestos 2 through her "being a Soviet immigrant," which she compares to "coming from a culture that has gone away" even though it is still on the map:

> I belong to a world that no longer exists. I wanted Sasha to be both a product of a Soviet event like festivals that brought people together and she came from a town that was gulag so it started from the Soviet times. . . . My dad was a mining engineer. So, he would go to business trips to this town called Asbestos, a Siberian city. . . . I wanted a ghost town, and I Googled Asbestos, and it is like a thriving city of three million people, and they are mining in Asbestos and everything is fine! So, I was like: "I can't do that. I cannot fictionalize a place I know nothing about." And I have never been to Siberia. So, I just made it up. I just called it Asbestos 2. . . . So, I just wanted a town that was Soviet. I wanted the story to start and end in Soviet times.[38]

Yet *Petropolis*—providing us with snippets of Sasha's family story—retraces not only the story of the quintessentially Soviet Asbestos but also key elements of the historically varying imperial symbolic geography of Siberia that reaches beyond Soviet times. Within Russian metageography, geographer Mark Bassin distinguishes three layers of meaning invested in "Siberia" since the eighteenth century: first, casting the Russian Northeast in positive terms as a national "gold mine" or economic powerhouse; second, in negative cultural terms, as the grim space of forced exile; and third, in revolutionary terms, as a promising frontier alternative to the imperial center, a space of renewal.[39] Bassin sees these three levels of geographical meaning as ordered somewhat chronologically. This is especially the case with the transition from economic wellspring to place of detention or banishment in the early twentieth century. Particularly in the twentieth century, these domains of signification overlap, thus creating a "multifarious" cultural space with a range of meanings depending on the ideologies in the center of the empire.[40]

These metageographical tropes converge in the protagonist's family story. Sasha's maternal grandmother, Evgenia Nechaeva, is deported from Leningrad and sentenced to exile in Siberia in 1941 as "the Wife of the Enemy of the People" after the death of her professor husband.[41] The penitentiary past of Asbestos 2— a former administrative center for the gulag and, at that time, one of many

Stalinsks in the Soviet Union—extends into the early 1990s, when the town was home to a strict regime colony.[42] This prison shapes the environment of Asbestos 2 because former felons, often together with their families, tend to stay in town after serving their sentence. It also shaped the romantic choices of Sasha's mother, Lubov. She dreamed of meeting an outsider—"a man without tattoos, a scientist on his trip"—whom she found in the person of Sasha's father, an orphaned Afro-Russian army recruit raised by prominent Muscovite Jew Victor Goldberg.[43] Renaming the town Asbestos 2 in the post-Stalin era itself points to the initial cultural and economic significance of Siberia as a trove of natural resources, a significance that had been renewed under Stalin himself.[44] Asbestos mining and milling define the town economy and, for a time, provide employment for Sasha's mother. Finally, the storyline of the Kotelnikov family—including Sasha's boyfriend and father of her daughter—embodies the failed promise of renewal in the borderlands. The Kotelnikovs, who had lived on a "miserable" collective farm in the European part of Russia, volunteered to come to Siberia to build the Baikal–Amur Railroad, but the construction plans never materialized and a group of 300 people ended up living in tents and then giant concrete pipes, "barrels" next to the town's trash dump.[45]

Consequently, Ulinich imbues Asbestos 2 with conflicting valences. On the one hand, it functions as a "postapocalyptic place" that "grew out of the demise of civilization," an "ugly little town with a miserable name," "a place unsuitable for living," even before its post-Soviet economic collapse, which we witness later in the novel.[46] On the other hand, Ulinich—narrating its story through the experience of an intelligentsia family—makes an effort to stage its cultural institutions and the engagement of its inhabitants, including Sasha, with the arts. As she puts it, "Occasional exiled dissidents and descendants of the postwar shipment of 'landless cosmopolitans' provided the necessary culture."[47] While Sasha's mother, a local librarian, is an element of this "necessary culture," so too are Sasha's art classes in the makeshift atelier AFTER EATIN, or the "world-famous" icon painter Alufiev living in one of the barrels at the dump.[48] One can read this as satire on the intelligentsia, with their inclination to recognize and nurture culture under any circumstances and against all odds: Lubov marries Victor Goldberg because he knows his Mandelstam. But this depiction of Asbestos 2 also seems to channel a utopia of the borderlands in which "necessary culture" and high art transcend class constraints.

Ulinich envisions Asbestos 2 as stratified rather horizontally with regard to social class, but the romance and marriage in the novel between Sasha's mother and the Afro-Russian Goldberg—as well as the product of this union, Sasha herself—serve as a focal point of racial and ethnic tensions. As literary scholar Dean J. Franco notes, "Though we typically think of ourselves as complexly composed of several identities, with each coming into relevance more or less depending on our situation, we are nonetheless bound by bluntly totalizing terminology that regularly fails to capture the fact of race."[49] In this vein, by giving Sasha her father's conspicuously Jewish-sounding surname, her parents hope to obscure in Asbestos 2 the fact that she is Black. Ulinich formulates her complex positioning and "bluntly totalizing terminology" of identity in the following way: "I wanted to make Sasha a kind of person who could be perceived in different ways. I was also interested in those imposed identities. When you are in Russia, being Jew is a category, but here in the U.S. it is entirely different. It is put on you in a certain way. 'You should do certain things if you are Jewish.' And being Russian. The Russian accent. . . . So, Sasha gets all of these random things that do not necessarily mean anything to her, but she needs to accept them and put them into places needed."[50] This may be a spoof of identity politics *à l'américaine*, but it still serves to expose naturalized norms of Jewishness and Russianness in both Asbestos 2 and Phoenix.

The utopian traces of an otherwise "postapocalyptic" Siberian frontier are crucial for forging a "trans-regional alliance" between Sasha's birthplace and her first destination in the United States.[51] After giving birth to her daughter, Sasha leaves the baby with her mother and departs to study art at a renowned school in Moscow. Her stint in the metropolis is embarrassingly short: she soon signs up for an international bridal agency called "Kupid's Korner," catering to Americans, and finds herself a "mail order bride," student visa in hand, on her way to a fiancé in Phoenix.[52] For Sasha Goldberg, Phoenix is "a perfect place to erase herself."[53] No one there can interpellate her as that which she was before, in Siberia. And what she sees in Phoenix is an urban utopia: "At a distance, a cluster of tall buildings stood wrapped in a brown haze, but roads dominated the scenery: straight, wide, impossibly even, flanked by equally perfect, empty sidewalks."[54] Sasha's ability to become "unseen" is also predicated on the ethnic makeup of this American border region, with its relatively small Soviet-born immigrant population and the discursive predominance of a racialized ethnic Mexican Other. In this milieu, Sasha can easily stay invisible, just "a very dark Jew."[55]

The confusion of assigning identity reappears multiple times in the novel and is based on unchecked metageographical assumptions. In one instance, it boils down to a false analogy that nevertheless illustrates a certain universality of othering. In Phoenix, reflecting on her fiancé's reaction to her appearance, and also referring to her fellow Soviet-born Jewish immigrant friend Marina, Sasha muses, "He probably figured Sasha was one of those black Russians, the way Marina's neighbors from the Palisades assumed Ukraine was full of Mexicans, asking Marina what language Mexicans spoke in Donetsk."[56] These apparently empathic lines of thought point to the domesticating of the post-Soviet space: they assume that the strands of imperial logic obtained there are not just parallel to the American pattern but rather exactly the same.[57]

Creating a Black Russian character that is read within the framework of Jewishness allows for multiple occasions where Sasha is misread. Ulinich, however, also comments on the novel and Sasha's character as a product of its times, penned from 2003 to 2004: "It was written by a young person who is not necessarily me. I do not have the same things to say now, but I do like how I think in some places of the book."[58] The crossover racial representation seems provocative today, but it foreshadows, for instance, academic interest in the Cold War battle over the Global South and, more specifically, interactions, exchanges, and solidarities between the USSR and African countries, here manifesting as the festival of nations that literally produced Sasha's father, Victor.[59] While today self-narratives by Afro-Russians occupy virtual spaces and social media, using their political potential, Ulinich reflects on their dearth in the early 2000s when a novel might have ventured to do such cultural work: "Maybe, somebody needed this white Muscovite person writing about Black Russians then. But now, everyone can write their own selves, their engaging stories."[60] This underlines the affordances of literature as a vehicle of imagining and textualizing marginalized positionalities that have not yet enjoyed the privilege to be narrated to life.

Casting Sasha as a transatlantic mail-order bride, Ulinich may be playing with the notion of Russian women as commodity, but this prearranged relationship follows a broader logic of regional affinity and gender non-normativity at national geographic peripheries. As the bridal agency employee predictably suggests, her future fiancé, Neil, and other Americans come to Russia to find unspoiled traditional femininity in their potential future wives. Sasha is advertised according to their expectations, as an Orientalized "Passionate Dark Beauty."[61] Yet gender relations in Asbestos 2 are far from the eternal femininity of the bourgeois ideal, and "the failure of domesticity" is but one of their manifestations.[62] For various historically conditioned reasons, and with the short-lived exception of her father, Sasha's multigenerational family in Asbestos 2 consisted of female members only. Moreover, this gender imbalance extends further to encompass seemingly all men in Asbestos 2, none of whom are destined to survive. It is a reverse of the standard gender imbalance in early settler communities, which sometimes results in the need to systematically import brides.[63] By sending Sasha off to Arizona, Ulinich narratively echoes—however satirically—the process of importing brides to once male-dominated peripheries. At the same time, this development parallels, to an extent, Sasha's own mother's accidental union with her father, a non-native Asbestonian who almost literally fell into her lap.

By setting her novel partially in the imaginary Siberian city Asbestos 2, and by placing an Afro-Russian, contingently Jewish character as its protagonist, Ulinich defamiliarizes the starting point of Soviet Jewish emigration, both geographically and ethnically. Similarly, since Sasha's destination is Phoenix rather than New York or another well-known Russian enclave, Ulinich defamiliarizes the place of migrant Soviet arrival in the United States. Because readers are unaccustomed to the representation of these places in Jewish American fiction, they can approach the narrative free of the assumptions that inevitably attach to this literature's classic locales. By means of its spatial novelty and literary constructs, *Petropolis* collapses the "before" and "after" of migration, especially in its initial part set in these two borderland locations. In the novel, through a comparative approach to borderlands, the three-world schema breaks down through the staged affinity of these smaller geographical units in the United States and in Russia, but also through a multilayered protagonist who is the product of Soviet encounters and cultural diplomacy with the Global South.

While *Petropolis* starts in Siberia and then moves to Moscow, Arizona, and other metropolitan spaces in the United States, Akhtiorskaya's *Panic in a Suitcase* starts in Brooklyn, New York, only to later shift its setting to Odessa, Ukraine. And while Sasha does eventually travel back to Siberia in *Petropolis*, post-immigrant tourism becomes the focus of the entire plot of Akhtiorskaya's novel. Moreover, this tourism extends in both directions: Frida, who immigrated to the United States with her parents as a child, visits Ukraine, while earlier her uncle is shown visiting his immigrant family in Brighton Beach, Brooklyn. Like Ulinich, Akhtiorskaya bridges the United States and the post–Cold War "Second World" by creating parallels in local landscapes—namely, by exploring the meanings that can flow from coastal settings. Here, however, the reciprocity of post-immigrant tourism further challenges the separateness of post-Soviet space and of immigrant "Second Worlds" in the United States, especially before the Russo-Ukrainian war.

Reciprocal Post-immigrant Tourism in the Time of Peace: Yelena Akhtiorskaya's *Panic in a Suitcase*

Yelena Akhtiorskaya's *Panic in a Suitcase* spans two localities that are linked even by their names: Odessa, in Ukraine, and Little Odessa, also known as Brighton Beach, in New York's South Brooklyn. While in *Petropolis*, unlikely post-frontier regional affinities are forced into a confrontation with Jewishness, Jewish genealogies link places central to *Panic in a Suitcase*. Historically, Odessa was the largest Jewish city in the South of the Russian Empire, a multiethnic Black Sea hub; Brighton Beach, meanwhile, is a former resort turned immigration destination for successive waves of Jewish immigrants in the twentieth century, becoming one of many such "ethnic enclaves" or "insular demi-worlds" in New York.[64] A sea-facing topography defines Brighton Beach and forms part of its affinity with peacetime Odessa: photographs of the boardwalk and sandy beach feature prominently in sociological studies as well as journalism and artistic projects on Soviet immigrants.[65]

In a photo essay she coauthored, Akhtiorskaya also commented on the centrality of the ocean: "The thrill and panic of being in a foreign place was cut by the immense relief of rediscovering what was feared lost, and not just rediscovering but recreating, with some minor but notable substitutions, such as the Atlantic Ocean for the Black Sea, and the boardwalk for Primorski Boulevard."[66] Although the link between these two locations seems to be self-evident, immigrants not only automatically "rediscover" but, as Akhtiorskaya insists, uniquely "recreate" these affective parallels. "Rediscovery" signals what I call the Cold War immigrant metageography that depends on spatial parallels between locations that exist in an ambivalent, hierarchized arrangement: due to limitations on mobility, the place of origin was radically different, unreachable, and subject to nostalgic attachment. Such, for example, is the still lingering resonance created by the caption to a beachfront photograph in a sociological study from the early 2000s: "For elderly Ukrainian Jews, the Brighton Beach Boardwalk, with its wide open views of the sea, helps to assuage pangs of nostalgia for the Black Sea vistas they remember from home."[67]

In contrast, *Panic in a Suitcase* restyles these connections between Brooklyn and Odessa, introducing a different dynamic between the sedimented meaning of these geographical localities. Here, these post–Cold War worlds are interconnected by phone, email, and relatively easy travel. Consequently, immigrants visit, or revisit, the place they think they are from, as Frida notes to her mother,[68] and nonimmigrant family members come to visit those who have left. Post-2022 the constraints on mobility are valid again, but Akhtiorskaya records a moment when a different special dynamic across "worlds" was imaginable.

The novel's division into two parts, set about fifteen years apart, with different protagonists and mostly different locations, allows it to speak to geographical mobility and results in a particular understanding of space. The novel's first part follows Pavel Nasmertov, or Pasha, as he visits his three-generation émigré family in Brighton Beach in 1993 and 1994; its second part, set in 2008, centers on his Odessa-born Brooklynite niece, Frida, who makes the reverse of Pasha's journey, traveling to Odessa from the United States. Formally, the novel's division into two parts may result from Akhtiorskaya's narrative penchant for catching the story at two distant moments and forcing readers to fill in the gaps themselves.[69] In relation to geographical mobility, the plot's discontinuity encourages readers to contemplate possible connections, consider tourism and immigration together (and think too about Pasha's decision not to immigrate), and interrogate the immigrant primacy of belonging and the meaning of the "Second World." As one critic put it, "Everyone knows that you can't go home again; what Akhtiorskaya suggests is that staying at home is no longer an option either."[70]

Pasha's tourist and defamiliarizing perspective on Brighton Beach provides an important counterpart to Frida when she later travels to Odessa. Akhtiorskaya goes to great lengths to characterize Pasha as an outsider. In the text, he literally embodies Odessa: "Pasha's physique resembled Odessa's habitations."[71] He discovers his place in Brighton Beach only when and where it is unlike itself: during an "epic storm" on the beach when he finds shelter among the unhoused under the boardwalk.[72] From Pasha's point of view, this Brooklyn neighborhood represents a satirical copy of a Soviet town: "His fellow countrymen hadn't ventured bravely into a new land, they'd borrowed a tiny nook at the very rear of someone's else's crumbling estate to make a tidy replication of the messy, imperfect original they'd gone through so many hurdles to escape, imprisoning themselves in their lack of imagination, forgetting the original had come about organically and proceeded to evolve, already markedly different from their poor-quality photocopy."[73] Even though immigrant "enclaves" are known for preserving otherwise extinct cultural peculiarities, this passage actually reverses the typical Orientalizing attitude toward Eastern Europe.[74] While Eastern Europe is often rendered as static, beyond time and eternally underdeveloped, here Brighton Beach is frozen in a form Odessa once had. Akhtiorskaya formulates this observation similarly, but with a more ambiguous valuation, in her coauthored photo essay: "Brighton Beach is a universe unto itself, with its own time, its own language, its own customs, for which it makes no apologies."[75]

Akhtiorskaya imagines Pasha, this critic of the immigrant enclave at Brighton Beach, as unapologetically focused on the émigré Nasmertovs and their characteristic traits, including their Jewishness. *Panic in a Suitcase* follows much Soviet-born fiction in exemplifying what I call contingent Jewishness: Jewishness that was a fact of ethnic belonging or so-called nationality in the former USSR, but which barely registers as Jewishness in an American context. In Ulinich's subversive approach to group identity labels in *Petropolis*, for example, Sasha Goldberg can hardly be even nominally associated with Jewishness, for the association comes only through the adoptive family of her Afro-Russian father. In *Panic in a Suitcase*, Esther Nasmertov, Pasha's mother, gestures toward Jewishness only when she encounters its obliteration; namely, when she is faced with Pasha—a convert to Russian Orthodoxy—wearing a cross necklace, she vehemently protests this irreverence. For his niece's sake, for little Frida, he should take it off, his mother urges him. Pasha's conversion is "an open wound on the family flesh."[76] In an interview, Akhtiorskaya expands on how Soviet-born Jewishness is read in the United States that it appears present mostly as an absence: "That is how I feel about it personally, and that is why it is so hard for me to talk about it. I could have longings that it would have been more of a presence, but I know it as an absence that in some way you get defined around. It is like a huge ghost or something, like a huge hole."[77]

The connecting tissue between the novel's two parts, central for interpreting metageographical interventions, first emerges in a scene that illustrates parallels between the main protagonists: the young, similarly contrarian Frida and her uncle Pasha. A Harvard professor of Slavic studies, John Lamborg, who is interested in translating and publishing Pasha's poems, visits the American Nasmertovs in their home in 1994. After "the routine immigration narrative that they were replaying for their guest," Lamborg engages ten-year-old Frida with an unreflective, nonchalant question: "[D]o you like it here?"[78] Akhtiorskaya's narrator is offended for Frida, who remains silent: "It was difficult to fathom a more catastrophically off-the-mark question. Here—as opposed to where? If there had been a somewhere else, Frida was currently engaged in an immense struggle to extract every last trace of it from her DNA."[79] Lamborg resembles other recurring figures in American immigrant fiction, such as the sociologist Frank Baker in Anzia Yezierska's short story "Children of Loneliness": an educated outsider, often a professor, thirsty for knowledge about immigrants, and patronizing. Lamborg's attitude points to a set of blanket assumptions about migrants, about how, regardless of their age, they are determined by their pasts elsewhere, their pre-immigration existence. Frida's intuitive silence calls into question the idea of immigrant "Second Worlds," but it also conjures up the elsewhere that, apparently unextractable "from her DNA," propels the second part of the novel.

The change of locale, about fifty pages into the second part of the book, is not a decorative move but rather signals a change in the underlying structure of the plot. The narration advances in an orderly manner in the first part of the novel and in the section of the second part that is still set in the United States. The plot here predictably follows the typical family and life-stage events. In the first part, these include Pasha's first visit, the grandmother's birthday, a family vacation, the grandmother's illness, another Pasha visit, and the grandmother's death; meanwhile, the U.S. section of the second part reveals a general marital malaise between Pasha's immigrant sister Marina and her husband Levik, punctuated by appearances of their disgruntled daughter (and Pasha's niece), Frida. As many readers complain, there is not so much a plot as a composite of vignettes;[80] the scenes that appear all the more tedious because they are fed by the normative middle-class family life with its imperfections that the Nasmertovs successfully model. Pasha's distanced perspective and Akhtiorskaya's linguistic flexibility and inventiveness groom these well-known grooves for an impending breakthrough, which, however, does not adhere to the usual immigrant genre expectations. For Akhtiorskaya such a mixed popular reception is linked with market expectations of what immigrant writing is: "Any kind of given about the plot has to do with marketing. There is an idea for what an immigrant story should be and I do not think *Panic in a Suitcase* is that."[81]

Indeed, later chapters set in Ukraine's Odessa refuse to develop along previously established lines. Frida's discomfort with the assumptions governing the American lives of the Nasmertovs is legible in her desire to attend her cousin Sanya's wedding in Odessa. It includes a critique of heteronormative middle-class respectability: Frida is attracted by the short-term announcement of the Odessa wedding, which marks a stark contrast to "a decade [spent] orchestrating an apocalyptic celebration with registries and flower arrangements and twenty-piece band."[82] Yet the plot doubles down on Frida's critique of normalcy: the moment she arrives in Odessa, the wedding is promptly canceled. It is merely an introduction to how the plot—seemingly irresponsibly—stalls, unravels, and then restarts. For example, only a few days later, the wedding is re-announced. And although the trip is purportedly to visit family, Frida never meets Sanya in the narrated time, despite plans having been made. Similarly, after a couple of days, it turns out that the uncle who was supposed to be hosting her in Odessa together with his younger life partner Sveta declares that he is leaving the town for a poetry festival, without telling Frida that Sveta's relatives are soon arriving at the apartment in Odessa for their vacation. The *dacha* that the American Nasmertovs romanticize is not the pastoral haven of their past with raspberry bushes and apricot trees, "an Eden from which they could be evicted,"[83] but a grim refuge for Pasha's estranged wife and her relatives who suffered from the Chernobyl catastrophe. Yet in this setting where there are no expectations of Frida, where events do not occur as expected and where the nuclear family fails to serve as the basic social unit, Frida acquires the agency that she was stripped of in Brighton Beach. This setting is generative for Frida, who feels empowered to question, if not abandon, the career path in medicine she was forced to take, as well as the expectations of the label "model minority," and to follow the now nascent creative impulses that she discovers through her exposure to her uncle Pasha.[84]

Travel is known to be a plot device that has a heightened liberatory potential;[85] in this narrative, read within the metageographical framework, it is also a comment on how we ascribe meanings to space and construct their hierarchy. Akhtiorskaya offers travel stories that make statements about migrant spaces. Like other works of "The Literature of New Arrival," to use Bharati Mukherjee's phrase, *Panic in a Suitcase* is a post-assimilationist narrative—that is, a narrative that challenges the primacy of the immigration destination.[86] While Uncle Pasha introduces the intellectual and affective arguments against emigration, Frida challenges the sedimented perception of the oppressive "old country."[87] Her positionality is key here: a young child émigré whose memories—unpopulated by stories and images of Odessa but for a sliver of playground topography—are barely triggered by photos and family stories. She may not remember much, but she is interested in visiting the place as it is: "I'll make more memories now."[88] As a counterpoint, Akhtiorskaya satirizes the

"Odessa instructions" provided by Frida's mother, these Soviet and early post-Soviet memories translated into pieces of advice.[89] Frida does not "return" to Ukraine, a frame that third-generation Holocaust survivor stories use, because there is no memorial template that she acknowledges as hers. She does not visit her great-grandparents in the Jewish cemetery of Odessa, despite her parents' guidelines, but rather engages in her genealogy through her uncle, whose attitudes she clearly espouses. The narrative concerning Frida and her visit to Odessa is not an attempt to compete with the memory of Jewish life in pre-Holocaust Europe; instead, it endeavors to fill in the gaps in the memory of the remaining Soviet and post-Soviet Jewish life in Eastern Europe—here, specifically Ukraine. Akhtiorskaya's mention of the Chernobyl disaster foregrounds a memory path that may at times be obfuscated but that complements and overlays earlier Eastern European traumatic events, as will become apparent in the next chapter, covering the memory of World War II and the Holocaust in a Soviet context.

This reciprocal post-immigrant tourism of the late 2000s challenges the distance in time and space that has constituted the backbone of so many narratives about immigration and its finality. Akhtiorskaya hinted at this changed dynamic in an interview: "When everyone was going, there was the idea that this was a final break. There was an idea that there was never going to be a return. It is a kind of a practical joke that then happened where everything got connected back again [after the fall of communism], and none of that finality was there."[90] Post–Cold War post-immigrant tourism differs greatly from the experiences of Soviet refugees who arrived in the United States in the 1970s, not to mention those of Southeast Asian refugees at the same time nor Russo-Ukrainian war refugees after 2022. With its reciprocal possibilities and its linking of migration and tourism, the phenomenon represents a "light" version of post–Cold War migration and mobility, in contrast to both Ulinich's *Petropolis*, in which only the single mother protagonist is able to travel, and post-2014 narratives concerning the annexation of Crimea and full-scale invasion on Ukraine in 2022.[91] At the same time, the intertwining of migration and tourism in Akhtiorskaya's texts provides a commentary on post–Cold War third-generation Holocaust survivors' "return journeys," with their circularity of memory predicated on a greater generational distance and a different understanding of space and place.[92]

By focusing on the movement between the Odessas of family members of different genders and generations, Akhtiorskaya is able to present a much more dynamic picture of the mutually dependent similarities and differences of these worlds. Her focus on the ocean as framing both of these locations signals not only a continuity between them, but also—however idealized—their fluid bidirectional and global relation. Characteristically, the novel's cover photo of a calm, steel blue ocean blending almost imperceptibly into the cloudy sky, with

FIGURE 3 Emine Ziyatdinova, from *Brighton Beach Photo Series*, 2012.

an elderly female bather in a bright orange swim cap, could have been taken in either Odessa or Brooklyn in the 2000s.[93] After reading the novel, the cover image and its title make us think: Whose suitcase is marked by the titular panic? What is the destination of this luggage? It could be the suitcase of the Nasmertovs at the time of their immigration, Uncle Pasha's when he visits them in Brighton Beach, or Frida's when she travels to Odessa. Through the post-immigrant reciprocal tourism presented in the text, Akhtiorskaya opens up these various interpretative possibilities. Narrative connections and continuities between Odessa and Brighton Beach challenge assumptions about immigrant notions of place and disrupt the supposedly rigid hierarchical difference of the "Second World," just as the cover photo does (figure 3). The post-immigrant reciprocity of movement—Pasha visiting Brooklyn and Frida traveling to Odessa—also helps actualize Ukraine as a living space and intervene with the metageographical assumptions concerning that world's pastness and separateness between the end of the Cold War and the beginning of the full-scale Russian invasion in Ukraine.

Post-Soviet Diasporic Connections

Literary settings created by Soviet-born Jewish writers in English vary greatly: some texts take place exclusively in the United States or Canada, while others negotiate various places of the (former) Soviet Union or span different locations

32 • Soviet-Born

to emphasize forms of mobility—namely, migration and tourism. With such varied Euro-Asian settings, this literature challenges the sometimes-imagined unity of "(post-)Soviet" and invites reconfigurations, or even rejections, of the post–Cold War three-world model. The texts gesture toward diasporic thinking, enter into a dialogue with other literatures of migration, and recreate post-Soviet Jewish spaces.

In *Petropolis*, on the other hand, Ulinich mimics the dominant imperial metageography not only of Eastern Europe but of post-Soviet space more broadly, channeling the Americans Sasha encounters in Arizona. But Sasha's character does point to transregional parallels between Arizona and Siberia based on their environments. In the few instances where Ulinich refers to the environment of the Southwest, she suggests that its natural conditions do not in fact seem natural. For example, Sasha "imagined that aliens had abducted the people here, while the wind from their spacecraft killed and mangled the plants, leaving an occasional squat cactus, a crooked palm tree, an evergreen hedge."[94] It is in this sense—the prodigious amount of human intervention and modification to an initially adversarial environment—that she perceives a resemblance between the American Southwest and the Russian Northeast: "Whose idea was it to build the city here? You can't open the windows, you can't go outside for five months."[95] When then asked by her friend Marina whether that makes it "worse than Siberia," she replies that it is not. Difference is thus produced only after a potential for comparison is suggested. Even though Sasha later travels to Chicago and New York, which are perceived as being much more traditionally Jewish places in the United States, the novel focuses on Jewishness in these other, more unlikely settings in both worlds. Creating environmentally based transregional affinities of the borderlands allows Ulinich to forge narrative connections between the two regions, which in the novel are also linked by the protagonist's travels as well as media representations. Ulinich goes even further to emphasize how these connections could have been even stronger if edited differently: "I wish that somebody would offer me another title, and that somebody told me to stop starting stories in Russia, to start it in the U.S. to make it more relatable."[96]

In Akhtiorskaya's *Panic in a Suitcase*, the construction of main protagonists Pasha and Frida, as well as the unobvious links between the two Odessas, rely on networks characterized by multiple directionalities and connections. In contrast to Ulinich's novel, this one does start in the United States. However, apart from plotlines centered on different forms of mobility across borders and regions, this novel restyles metageographical meanings using the basic associative imagery of Brighton Beach present on the novel's cover—namely, the ocean. In a photo essay on Brighton Beach, Akhtiorskaya confessed, "We were part of the Odessa diaspora, unable to resist the allure of the water, so reminiscent of our beloved Black Sea home."[97] Following this "allure of the water" and a certain environmental sensibility, *Panic in a Suitcase* entices its readers to think about the regional affinities of "coastal peoples."[98] These affinities are unobstructed by geopolitical dynamics and the post–Cold War hierarchy of worlds. The novel articulates a specific logic of belonging that is based on proximity and relation to the ocean, also a hallmark of, for example, Caribbean writing, using the ocean to reformulate the concept of identity and belonging as anchored in territory.[99] "Coastal peoples" becomes a key category that runs across multiple delimiting and metageographical identifications—those of imagined nationness, ethnicity, or region. Ocean becomes an element, gains a pronounced planetary dimension, spanning the globe and idealistically connecting "coastal peoples." Akhtiorskaya's comments may seem hyperbolic or somewhat pompous, yet they sketch an alternative, nonlinear topographical connection among peoples living in the littoral space.[100]

This sense of a connective environment permeates the novel: as described above, just after Pasha arrives in Brooklyn in the first chapter, the family organizes a beach escapade to welcome him that prepares readers to think about geographical meanings; in the second part of the novel, Akhtiorskaya imagistically illustrates Marina's innate affinity with the ocean—her name literally means "of the sea"—when it envelops her on the beach at night; and finally, Frida's encounter with the Black Sea is a variation on the "epic storm" experienced by Pasha in Brighton Beach earlier in the book. The ocean is a force unmarked and undivided by metageographical distinctions into historically defined discrete bodies of water. I am not suggesting we read *Panic in a Suitcase* as radically questioning "sea as a metaphor,"[101] as it does not focus on the materiality of the maritime world, which is one of the postulates that can lead to questioning the dominance of continents in metageography. At the same time, Akhtiorskaya attempts to create a new sense of relatedness, a diaspora without a center, but linked through the ocean—the ocean "as constructed, but also as shaper," as one critic wrote in a different context.[102]

This idea of the ocean as defining the space and connecting the past, present, and future of the Nasmertovs works hand in hand with the complex connectedness of the two worlds. Akhtiorskaya expressed this connectedness through the ocean visible in the novel in contrast to the land: "It is such a primal connection to the ocean that it's almost beyond words. It's almost like it's hard to try to put it into words. On land, you kind of always feel so anxious, which I think is also such an immigrant kind of experience, like an immense kind of anxiety."[103] By spanning a period of more than twenty years and by focusing on linked immigration and, to some extent, reciprocal postimmigration tourism in the time of peace, the novel skillfully introduces confusion between the two coastal locations of Odessas with regard to their hierarchical position, temporal belonging, and originality, using gender and family norms to underpin these displacements. The vignette-like and imagistic quality of the text, with its sometimes-meandering sentences, slows down reading and reveals these constructed connections that unsettle metageographical habits. Akhtiorskaya's Брайтон Бич, as she transcribes "Brighton Beach" into Cyrillic in her photo essay, is not an "insular demiworld" or an "ethnic enclave." More specifically, it is not devalued like a "demiworld" and lacks the enclosed quality and separateness of an imagined "enclave." And as a metaphorical "island"—similar to Ulinich's Siberia—it is not cut off from other places but rather showcases how seemingly discrete locations are connected by human mobility into a network of belonging.

Nonimmigrant Jewish writers' "return narratives" cast the region as belonging to, and remaining mired in, the Jewish past. This separateness in time becomes also a broader, metageographical separateness: post–Cold War Eastern Europe is bracketed off as belonging to the "Second World." In *Petropolis* and *Panic in a Suitcase*, dramatizations of lived migrant connections between U.S. and post-Soviet places break down this separateness. Migration actualizes these spaces, as does characterizing the migrant homeland not as an imagined Eastern Europe but, less conceptually, as the very real USSR—a distinct, formerly existing state (however conglomerate). Because distinct settings give life to literary narratives, these novels localize and show variety in the former Soviet Union, exploring the specific environments of Moscow, Ukrainian Odessa, and Asbestos 2 (even if the last is fictional). Further, literary elements—plotlines, descriptions, dialogues—point to diasporic connections and underscore the similarities of these regional or local settings. Literariness shapes links between the post–Cold War "Second World," immigrant points of departure, and the biographical and literal "Second Worlds" of migrant arrival and life in new lands.

2

Redefining Survival

In the opening of David Bezmozgis's short story "An Animal to the Memory" (2004), narrator Mark Berman reminisces about his experience as a seventh-grade student: "I never heard dirty Jew," he recalls, but "dirty Russian tended to come up. Particularly in Hebrew school. Not very often, but often enough that I felt justified in using it as an excuse when I tried to convince my parents to let me transfer to a normal public school."[1] Berman, an immigrant from the Soviet Union, here points to a set of categories among which "Russian" is the marker of difference. Ultimately, his "campaign" to leave Hebrew day school fails because his parents insist that he stay to learn "what it was to be a Jew."[2] As becomes clear, moreover, this meaning of Jewishness was inextricably linked to the memory of the Holocaust. The story renders Berman's Jewish education as instruction in remembrance, and it further suggests that his Russian difference is responsible for his failure to properly celebrate Holocaust Remembrance Day at school.

When Mark comes down to the basement hall at school to see the commemorative exhibit, he is mostly interested in active Jewish resistance to Nazi persecution. A raucous teenager himself, he gets shoved and immediately retaliates with even more force. As a result, during the solemn ceremony led by the school principal, a rabbi, a Holocaust survivor, and the author of a published Holocaust memoir, exhibition objects are broken and the ritual of the ceremony is interrupted. In a physically and emotionally intense interaction, Mark is reprimanded by the principal in the candlelit basement exhibit and thus initiated and assimilated into a collective memory of the Holocaust. But his Russianness had been, and in many ways continues to be, his more salient identity of difference.

Bezmozgis's 2011 novel *The Free World* picks up on the themes of his earlier short story, exploring the difference that "Russian" makes in Holocaust remembrance and war memorialization. Indeed, for much recent fiction by Soviet-born writers, the adjective "Russian" often functions as a marketing brand or a category of difference within Jewish contexts. *The Free World* and the other two literary works discussed in this chapter focus precisely on "Russian" stories, mostly of Jewish Red Army soldiers and evacuation into the Soviet interior, and ask how they matter in the American memorial landscape. The figure of the Soviet war veteran populates much Soviet-born Jewish fiction in English. In Gary Shteyngart's foundational *A Russian Debutante's Handbook* (2002), the eccentric Russian who propels the plot is also a war veteran.[3] Moreover, as a young boy, the protagonist of the novel would routinely go with his grandmother to visit the Piskaryovskoye Memorial Cemetery for the defenders of Leningrad, including his grandfather Moysei and other civilian victims of the siege.[4] Indeed, the war is present in casual conversations throughout Soviet-born writing, shaping, for example, the dialogues between the protagonist and her grandmother in Maria Kuznetsova's *Something Unbelievable*.[5] The loss of Jewish lives in war and in the Holocaust is an omnipresent undercurrent in these works.

Among the many novels, short story and poetry volumes, memoirs, and graphic novels published within the "new wave" of Soviet-born writing, these three novels in particular—David Bezmozgis's *The Free World* (2011), Boris Fishman's *A Replacement Life* (2014), and Julia Alekseyeva's graphic novel *Soviet Daughter* (2017)[6]—contribute to what I call post-Soviet migrant memory of the Holocaust. This literature stages converging histories of the same events on a global scale by adding a story determined by the Soviet experience and by the Soviet strategy of curbing movement and migration—a story that now enters migrant writing in English.

Like Bezmozgis's protagonist in "An Animal to the Memory," this fiction, in its migrant condition, stands at the crossroads of American and Soviet genealogies of memory. It is informed by the Soviet cultural memory of "the catastrophe," as the Jewish genocide is often termed in Russian, and by the "imperfect silence" about this genocide in the Soviet Union.[7] The silencing, or erasing, of the event in Soviet memory occurred on political grounds. Namely, it was often subsumed under the murder of universalized Soviet citizens, which foregrounded the sheer immensity of Soviet civilian losses generally, estimated at around 18 million.[8] Political scientist Zvi Gitelman explains that the Jewishness of the victims was typically muted in the Eastern Bloc because it served the "friendship of the peoples . . . and proletarian internationalism"; in other words, workers' solidarity was to transcend any ethnic or religious designations.[9]

However, as historian Tarik Amar and others have demonstrated, this silencing was not the result of a coherent Soviet policy; it existed only as a general tendency and so remained "imperfect."[10] Accordingly, the Soviet memory of the Holocaust was not absent but rather less codified. Soviet literary and film representations of the Holocaust generated less victim-centered meanings,[11] especially because of their representation of Jewish Red Army soldiers.[12] Consequently, in the context of Soviet memory, we need "a broadened definition of what constitutes a Jewish response to the Holocaust," one that would counter tacit cultural assumptions as to what the Holocaust signifies in American and Israeli culture.[13]

Anglophone fiction by immigrants from the former Soviet Union not only locates its characters within the reach of Soviet and diasporic post-Soviet memory, but also, with the Soviet setting of some of these stories, expands geographically and conceptually the dominant American narrative of the Holocaust—which focuses rather narrowly on death camps, especially those in Nazi-occupied Poland—by adding tales about escape, hiding, shooting sites, and the ghettos in various locations in Europe. To put it briefly, the Holocaust is remembered differently, and it is a different Holocaust that is remembered. Parallel to Soviet Jewish writing on the Holocaust, these works illustrate what literary scholar Harriet Murav calls a "different trajectory" of the Holocaust in the Soviet Union.[14] Moreover, considering that up to 1.635 million Jews living within the 1941 Soviet borders either evacuated or escaped to the East,[15] examining this "different trajectory" means also expanding the definition of "survivor" to include those who fled to the eastern Soviet Union.[16]

These particular convergences of, first, the Soviet experience, the effects of Soviet memory politics, and migration narratives, and second, the American (post–)Cold War context foster a new mode of thinking about connective pasts. While such theorizing builds on earlier work on connective memories that uses postcolonial theory and critical race theory to contextualize antisemitic violence vis-à-vis other racially motivated oppressions, the intersections that these particular texts bring to the foreground differ for several reasons. First, they include diverse paths of historical violence, but all linked to Jewishness: the synergies and divergences that appear here stem from immigrant Soviet-born and American native-born Jewishness, and the mnemonic assumptions that are inherent in them. Second, they are predicated most centrally on a Cold War economy of Holocaust and war memory. Because of the Cold War dynamic, communist memory of the Holocaust did not help constitute the "global" Holocaust memory developing from the 1970s. Also, Soviet Jewish combat experience did not form a part of the well-known Jewish narratives of World War II outside of the Soviet Union. In this case, it is then the Cold War logic (and its afterlives) that privileges certain narratives as intelligible forms of victimhood—for instance, making them worthy of compensation. Third, these narratives center migration and refugeeness, with their bureaucratic as well as existential aspects. With these at the forefront, the "correct" Holocaust and war memory becomes a key asset—or a significant hindrance—not only in the fight for individual recognition but also within the bureaucratic processes of applying for visas or for restitution. Silencing Soviet-inflected memory may be the price of eligibility for refugee status: as human geographers Thomas Lacroix and Elena Fiddian-Qasmiyeh note in the context of migrant memory, "What, and indeed who, one chooses to remember (and to forget) derives from a political positioning towards the 'others,' be they sending and receiving state authorities, or other diasporic groups."[17] While the nation-state is often critically approached in memory studies, frequently held responsible for staging memory competitiveness, it becomes especially salient in its double role as both a "significant player" in memory politics and a creator of migration regulations.[18]

To a large extent, complex decolonial models of memory making attempt to illuminate intersections of oppression and expose structures of privilege at *one particular location*, often determined by the nation-state. As Max Silverman wrote in the context of Holocaust and colonial memory representation in France, texts create layers of signification or "palimpsestic memory": "a superimposition and interaction of different *temporal* traces [that] constitute a sort of composite structure, like a palimpsest, so that one layer of traces can be seen through, and is transformed by, another."[19] This model radically expands the singular context into a multidimensional matrix—a complex web of histories, hard to disentangle from one another, pulling in different directions.

Yet narrated pasts encountering each other in Soviet-born writing in English are predicated on not a temporal but a *spatial* convergence brought about by migration. The disparate elements are not superimposed on each other in a temporally stratified way, some peeking out through others. Rather, like the opening of Bezmozgis's story, these narratives occasion a meeting of elements that do not fit neatly into a single layer, as they might in Silverman's image. In these texts, they are instead the disparate pieces of an assemblage, an assemblage that may be imagined as a layer—unified, smooth—but in fact its various pieces compete for legibility and legitimacy.

These various pieces—that is, versions of both dominant and marginalized memories of the war and the Holocaust—collide, testing their malleability and potential for interaction. Even if theoretical models of collective memory call for general inclusivity, for migrants these versions compete with one another in matches of uneven strength due to the hierarchical relations between them. This competition may also have an existential value, be it advantage in applications for refugee status and compensation or legibility within a community. The texts here illustrate the price of Soviet-born stories, of Soviet-born memory, based on what is marginalized and disremembered because of a Cold War anti-Soviet bias.[20]

As memory studies scholar Julia Creet notices, "displacement intensifies investment in memory."[21] Migration encourages and pressures one into—often even necessitates—giving an account of oneself, remembering or disremembering the past in order to decide the present; it generates a constant pressure to say who you are in a context in which the meaning of experiences is far from obvious. Migration is but one aspect of Astrid Erll's concept traveling memory, which is characterized by "circulation among social, medial, and semantic dimensions."[22] Namely, it is the aspect linked to memory's "carriers" or, to stress their agency, its actors. Erll notes that memory's "movement across boundaries is always contingent on specific possibilities and restrictions, which can be of a medial, social, political, or semantic nature."[23] But migration, and especially forced migration and refugeeness, creates a setting for transcultural memory whose analysis barely comports with the metaphoricity of memory flows through symbols or global media. As demonstrated by the literary texts in this chapter, the encounter between nationally bounded kinds of mnemonic logic becomes especially salient in this context.

Further, migration not only influences how memory travels but is constitutive of the narrative patterns employed in the literary texts under scrutiny. The particularity of literary discourse in the works discussed in this chapter appears against bureaucratic discourse (visa and compensation applications), which literature amplifies and defamiliarizes at the same time. In Bezmozgis's *The Free World*, refugee statelessness in Italy and the need to write refugee application narratives trigger old memories of the eldest Krasnansky, Samuil, a veteran and "true believer" in communism.[24] Fishman's *A Replacement Life* traces the remembrance of war and the Holocaust in a distinctly (post-)Soviet migrant "enclave" in South Brooklyn, probing the legal and ethical ramifications of writing fraudulent Holocaust compensation applications. The affordances of the third text, a graphic novel, are only more visible after these readings: the book re-narrates a memoir written by a migrant in the United States who was once a Jewish Red Army soldier. The visual layer hyper-represents the Soviet-inflected displacement of American memory images. In this way, these texts are both memory-productive, since "they reinforce existing structures of cultural schematization, but also generate new ones,"[25] as well as memory-reflexive, revealing to us how memory is made.[26] The texts use various aspects of the memory of migration to produce the Soviet-inflected memory of war and the Holocaust in English and reflect how Soviet and post-Soviet migration reshapes these narratives.

Aspects of Sovietness related to the war, the Holocaust, and memory making are responsible, then, for a set of conceptual diasporic displacements that distinguish these texts. Migration inflects the narrative patterns employed and shapes what is representationally possible, which readers of Jewish American writing may be not used to. At the same time, these narratives renew older narrative patterns that characterized earlier Jewish American literary strands. Given the complex dynamics of memory, these novels further cement the close link between the war and the Holocaust that was characteristic of Jewish American writing in the late 1940s and revolved around the figure of the Jewish American soldier.[27] But unlike much of that literature, these texts revisit that link specifically in the context of the Holocaust in the East, allowing us to diversify the meaning of survival and think further about how the assemblage of remembering war and the Holocaust changes with the narratives of migration in diasporic writing.

Another set of displacements relates to the *nonimmigrant* Jewish American literary authors who also write on the Holocaust—a dynamic partly explored in chapter 1. All the texts considered in this chapter are written by the grandchildren of Holocaust survivors and nominally belong to American third-generation Holocaust literature. Formally, their writing exemplifies this literature's key features. In the words of literary scholars Victoria Aarons and Alan Berger, "afterknowledge [of the Holocaust], both real and fantasized, takes shape in the stories acquired by the third generation through competing versions, mired accounts, and in the interstices of fantasy."[28] Yet the generational distance feels smaller. In the diasporic texts, the postmemory of war and the Holocaust essentially intersects with the memory of migration on two levels: first, the stories of war, the Holocaust, and migration converge in the narrated stories of survivors themselves; second, the memory of migration shapes the lives of third-generation narrators and/or protagonists. This supplies additional lines of identification—beyond family bonds and Jewishness—with the characters' (and their community's) grandmothers and grandfathers, and it opens us to new narrative possibilities. Additionally, it complicates the chronological generational narrative, something I return to in chapter 5. These Soviet-born grandchildren of Holocaust survivors and/or war veterans write from a historical distance about stories of survival and simultaneously create their grandparents', as well as their own, stories of migration and diasporic memory.

Moreover, the novels I examine here redefine survival by including the Soviet trajectory of World War II and its communist memory. Yet these traces of communist memory only signal the deeper entanglements of this fiction in the whole spectrum of the memory of communism/state socialism, themes I explore more extensively in chapters 3 and 4. Especially in *The Free World* and *Soviet Daughter*, the war and its "concurrent" event, the Holocaust, take place within the larger story of communism starting in the 1910s.[29] Alekseyeva's *Soviet Daughter*, while somewhat concerned with the Soviet trajectory of World War II and the Holocaust in the East, centrally builds migrant leftist political affinities across generations of women within a family in an effort to reevaluate the memory of early Soviet Russia. These connections to Soviet, and particularly early Soviet, history provide an occasion to further showcase gendered entanglements of diasporic post-Soviet memory making.

Survival without "Survivors par Excellence": David Bezmozgis's *The Free World*

The phrase "Jewish survivors of the Holocaust" sounds redundant today, even if that was not the case in the 1980s.[30] Despite the broadening of its multiple legal and social definitions, "survivor" still most often denotes a "survivor par excellence,"[31] a person who lived through the ghettos and concentration camps, or survived by disguising themselves or hiding. In David Bezmozgis's first novel, *The Free World* (2011), the word "Holocaust" does not appear even once, but the book does contain Jewish stories of survival: the story of Samuil Krasnansky, a Jewish Red Army soldier, and the story of his family members, who evacuated to the Soviet interior from Riga ahead of the advancing Nazi forces. Bezmozgis has said he was guided by "a strange missionary feeling" as he wrote this prequel to his stories of immigration, narrating a Soviet Jewish experience in a way he thought to be pioneering in English[32]: "The idea behind Samuel was to present a type of Soviet Jew who I think has been lost to the popular memory in North America anyway, and is quite distinct from Jews of his generation in North America."[33] It tells the story of a Jewish revolutionary communist past and of the Great Patriotic War, of ambivalent success and oppression within the communist regime, and of one multigenerational family's immigration in the late 1970s. Samuil, an older World War II veteran applying for refugee status in Europe, serves here as a representative of Jewish combat experience. His memories of war and the Holocaust, elicited by the need to write a narrative for a refugee application decades later, convey the tension between his former status as a celebrated veteran and successful communist operative and his current, often humiliating position as a migrant and a refugee applicant. At the same time, the elements of remembrances, with their different valences and levels of legitimacy, implicate Samuil in the functioning of the late Soviet regime. The bureaucratic process of migration and refugee application places pressure conducive to a strategically selective remembering: it creates the conditions for writing over one's own memories and at the same time makes earlier erasures visible.

The Free World takes place in 1978. A sixty-five-year-old "true believer" in communism has just arrived with his large family in Ladispoli, Italy, having come from Riga, Latvia, on their way to cross the ocean.[34] In his view, Samuil Krasnansky is an "old useless man."[35] As the family settles in Italy, waiting for three months to go through the asylum application process, Samuil's main preoccupation is recollection. "This concerted effort at remembering,"[36] sparked by the "persecution statement" required for his refugee status application, takes him back to prerevolutionary Russia, the Russian revolution, and World War II, known as the Great Patriotic War. Because he is consumed by writing an "account of his life,"[37] everything Samuil sees around himself appears as traces of the past. A decorated veteran, he scrutinizes the medals worn by older immigrants with the zealous passion of a detective: "Samuil paid close attention to the decorations he saw other men wearing. He saw one man with an Order of the Red Banner, extremely rare for a Jew if it was authentic. He saw another man with a chestful of campaign ribbons, attesting to a prolonged, almost miraculous, frontline tenure. Most, however, possessed the standard commendations that accrued to anyone who survived the war: combatant medal, bravery medal, victory over Germany medal, and the commemorative decorations issued to mark the jubilees of triumph: one decade, two decades, a quarter century."[38] Samuil reads these decorations as indications of how these veterans "survived the war," having internalized an understanding of "survival" as surviving *combat* and not—as English speakers might assume—surviving *the Holocaust*. War medals pinned to the chests of veterans function as a symbolic reminder of the status Samuil enjoyed in Riga. Sections of Rome and its environs teem with older men wearing Soviet war medals. They remind him not only of his own combat experience—"there were only several that were more decorated than he"[39]—but also of the hardships of the migration pipeline: as the property of the Soviet Union, his medals had been confiscated at the border. At the border, then, Samuil symbolically transforms from decorated war veteran into "traitor Jew,"[40] as the customs official had called him while tossing his medals into a bin full of the miscellaneous possessions of émigrés.

Among the older migrants in Ladispoli, the transit visa processing site close to Rome, medals take on new emblematic functions, signaling common pasts and the potential for further solidarity. Encouraged by the man's decorations, Samuil befriends "a small, one-legged man with an Order of the Red Star."[41] This fellow veteran, Roidman, becomes Samuil's friendly companion, playing chess with him, complaining about the Canadian immigration process (which was biased against older persons), and distracting Samuil from his thoughts of suicide—thoughts that ultimately led to nothing because "after a lifetime spent evading death, the habit of survival was deeply engrained."[42] Toward the end of the novel, Roidman lends Samuil his medals for the Canadian embassy interview. Even though such military decorations were known to ensure preferential treatment in the Soviet era—for example, helping one gain admission to a university—for Samuil, using medals as currency on the immigration market confuses epistemic orders: "How could he explain to his wife, Emma, the disgrace of using the medals of a Red Army soldier to curry the favor of some petty capitalist official?"[43] Both within the Soviet citizenship hierarchy and to Samuil personally the medals indicated status, desirability and in the end veteran solidarity that here also pushes Roidman to lend his medals to the elder Krasnansky. These previously obvious symbolic characteristics of the military decoration now became potentially necessary in order to painstakingly explain and defend to an embassy bureaucrat at the risk of being not compatible with and rather hardly translatable into the pragmatic exigencies of consular processes.

Samuil's narrative voice—one of three that alternate throughout the book—is representative of a number of older Soviet immigrants, both men and women, whose life stories have intervened into the transnational memory of World War II, especially in four countries that served as major destinations of Soviet immigration: Germany, Israel, Canada, and the United States.[44] Of the 300,000 to 500,000 Jewish soldiers who served in the Red Army during World War II,[45] an estimated 26,000 moved to these countries in the 1990s.[46] As Anna Shternshis noted in 2011, Soviet veterans "regarded their participation in the war as the most important part of their Jewish identity, and they were often shocked to find out how *little* the war meant to the Jewish identity of the local populations they encountered."[47] For these men, their veteran status was more central than "their Jewish ethnicity."[48]

Why would immigrant Soviet Jewish veterans perceive themselves in such different terms if the participation of over half a million American Jewish soldiers in World War II had also "changed a generation," to use historian Deborah Dash Moore's famous phrase?[49] With reference to literature, after an initial flurry of war novels by Jewish American ex-soldiers, their retrospection on the war was largely pushed to the side.[50] Simultaneously, Holocaust memory has become a key coordinate of American Jewishness, and "surviving" has sedimented as essentially linked to the Holocaust.[51] The memorial paths of Jewish soldiers in the Soviet Union were rather different. Even though Jewish Soviet soldiers were first to witness the atrocities of the Holocaust,[52] the memory of the catastrophe as an atrocity against Jews was veiled by "an imperfect silence" in the Soviet Union. Simultaneously, veterans of the war, including Jewish veterans, were celebrated for decades as Soviet heroes, which elevated their combat experience to the central element of who they were.[53]

Because Red Army experience could be considered part of a universal Soviet experience, unconditioned by antisemitism,[54] the figure of the Soviet Jewish soldier does not sit comfortably within the early twenty-first-century American memorial landscape. Soviet Jewish veterans represent "migrant memory,"[55] meaning here that they come from a different national memorial lineage, where "surviving" extends its field of meaning to include, in this case, surviving combat. They are the decorated war heroes, widely commemorated for decades in the former Soviet Union, who even today celebrate the Soviet Victory Day (May 9) in the migrant neighborhood of Brighton Beach, holding a parade for the event as recently as 2015.[56] Their migrant status is underscored by the marginalization of their particular memory of World War II, a memory that—like the May 9 Victory Day—is not recognized outside their community. Their particular memory of the war further intersects with the memory of migration because—as Bezmozgis makes clear in his novel—in the context of the visa application process, their celebrated status within communist memory and their potential affinity with the communist system were transvalued and could become liabilities.

While war memories are central to Samuil Krasnansky's narrative, they are elicited by the current context of migration and immersed in postwar remembrances of the communist regime. Together, they form conflicting elements, tenuous in the migrant legal limbo at Ladispoli, this "Italian purgatory."[57] Migration prompts the erasure of communist memory, but at the same time adds another valence: it reveals the earlier erasures of Holocaust survival stories, or early twentieth-century Zionism, under communism. This connection between migration and memories of war appears promptly in the first chapter, focalized by Samuil as the family's train from Vienna approaches Rome. The memories are triggered by the specific circumstances the Krasnanskys find themselves in and underscore the tension between Samuil's former and current status: "When last he had seen Austrians like these [in green uniforms], they had been marching in long, dejected columns under Soviet command. He had been a young officer then."[58] Memories of the war color his perception of migration. His bitterness comes from experiencing radically shifted (gender) hierarchies in comparison with the times just after Soviet victory: "Men still chose their words carefully when addressing him. Fussy women with clipboards had not felt entitled to pry into his thoughts and personal affairs."[59] A decorated war veteran and former Soviet factory director, Samuil acutely feels what he perceives as a lack of respect. The gender-discriminating language he uses throughout the novel may be a marker of his age. At the same time, it also speaks to the loss of those privileges he enjoyed as a member of the Riga elite, indiscriminately pursuing romances with—or, to put it in a different discourse, perhaps sexually harassing—his female employees, as suggested by his daughter-in-law. Even if we acknowledge the theses about the Soviet and late Soviet masculinity crisis, migration only makes it more acute.[60] Samuil's memory flow as he nears Rome that contrasts the combat past and migrant present serves as a soft prelude to the immigration application process in Rome where the communist past and present are not only in contrast, but his partly even glorious communist memory needs to be displaced to fit the dominant blanket anti-communist Western narrative.

Belief in communist ideals and participation in the communist system are liabilities during the Cold War when bartering for American refugee status that was predicated on the persecution of Jews by this very regime. One of the characters tells us that "Americans regard Communists the way Canadians regard invalids."[61] The forms leave little space for ambiguities, which might easily become traces of damning complicity. No wonder, then, that a friend encourages Samuil to camouflage his communist past and regard the Party story section of the application form cynically, as something that does not need to be honest since it is "only between one's self and the American immigration service."[62] Yet Samuil is unnerved by thoughts "of the dozens, the hundreds if not thousands of Party stories being written by traitors and prevaricators to please the Americans."[63] This is the clearest moment in this novel that exposes the erasure of memory that migration bureaucracy necessitates. Bezmozgis put it in a different existential register, pointing to the crisis it poses for a subject: "What I tried to do in the book is to put Samuel in a situation really at the end of his life where he finds himself in a place he never wished to be, forced to leave the Soviet Union, and to have him reflect on his life. The character in the book poses the greatest source of existential and moral questions than anyone else does. For him, he really is questioning the whole purpose of his life."[64] Yet, while erasure of communist memory generally seems to become necessary to successfully immigrate, it also creates an occasion for these memories to be uttered, formulated, before they need to be displaced.

Samuil's principled attitude toward the Soviet commemorative symbols of combat and his party membership that rather deprives him of symbolic capital foreshadows the clandestine stories he remembers of his prewar communist past. These are other elements of memory that resurface under the current pressure of erasure. Indeed, Samuil with his commitment to communist ideals and anti-Zionism is close to the stereotype of the Red Army Jewish veteran:[65] he is a "true believer" in communism, a person "where the real events of proletarian struggle and triumph were housed like a breathing archive."[66] Stories about his communist coming-of-age are strewn across the novel, linked with youth and fervor: "He remembered hunger, cold, filth, penury, and, worst of all, the smothered hopes of gifted proletarian youth. None who had not experienced these things could legitimately judge the Communist state."[67] As Bezmozgis indicated in an interview, Samuil is already "torn within" in his youth because siding with communists means the first instance of erasure: Samuil is in "conflict with himself because the bargain the Soviet Jews were presented with was to be liberated from the settlement and the oppression that it represented, but to do that you basically had to recant and repudiate your language or history or tradition. Samuel is a character who feels like that is the bargain that I must strike."[68]

Krasnansky may be a "die-hard communist," as we see from his memories of being in a communist cell in Riga, but he is primarily an ardent atheist.[69] Immigration organizations in Ladispoli offer Jewish religious services and events, but Samuil scorns them. In fact, these are the few moments throughout the entire novel that his character uses humor: "Eagerly, in their singsong voices, his grandsons chirped away in Hebrew, and turned back two generations of social progress."[70] For him, religion is backward, and when asked if it is Israel that he has in mind as a "contingency plan" if Canada rejects him, he offers a blunt correction: "The grave."[71]

Here Samuil himself seems not a simple narrative shorthand or stereotype. His character functions as a conflicted memory vessel, his remembrances encompassing revolutionary communism, Jewishness, war combat, and official communist political culture, narrated in the immediate, evolving context of migration. These elements may be momentarily distinct, but they constitute multiple elements that can and do connect in various, sometimes unexpected ways. One critic complained that Samuil is a "troublingly static character [whose] main personality trait is his rigid ideological adherence to Communism," pointing out that such lack of development was "implausible" and "makes Samuil uninteresting."[72] Yet the character is a reservoir of the past, a necessarily static archive and thus a key foil on which the plot develops. If, narratively speaking, almost nothing happens to him in the space of the novel, it is because almost everything has already happened. In this vein, he himself wonders how, paradoxically, his memories are more palpable than the reality around him: "How had it happened that the people in the past, all long dead, now seemed to him to be the real people, and the people in the present, including his own children, seemed to him evanescent, so nearly figments that he could imagine passing his hand through them."[73] What appears as a flaw of a literary construct is instead a comment on how certain memory traces bear a limited legitimacy within a specific context—here, the Italian context of an older refugee applicant. Not all of these elements bear equal systemic legitimacy. And more importantly, individual elements are quite differently legitimate than in Soviet Riga. Bezmozgis wants us to believe that this generation is "obsolete, a travelling museum exhibit of a lost kind: Stalin's Jews, unlikely survivors of repeat appointments with death."[74]

In *The Free World*, Samuil's narrative effectively weaves together the overlapping meanings of "migrant memory." His self-proclaimed "uselessness" as a migrant in Italy elicits memories; he makes sense of migration through memories of his early communist past and combat during the war. These memories highlight his peculiarly displaced status: the material privilege he enjoyed just a few months earlier as a communist factory director has disappeared, the symbolic recognition of a veteran (that is, medals earned during the war) now holds significance mostly just within the veteran community, and his Jewishness demands redefinition along a religious axis that he negates and refuses. Migrant memory also changes the meaning of his remembrances: the "Party story" section of his visa application requires marginalizing the role communism has played in his life. Strategic selective remembering that the refugee application process produces ends up at an impasse and crisis, unproductive for him. The ironies of migrant memory as well as Samuil's statism and pastness eventually become narratively untenable; namely, after months of recording his memories, he dies of a heart attack in Italy. With Samuil's multiple ailments out of the picture, the other Krasnanskys' Canadian visa application is approved. They gather up the pages of the migrant memoir that Samuil had begun when he arrived in Italy and prepare to leave the transient condition of statelessness. With Samuil's death, the door to the Krasnanskys' immigration is opened.

Samuil Krasnansky might not have directly witnessed the atrocities of the Holocaust, but his migrant remembrances include not only the memory of his brother Reuven's death—killed by a German bomb at the front—but also moments of grief for his mother, his uncle, and the family members who could not evacuate from Riga. The migrant memory of Soviet veterans puts in staggeringly close proximity different modes of survival: in combat, in flight, and in Nazi genocide. In his case, however, the potential memorial opportunities that arise from migration and that could propel another economy of memory are silently written, but finally packed up in the boxes that only may make it across the Atlantic. Bezmozgis explains this using structural aesthetic arguments: "In the story, you do not read what Samuel is writing because it would have felt too stilted—we just know the story. Otherwise we would have felt like reading a book within a book, which I was not interested in. We do already get with the letters between Polina and her sister, and we do get it with the letters that Samuel's brother sent from the front. It was way too much."[75] Even if Samuil is a key figure in this novel, two other narrative lines by his younger family members—his above-mentioned daughter-in-law, Polina, and her husband, Alec—take up space and dilute the possibilities of his story and its consequences for subverting more codified stories of survival. It reads like this even in the final published version, which is only half of the initial 700 pages that Bezmozgis wrote over seven years.[76] These connected but still separate narrative lines give insight into the diverse challenges migration poses, which in the end produces the memory deadlock Samuil finds himself in. In Boris Fishman's *A Replacement Life* another legal process, that of compensation application, produces an occasion for collective and intergenerational memorial assemblage that promises to relieve the impasse.

Translating the Hierarchy of Suffering: Boris Fishman's *A Replacement Life*

Like Bezmozgis's *The Free World*, Boris Fishman's widely acclaimed 2014 novel *A Replacement Life* focuses on the crafting of narratives in a legal context:

writing the life stories required for application forms. But while ruminations about bureaucracy and qualms about dissimulating a Communist Party story in refugee applications took only half a page in Bezmozgis's novel, the falsification of Holocaust compensation claims—specifically, by members of the Soviet-born community of Brighton Beach—is the driving force of Fishman's book. Although the two applications had radically different rationales, both cases illustrate the entanglements of memory and migration regimes: just as survival and its consequences played a key role in Samuil's visa application, the post-Soviet migrant attitudes lead to forging of Holocaust compensation claims in Fishman's *A Replacement Life*.

Fishman has called his novel "a pained love letter to my people."[77] Noting the centrality of the novel's Soviet migrant background, he emphasized that the book is, more precisely, a love letter *à rebours*: "Haven't we lived this way—meaning, corruptly—for long enough? Isn't it time to welcome the future?"[78] As an insider with a keen, critical yet loving eye for detail, Fishman provides in the novel a commentary on the aging community of Soviet migrants and its murky dealings. Like *The Free World*, the book sympathetically re-centers those who survived by fleeing, Jews who evacuated to Soviet Central Asia, and Red Army soldiers, particularly focusing on the legal hierarchy of suffering and, consequently, the hierarchy of compensation. It also extends this critique to larger questions about law, justice, and restitution that transcend this particular Soviet Jewish migrant locale. This broader impetus is a remnant of the original design of the book: a comparison of false claims in two communities, (post-)Soviet Jewish Brooklyn and post-Katrina New Orleans.[79] While this second context was ultimately removed (though the 2006 setting was retained), the story remains implicitly open to historical connections and comparisons that go beyond analogies.

The fake narratives written by Slava Gelman, the novel's protagonist, reveal different strategic silences within Soviet and American memory. An aspiring bilingual Manhattanite journalist, Slava has language and writing skills that allow him to become a secondary witness, to use Aleida Assman's term, for the person listening to and collecting testimonies from older Russian speakers.[80] Ultimately, of course, he creatively rewrites these testimonies to fit the requirements of the application, but in the meantime, he collects Jewish wartime stories from the former Soviet Union. He is the local archivist gathering "tales of woe and deceit."[81] Slava listens to stories of evacuation into the Soviet interior, stories that have remained untold because they were deemed not heroic enough to be worthy of memory in the Soviet Union and not tragic enough to merit a place alongside the Holocaust in the West.[82] Fishman's use of internal dialogue makes us think about the internalized way in which we speak, in English, about survival and what this way of speaking implies: "Grandmother had been in the Holocaust—*in* the Holocaust? As in the army, the circus? The grammar seemed wrong. *At* the Holocaust? Of it, with it, from it, until it? The English preposition, stunned by the assignment, came up short."[83] This automatism in language—rather than its infamous incommensurability, so often written about since the end of World War II—is at the foreground here. It is not only the rules of language that fall short but also the legal regulations about whose suffering is worthy of compensation and what that compensation should be.

What becomes a minor criminal money scheme run by Slava's grandfather starts with a feeling of incomprehensible bureaucratic unfairness upon receiving the Claims Conference compensation paperwork just after Slava's grandmother Sofia has passed away: "'Sixty years they had,' said Slava, 'they do it the moment she dies.'"[84] After Sofia's funeral, family and friends gather for a feast of Soviet cuisine, and with moving toasts they commemorate her and express hope for the next generations: "What we have been through, may they never."[85] Following the big get-together, Slava's grandfather approaches him with the paperwork and suggests that he use his grandmother's story of escape from the Minsk ghetto and survival with partisans in the woods to apply—illegally—for a Claims Conference pension to be collected by him, her widower. For Slava, stitching together these "narratives" from remembered fragments of his grandmother's memory constitutes a work of mourning. At the same time, in an unsurprising turn of events, the scheme evolves into a business opportunity for his resourceful grandfather, who enlists Slava to falsify claims narratives for other community members. The grandfather's character brings to mind the early Soviet Jewish masculine figure of the trickster, being able to work at the interstices of the always evolving system, and "prefigures the development of a rich tradition of tricksters, swindlers, and conmen in Soviet culture."[86]

The grandfather's bid to enlist Slava as his accomplice in forging the application illustrates how two ostensibly conflicting ethical approaches toward reparations can overlap—here, specifically in the context of grieving. Scholars have extensively analyzed the perception of compensation by survivors and their heirs, revealing a broad spectrum of motivations—beyond financial need—influencing their willingness to seek compensation. At one end of this spectrum is a total refusal of "blood money" that is repulsive because it implies "the calculating, materialist, instrumental monetization of . . . sufferings" and thus is "morally earmarked," as anthropologist Susan Slyomovics succinctly puts it.[87] Meanwhile, at the other end of the spectrum stands a deliberate, meticulous pursuit of indemnity programs with their peculiar eligibility quirks, which is very differently motivated.[88] Sociologist Natan Sznaider suggests that "at the level of individuals, the act [of receiving restitution] is one of closure. Money symbolizes the irrevocable admission that a crime has been committed."[89]

Early in the novel, Fishman stages a situation in which these two seemingly opposing attitudes intersect in the person of the grandfather, which leads him to consider forging the claims application. Yevgeny Gelman's mourning over his spouse, which itself requires closure, is deepened by the frustration of receiving the paperwork belatedly, which for him constitutes a further injustice done to her that needs to be countered. At the same time, *A Replacement Life* reveals the grandfather to be generally money smart, managing shady businesses and procuring hard-to-find technical novelties. It is all very reminiscent of the ingenious arrangements for securing products within a Soviet regulated market economy—arrangements that appear to exist in Brooklyn, too. When the grandfather asks Slava to write a ghetto escape story for him based on his wife's experiences, the novel seems to be asking: If the world is fundamentally skewed and unjust, full of arbitrary rules to be tampered with, why be honest in the claims application? And if, in addition, compensations are fundamentally "morally earmarked," why follow the instructions verbatim? Why not manipulate the process to try to find this much-needed closure, as Sznaider above terms it? These questions decidedly push the logical contours of fundamental injustice related to memorial hierarchies. Codified memories not only marginalize others. This codification becomes translated into legal and then financial legitimacy not accessible to the nonsubjects of "correct" memory.

Conversations between Slava and his grandfather reveal further how the strict regulations governing compensation seem inadequate when juxtaposed with the messiness of history and human life. While the grandfather could apply for compensation for fleeing to Uzbekistan from Minsk, he insists that it is "dicey" and would entail less money in any case.[90] His claim is more universal—namely, that as much money as possible should be paid by the German government to all who suffered, regardless of eligibility criteria: "Maybe I didn't suffer in the exact way I need to have suffered . . . but they made sure to kill all the people who did. We had our whole world taken out from under us."[91] Eligibility requirements for certain types of compensation produce a hierarchy of survival. The monetary value linked to the "proper" survival stories threatens to marginalize, if not erase, other experiences of survival.

In the novel, in a slightly different graphic formatting, Fishman includes in full three out of the twenty-two stories that Slava writes for Soviet Jewish migrants. In this form, the stories give us a sense of textual materiality and simultaneously force us to reconsider how memory works and how testimonies are written. The first full story of survival rehashes the few tales about the ghetto and about living in hiding that had been reluctantly shared by Sofia Gelman and, following the plan, assigns these experiences and their memory to Slava's grandfather Yevgeny. One of the grandfather's friends, Israel Abramson, who with Slava's writerly assistance plans to become another claimant, has a very pragmatic critique. He protests that Slava's evocative mode of writing is unfit for the task at hand: "You've got this movie scene.

Beautiful moment, written, the cows. The Minsk ghetto was formed on such and such date. We lived at such and such address from this date to this date. This is where we moved when they put up the wire. And then you can do your beautiful sentences."[92] Israel's criticism about the lack of detailed factual information embodies the main questions of scholarly debate on such testimonies. Testimonies are located within two spheres of different relevance, functioning as both "a highly public story (and a dilemma of justice) and a highly private story (and its biographical dilemma of justice)," as literary scholar Shoshana Felman put it.[93] In other words, they serve as evidence in legal procedures and as self-expression conducive to healing. The perceived conflict between these functions, the tainting subjectivity of first-person accounts, led to the reluctance of Holocaust historians before the 1990s to use them as sources because of how hard it was to verify their accuracy.[94] Israel's insistence on facts may also be influenced by what has since become the genre of video testimony, which is highly formulaic with a predetermined script presented by the interviewer.[95] Even though, as Slava insists, "someone applying for restitution is not a historian. . . . The people in the ghetto didn't get the fact sheet,"[96] Israel insists on "a little boring story,"[97] filled with the dry facts that readers are used to, rather than a suspicious literary tour de force.

The other two survivor stories that are included in full in *A Replacement Life* also rework details from the grandmother's life during the war as well as her subsequent love story with Yevgeny. Compared with the first testimony, they feel repetitive, centered on the Minsk ghetto and escaping from it; indeed, they are as monotonous as Israel Abramson wanted them to be. For Slava, the recycling of his grandmother's memory fragments through the production of texts seems to serve the above-mentioned healing function. On a broader, cultural level, the repetition of a constellation of the same elements underscores the sameness of the muted experiences that are not eligible for compensation. *A Replacement Life*, like *The Free World*, returns to Soviet Jewish veteran stories, which—as we are told in the novel—do not translate into receiving an indemnity.[98] Slava hears stories about Kharkov and Stalingrad in the households he visits. Israel Abramson parades in the summer heat wearing his decorated Red Army uniform.[99] Lazar Rudinsky marvels that his family member was a tank commander, asking rhetorically, "How many Jewish Red Army tank commanders do you think there were?"[100] When, toward the end of the novel, it becomes clear that Slava was denounced to the Claims Conference by an insider to the scheme, and he is interviewed by its German employee, this repetitiveness of the narratives he fabricated provides a cover. Claiming that he forged only his grandfather's story and not any other, he builds his defense on the set characteristics of the established literary genre of testimony: "Even if their stories were real, I would not do it. But I would teach them how to write. That's why you have the similar phases, the maneuvers."[101]

As more Soviet senior citizens called on his grandfather's recommendation, Slava learned to tailor the stories: "It fell to Slava—half listening to what those gathered around him had actually gone through during the war so that he could pillage it later for the oddly specific details he had to come to learn made a narrative feel *authentic*."[102] Visits to their households to get to know them or to conduct research seem to have fulfilled a social function within the community of Soviet immigrants. They created or re-created relationships, a personal bond between them beyond the Russian language they shared. This holds true despite the fact that, without Slava's knowledge, applicants pay a fee to Slava's grandfather, and despite the fact that one of them denounces Slava to the Claims Conference.

Through Slava's encounters with multiple families in South Brooklyn—a "foreign city if you were coming from Manhattan"[103]—the novel gives us a sense of the makeup of the community of migrant Soviet-born Jews, much like the texts I discussed in chapter 1 do. Slava's U.S.-born Jewish American girlfriend sees South Brooklyn, saturated with Soviet paraphernalia, as "another act in New York's great ethnic circus."[104] Yet Fishman counters this by expanding the sense of empathy and solidarity that Slava feels for the aging community, a sense of family that transcends blood relations: "I am going to be arrested for forging restitution claims for my grandfathers."[105] This inclusive tendency is restated in different terms at the close of the book's acknowledgments, where the novel is dedicated "to the walking wounded who survived the degradations of a life in the Soviet Union. For all their warts, they, too, are survivors."[106] Implicitly countering the idea of "an erosion of the term survivor,"[107] which critics claim has expanded to include those who have lived through a variety of crises beyond atrocities, Fishman stretches the term to encompass the less obvious, undervalued, and under-narrated suffering within the Soviet system. The "walking wounded" are a generation of grandfathers—and grandmothers—who served in the Red Army or evacuated to the interior; they are encountered not only in *A Replacement Life* but also in *The Free World*. This fiction illuminates the apparent void in the memorial landscape occupied by those who survived their parents' death in the Holocaust—memory of whom is so often silenced in the Soviet Union—and asks how to do justice to their past, a past that fuels the migrant present.

By showing the process of Slava's forging—understood as both "producing" and "falsifying"—*A Replacement Life* reflects not only on how to write effective testimonies for compensation applications but also, more generally, on how to write about the Holocaust in such a way that it does not compete with the memory of other concurrent or subsequent events. The novel addresses the question of how descendants—meaning both familial descendants and inheritors of cultural memory—are able to represent the atrocity, and to what ends. With the passage of time, the term "survivor" evolves to include, in the words of Susan Slyomovics, "surviving fifty years after the atrocity event, able to make claims and willing to tell the story."[108] The span of fifty years—or the period of time narrated in *A Replacement Life*, or indeed the time from the events in question to the present—adds to the story and its memory. As Fishman shows, Soviet migration generates a different vocabulary to supplement how we theorize surviving World War II and the Holocaust. There may be an erasure of combat and evacuation stories in the application narratives, but in the novel, taken as a whole, we hear snippets of these stories, some of which—the stories of evacuation–were also pushed aside under communism as not heroic enough. Stories like the grandmother Sofia surviving the Holocaust in hiding, stories not given systematic prominence under communism, are also memorialized by Slava multiple times in the restitution narratives written for others. Fishman creates coexisting elements of memory that may reveal past and present erasures and hierarchies, but here within the plotlines seem to depend on each other: the compensation application creates a model that exceeds the violence of erasure. This conglomerate of stories for this community is also horizontal, additionally tampering with linearity, as it consists of records of various forms of survival. If Samuil in *The Free World* was alone and at a memorial deadlock, here the mnemonic productivity is made possible through intergenerational investment in memory: the agency of a grandson. In Julia Aleskseyeva's graphic memoir *Soviet Daughter* this intergenerational investment is not only empathetic but even identificatory, resulting in multidirectional transgenerational affinities. This text further expands available vocabulary, adding feminist lines of inquiry, and projecting diasporic communist-tinged postmemory into a visual medium.

Migrant Transgenerational Affinities: Julia Alekseyeva's *Soviet Daughter*

Soviet Daughter: A Graphic Revolution is the only published longer work of fiction by Julia Alekseyeva, a scholar and graphic artist who in her output merges her academic work with artistic production. "It is a story of our two generations separated by 80 years—but somehow united in spite of everything," Julia narrates in the opening of the semi-autobiographical graphic novel.[109] It is a tale about the unexpected yet ultimately obvious affinity between great-grandmother Khinya Ignatovskaya, nicknamed Lola, and her great-granddaughter Julia, who together with other family members immigrated from the former Soviet Union to Chicago in 1992. After Lola's passing, Julia inherits her memoir, which results in this graphic narrative, creating transgenerational links between women with regard to leftist politics, survival, and immigration. *Soviet Daughter* consists of two entangled storylines, both drawn in the same dynamic style, with soft black lines and gray watercolor shading. The main storyline proceeds in chapters and follows Lola's life from her youth in tsarist Russia to her death in 2010, taking the reader through the Russian Revolution, World War II, her evacuation to Central Asia, and her immigration to the United States. But these chapters are interrupted by "interludes" devoted to Julia when she was a graduate student at Columbia.

While the text often focuses on specific Soviet historical contexts during World War II—for example, evacuation to the interior and service in the Red Army—its central concern is the memory of migration that unites these two women across their generational distance. Like Bezmozgis's novel *The Free World*, *Soviet Daughter* narrates an individual's prewar involvement with Soviet communism. Here, however, this is not a hazardous past that might put at risk one's refugee application; rather, in the transgenerational dynamic of the story, it is resignified and functions as an occasion for Julia to identify with her great-grandmother. Consequently, in order to create a space for such identification and to read Lola's story as one of emancipation, Alekseyeva idealizes some of her great-grandmother's communist experiences or fails to present their full context. In *Soviet Daughter*, surviving the war and the Holocaust is configured as part of a broader twenty- and twenty-first-century Soviet Jewish story, framed at one end by tsarist Russia and the Russian Revolution, and at the other by post–Cold War migration. Fishman's narrative, in contrast, did not use such a broad temporal perspective and his focus on the external contemporary challenges of Holocaust compensation did not facilitate the kind of identificatory reading that interests Alekseyeva.

The tightly constructed entanglements of Julia's and Lola's lives call to mind some familiar traits of Holocaust literature by U.S.-born granddaughters and grandsons of survivors, or so-called third-generation Holocaust literature.[110] Yet, in Alekseyeva's work, the shared migration experience decidedly binds Julia and Lola, reconfiguring the dynamic of memory they share and allowing Julia to narrate her own story. They are first- and third-generation survivors of the war and the Holocaust, but first- and 1.5-generation migrants.[111] Both immigrated to the United States in 1992, though Julia was a four-year-old girl at the time. Accordingly, early in the narrative, in a family picture panel, we see five family members, including Lola and Julia, at the time of their immigration to the United States, which emphasizes their shared experience.[112] Since Julia's mother and grandparents had to work, it was Lola that took care of little Julia: "Thankfully there was Lola, the only refuge in the land of monsters," we read in a panel that is the first of the series of Julia and Lola's common portraits.[113] A few years later, Lola's company offers a shelter from Jewishness in the United States, which little Julia compares to a "ball and chain."[114] Julia grows up under competing pressures to fashion herself in different ways. Her parents, even though they are living in the United States, are still guided by the mindset of institutionalized Soviet antisemitism and accordingly tend to obscure their Jewishness. The narrator elucidates the background for this position: "Some people think there isn't any anti-semitism left in the US. / But they didn't grow up in the working class in school with no other Jewish kids."[115] At the same time, at school Julia's Jewishness functioned as a handy shortcut to "explain everything—good grades, bullying, certain interests and hobbies."[116]

Only with her great-grandmother does Julia not feel the burden of these rigid, seemingly conflicting frameworks. This perspective is not common in other Soviet-born Jewish narratives in English about childhood and adolescence. For the young protagonists in New York City in Gary Shteyngart's *Little Failure*, or in Toronto in David Bezmozgis's *Natasha and Other Stories*, growing up involves attempting to fit into the sociality created by American religious Jewishness and its educational institutions.[117] We may at first think this is a gendered narrative, but in Anja Ulinich's *Petropolis*, her young protagonist, Sasha, is somewhat similarly taught to be a religious Jewish woman by the well-off American Jews for whom she works, who were engaged in the movement to free Soviet Jews.[118] In contrast, the axis of religious Jewishness is absent in Maria Kuznetsova's *Oksana, Behave!*[119] The tendency to move away from the religious coordinates of original migration contexts—while certainly a function of the new social contexts staged in these novels—may be a sign of a recently developing theme in this literature, potentially influenced by the gender of the protagonists.

Alekseyeva traces Julia's feeling of ease around her great-grandmother back to prewar communism. In Soviet Russia and the prewar Soviet Union, Jewishness—though present—is rather invisible, disappearing beneath an ideal, universalized citizen on the path to a better socialist world. Lola's prewar activities as a member of the Worker's Union and the Komsomol, marked by the postrevolutionary changes in the political system, pose as lines of transgenerational identification for Julia. For Lola, her work in a factory and then membership in the Worker's Union form a path toward emancipation, which Alekseyeva reads as leftist and feminist. If "[t]he Komsomol member was expected to help liberate women from the supposedly 'oppressed and enslaved' conditions they had suffered under the capitalist system,"[120] Lola's case seems to confirm this reading. First, to build a contrast, Alekseyeva meticulously illustrates Lola's childhood in a large, poor Jewish artisan family in Kiev, a well-known trope in many Eastern European Jewish narratives. As Lola dryly remarks, she bore much responsibility from a young age: "My mother was often sick, and as I was the eldest girl, I became head of the household."[121] With this background, it was a positive breakthrough when she landed work as a factory machine operator in 1926 and then joined the union.[122] Her work, even with a gender pay gap,[123] frees her from having to work as a seamstress

56 • Soviet-Born

and allows her take care of her large family. Such an optimistic reading of the great-grandmother's history parallels how many young Jews—highly critical of traditional shtetl life—felt about the gains of the Bolshevik revolution.[124] Narrating such a markedly emancipatory trajectory identifies Julia with her great-grandmother and intergenerationally grounds hope underlying Julia's own narrative.

Lola's activities in the Profsojuz, or worker's union, from 1927 and soon after in the Komsomol are paired with Julia's political engagement in the early twenty-first century—her attempts at unionizing and her participation in the "Occupy" movement. For example, in the panel closing the novel, we see Julia at a union meeting just after Lola's death.[125] The last passage of the text resonates with Vladimir Mayakovsky's idealistic poem "At the top of my voice," quoted in the section of the novel covering Lola's Komsomol activities, as well as with Lola's deep belief in the collectivist ideals of communism: "After all—governments may change, the historical period may shift, generations may differ. But nothing, not all the guns and pepper spray and police batons in the world, not even time can kill a true idea."[126]

The transnational recirculation of the memory of Jewish life in Eastern Europe and leftist engagement before the Holocaust, which we see here in Alekseyeva's graphic novel, constitutes an important turn in recent auto/biographical literature. It can be found, for example, in historian Ivan Jablonka's influential personal narrative about his grandparents, originally published in French in 2012.[127] A similar framework shapes Bund historian David Slucki's recent memoir, in which he relates, among other things, his grandfather's activities in the Bund in postwar Poland, and then in Australia.[128] Alekseyeva does not bring the toolbox of a historian to the table and works with a different genre. Rather, with her comparative literature background, she constructs visual intertextuality, expertly juggling the more or less recognizable inventory of historical images to demonstrate the relevance of her great-grandmother's experiences for herself and, by extension, for her reader. As such, this design includes elements of memory that are "beyond the traumatic," focus on transgenerational continuities between women, are based on political engagement, and participate to an extent in "the transmission of positive forms of attachment."[129]

Both the affinities between Julia and Lola—based on their shared migration experience and political proclivities—and the different historical circumstances of their lives come to the fore on the cover of *Soviet Daughter* (figure 4). At its center is an oval-framed color portrait of a young Lola in a military uniform next to Julia, who is approximately the same age. Julia gazes directly at readers from behind Lola, who looks up at something unspecified. While the hammer and sickle next to the title gesture toward the Soviet setting, the rusty reddish background images come from the staple repertoire of Holocaust

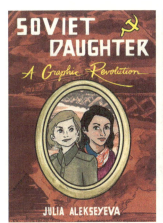 

FIGURES 4 (LEFT) AND 5 (RIGHT) Julia Alekseyeva, *Soviet Daughter: A Graphic Revolution* (Portland, OR: Microcosm Publishing, 2017), 142. Designed by Joe Biel.

representation in the West; namely, the train crossing a bridge resonates strongly with deportations and camp imagery.[130] Yet just like she had refreshed the connotations of early Soviet state socialism, so too does Alekseyeva redefine this imagery. When juxtaposed to the panels in the novel, these images capture the various trajectories—both hopeful and tragic—of Lola's Kiev family. The train on the cover appears within the novel as a part of the panel depicting Lola's evacuation to Aktyubinsk, Kazakhstan, in 1941 (figure 5).[131] In contrast, when the burning barn from the cover reappears in a panel, it illustrates that not all evacuation scenarios were successful; it is part of the story of Lola's parents' murder in Vladikavkaz by Chechens.[132] At the risk of interrupting narrative continuity, Alekseyeva juxtaposes these lesser-known stories of survival and death in the Soviet Union to the Babi Yar massacre by Nazi shooting squads (*Einsatzgruppen*). The event fills a double-page spread,[133] a format unique in this graphic novel, which speaks to the emblematic nature of the event for the Holocaust in the East and implicitly may be read as alluding to the earliest Soviet Jewish texts on the catastrophe.[134] At a broader level, the visual resonates with the American memorialization of the Holocaust in the East: the large Babi Yar Memorial Park (1982) in Denver, for example, or the smaller Babi Yar Triangle (1981) in the midst of the Soviet Jewish neighborhood in South Brooklyn, both of which were established after the initial influx of Russian-speaking Jewish migrants.

Like *The Free World* and *A Replacement Life*, however, Alekseyeva's *Soviet Daughter* also represents what Jewish studies scholar Olga Gershenson termed an "alternative track" in Soviet Holocaust memory or the experience of Soviet Jewish soldiers.[135] A panel devoted to three soldiers who were brothers shows their oval-framed photographs lying on what appears to be a checkered tablecloth. This intimate setting brings the official history back home, makes it familiar, especially since the text mentions only their service, without foreshadowing their fate: "I would think about them often. . . . I had no idea where anyone was, whether they were safe, whether they were even alive."[136] In a later section, we see Lola receiving a message about her husband's death on the frontline, followed by details about the deaths of her two brothers in combat.[137] Adding these stories of service in the Red Army, next to the panels depicting the evacuation and the emblematic atrocity event in the Soviet Union, reveals an uneven dynamic in much of the American memorialization of the Soviet Jewish experience during World War II.

The titular "Soviet daughter" points toward a political genealogy and refers primarily to the great-grandmother, a woman metaphorically born of and shaped by the political system. At the same time, the appellation refers also to Julia, who compares herself in multiple ways to her great-grandmother and writes her own autobiography from the perspective of a particular migrant and diasporic Sovietness, a kind of Sovietness conceptualized with the help of her great-grandmother's memoir and on the basis of inherited photographs.[138] Like Bezmozgis in *The Free World* and Fishman in *A Replacement Life*, Alekseyeva extends the meaning of survival in the context of World War II in the Soviet Union. Further, as the graphic novel illustrates the parallel lives of generationally distant women, she also shows how Soviet history shapes Julia's life: her health crisis is caused by thyroid cancer resulting from the disaster at Chernobyl. Instead of constructing often false and flat analogies about different, unrelated kinds of survival, this post-Chernobyl narrative element rather demonstrates how the memory of different periods of Soviet history presents itself in this transgenerational migrant narrative.

Assemblage Memory

North American diasporic post-Soviet settings entail a different emplotment of Holocaust narratives and Holocaust memory.[139] Diverse historical contexts force authors to stray from the known mold, to exceed narrative patterns and explanation grids that readers in English have become used to, by adding stories of Jewish Red Army soldiers and stories of evacuation and escape. These scenes in *The Free World*, *A Replacement Life*, and *Soviet Daughter*, centered on Jewish Soviet veterans, can serve as background to Mark Berman's heartrending reaction to Holocaust Remembrance Day. By expanding— geographically and conceptually—the repertoire of Holocaust narratives into the Soviet and diasporic post-Soviet domains, these texts intervene in understandings of survival and the survivor, as well as understandings of third-generation Jewish American Holocaust writing, and they illuminate what affordances migration plotlines create for memories of war and genocide.

When we hear "Never again," we do not think about the Soviet-inflected stories explored in this chapter, in which the Holocaust in the East intersects with experiences of evacuation and combat. There is a frozenness to the global, mainstream post–Cold War memory of the Holocaust that grants it relative coherence. As such, it can be rendered incomparable on any level to other genocides and misused as a tool to compete with other traumatic group memories. Yet, if one looks closely, it is more epistemologically and politically beneficial to approach Holocaust memory as an assemblage of various stories that question each other and, in some contexts, compete for legitimacy *within* the larger framework of Holocaust memory. In the words of Holocaust scholar Zoë Waxman, "There is no universal survivor experience. Many survivors never experienced a concentration camp or a labour camp but survived by hiding (some with false Aryan papers and some without), some alone, some with family members."[140]

The various disparate and contextual strands of Holocaust memory interact with each other in a hierarchical relationship. In short, together they are rather an assemblage that with all its elements constitutes the never *fully* known field of Holocaust memory. Such a recognition of the radical multiplicity of stories inflected by quite different settings and contexts may decenter the single, hegemonic Holocaust memory that pervades the global cultural sphere. Yet, in the long run, such inclusivity allows for greater connections and intersections with memories of other traumatic events experienced either by the same group, such as the memory of communist violence, or by other groups within the same setting—a multiplicity that may amplify Holocaust memory.

Soviet and diasporic post-Soviet thematic elements produce a remembrance of World War II and the Holocaust in specifically migrant contexts: refugee statelessness, insular migrant enclaves, and migrant political affinities. Migration determines the manner in which these entanglements are narrated, which reveals how memory is accorded different levels of legitimacy in various geopolitical and legal settings. The diasporic post-Soviet economy of remembering Soviet Jewish survival may further contextualize the "sacralized uniqueness" of the Holocaust[141] and, alongside entanglements with migration regimes, facilitate localized dialogues that move beyond a competition of memories.

To be sure, the Soviet diasporic redefining of survival is one of many responses highlighting the heterogeneity of survivor experiences, and it contributes to a Holocaust memory characterized by assemblage rather than homogenization. From the late 1980s, scholars began using women's experiences (previously ignored) to challenge the "the hegemony of collective memory."[142] The next step in dehomogenizing these narratives involved unearthing queer testimonies.[143] In parallel, narratives concerning other racialized identities and marginalized settings started to emerge. While earlier research more often than not included disclaimers that testimonies by Sinti and Roma did not fall under its purview, recent studies engage such evidence in comparative analysis or are even fully dedicated to the Porajmos as an understudied chapter of the Holocaust era.[144] The redefinition of survival includes a new focus on non-European settings, such as North Africa, as well as Black individuals who found themselves within the boundaries of the expanding Reich—all of which are pieces of the assemblage.[145]

Literary forms are instrumental in turning our attention to the making of memory. Soviet postmemory texts—even though their content and mnemonic contexts are markedly different from nonimmigrant texts—display narrative features that zero in on these mechanisms of memory. The memory-reflexive function of literature, to invoke Astrid Erll's term, notably emerges in these narratives, with their "mired accounts."[146] As demonstrated, these texts are structured by fragmentary knowledge and a detective-like search to find stories. In *The Free World*, Bezmozgis describes Samuil Krasnansky's writing of his "secret memoirs" in Italy, which are packed up in boxes after his sudden death, to be discovered—we may speculate—by his grandchildren, who would be of Bezmozgis's generation.[147] While this novel ends with the passing of the patriarch, Fishman's *A Replacement Life* begins with grieving the loss of a grandmother in Brooklyn. Her death generates a new sense of connection between her surviving husband and their grandson and leads to the recording of her memories, however skewed they become in false claims narratives, that serve also as memories *of* her. In *Soviet Daughter*, meanwhile, Lola's memoir becomes the basis for a story about her and her great-granddaughter, Julia, who inherited the text. All of these novels rely on other texts, be they bureaucratic or life writing, and thus reflect on the knowledge-producing qualities of these original texts and, by extension, their own memory-making features.

However, in Soviet-born Jewish writing in English, the war and the Holocaust make up only part of the story; the memory of migration also plays a key role. If we perceive "generation" not as a genealogical calculation, a broadly shared birth date, but rather as a shared lived experience, as Astrid Erll suggests, the diasporic (post-)Sovietness of these writers and their protagonists encourages us to look critically at a specific, localized genealogy of memory (with English as "the authorized language of Holocaust memory"[148]), explore different meanings of "generation," and reconsider the role played by migrant regimes, narratives of migration, and communist and Cold War memory in shaping this fiction and its memory of survival. Redefining survival encompasses a redefinition of *third-generation Holocaust writing*, too. These differences of positioning between immigrant and nonimmigrant "third-generation" writers are even more pronounced when reading Soviet-born texts that focus on communist postmemory, which the next chapter examines.

3

Afterlives of Communism

In November 2021, the U.S. Senate witnessed bickering about a long-defunct Soviet organization known as the Komsomol. The Komsomol, a hallmark of the Soviet Union throughout that state's existence, was an abbreviation for the Russian Young Communist League, a helper organization of the Communist Party. The protagonists of the widely watched and commented-upon hearing-turned-spectacle were Republican senator John Kennedy and Soviet-born Ivy League professor Saule Omarova, Joe Biden's nominee for a key banking regulator. In his highly personal attacks, Kennedy tried to paint her youth in the Soviet Union as fundamentally disqualifying her from serving in the president's administration. For Kennedy, "communist" appeared to be an almost inborn trait: once born and educated in the Soviet Union, one was—and always remained—communist. He famously quipped, "I don't know whether to call you professor or comrade."[1] Omarova soberly protested his illogical speculation. Many criticized Kennedy for his "Red Scare Tactic," reminiscent of the anti-communism of the McCarthy era.[2] Yet, in the end, his strategy worked and Omarova withdrew her candidacy.[3]

This surprisingly recent scene contains all the elements of American stories in which individuals suffer scorn or ostracism merely because they were born and raised in the Soviet Union: their essential and radical difference as a person and their incompatibility with U.S. culture and politics, all of which is based on the straightforward identification of "Soviet" as "communist" and the demonization of the latter. Typical gendered and racialized logic only amplifies this message, framing the stage along dominant hierarchies as a white cis man berates a woman of color. Moreover, the dichotomy "professor or comrade" suggests the persistent ideal of the supposedly apolitical, "objective" nature of research and academic instruction.

Even though McCarthyism was eventually discredited, its anti-communist message has remained a staple of politics, whose participants and pundits rendered American communists as "uncritical and irrational followers of the aggressively expansionist and antidemocratic Soviet Union."[4] In this Cold War spirit, communist Jewish writers found themselves sidelined, and this genealogy of Jewish American writing is rarely foregrounded within literary histories. In a complementary move, Soviet-born individuals were assumed to be essentially communist. In his memoir *Little Failure*, Gary Shteyngart reminisces about how "after one Commie comment too many" while he was in school in the 1980s, he declared that he was "actually born in Berlin."[5] The absurdity of the situation is not lost on the narrator: "So here I am, trying to convince *Jewish* children in a *Hebrew* school that I am actually *a German*."[6] Anti-Soviet and anti-communist sentiment in the United States looms so large that in this rendering it has obfuscated the demons of World War II and the Holocaust. At that point, Shteyngart declares himself a "10-year-old Republican" who "love[s] America more than anyone loves America."[7] His transformation toward progressivism starts in college, but first he became assimilated into wholesale anti-communism.

These prevalent narratives fusing former citizenship and current political affinities influence the literary market. They lie behind the marketing choices of publishers, who, despite the protests of authors, push for red covers or red lettering on Russian-themed books.[8] Just like Shteyngart remembers how his schoolmates interpellated him as a "Commie," forcing him to take a stance, *Soviet*-born writers enter a similar cultural field, one that loves to say "red" to denote Russian/Soviet/communist, a seemingly inseparable triad. Earlier literary works in English by Soviet-born writers often satirized this received American knowledge and faulty perception of post-communist Central and Eastern Europe, with Gary Shteyngart serving as the prime example.[9] For example, in Shteyngart's *Russian Debutante's Handbook*, the author's photo shows him wearing a fur-lined coat (stereotypical attire for communist Central and Eastern Europe) alongside a baby bear (a stereotypical attribute of "the wild East").

Characteristically, in early critical interpretations these hyperbolic takes on post-communist Central and Eastern Europe—such as the imaginary city Prava in *Russian Debutante's Handbook*, or the fictional regions in Shteyngart's later work *Absurdistan*—and on Eastern Europeans in North America represented a "new immigrant chic" that was bold and proud of its difference.[10] Critics viewed these texts as ironic responses to how immigrants had "so easily assimilated," as a perhaps unintentional "parody [of] previous narratives of Jewish immigration and assimilation."[11] Even with these texts' modified post-assimilatory impetus, "the deprivations of late-twentieth-century communism" within this literary wave apparently functioned as a mere substitute for the original estrangement of Eastern European shtetls a century earlier. These transhistorical comparisons between early and late twentieth-century immigrants from the Russian Empire and from Soviet and post-Soviet space collapsed the central difference in how the migrants and, consequently, their literature could be perceived: Soviet-born writing plunged into a landscape of latent anti-communist sentiments.

Some Jewish American fiction by Soviet-born authors precisely centers on communism, its memory, and its American afterlife, revealing yet another set of meanings of Soviet-inflected Jewishness in the United States today. The novels discussed in this chapter, Sana Krasikov's *The Patriots* and Keith Gessen's *A Terrible Country*, point toward the once lost and now rediscovered American ways of narrating emancipation from state socialism or communism without leading to their automatic demonization or to an embrace of conservative political positions. These texts traverse a broader time period, both stretching back further, to before World War II, and reaching closer to the present, entering the twenty-first century. Through their sweeping narratives relating to the Soviet Union and Russia, both complicate genealogies of leftism and the United States. Krasikov's main character leaves for the USSR in the 1930s, allowing the author to explore American leftism before World War II and its links to the Soviet Union. Complementarily, Gessen, focusing on a Soviet-born American academic, locates today's American progressivism in relation to local post-Soviet anti-capitalism. Together, they touch on or at least allude to tensions within the memory of American leftism, Americanism, and Jewishness, as well as critically highlight the power dynamic in Vladimir Putin's Russia.

While the opening anecdote of this chapter highlights today's (latent) anti-communist sentiment, its Cold War forms motivated the relative disremembrance of prewar Jewish radicalism. Jewish involvement in the labor movement and early twentieth-century socialism in the United States was significant, with Jews being the largest immigrant group in New York's Socialist Party throughout the first two decades of the twentieth century.[12] The phenomenon lasted particularly long because, in contrast to other immigrant groups, second-generation immigrant Jews carried on the "radical legacy" of their parents, including within the Communist Party.[13] As historian Tony Michels makes clear, they harbored "the desire to trade Jewish ethnicity for the international Jewish proletariat."[14] Consequently, "ethnicity . . . served as both a formative influence and a target of rebellion."[15]

This high participation in the Communist Party, with an estimated 50 percent of the Jewish population participating in party-affiliated cultural organizations, became especially salient during the Cold War era.[16] Susan

Glenn has suggested the idea of a "Jewish Cold War" to mark, among other things, the tendency of Jewish intellectuals to distance themselves from the Jewish prewar radical past. Namely, Glenn writes, the Cold War "led to the censure and isolation of Jewish Communists," but more broadly, "the rejection of Stalinism and totalitarianism by liberal Jewish intellectuals triggered a complex debate about postwar pressures for Jewish group loyalty and conformity."[17] While scholars have begun to consider this history critically, a revisionary post–Cold War Jewish history—and literary history—is still needed.[18] Krasikov echoes such a sentiment, affirming the need for more diverse storytelling around communism that would serve de-mythologization: "This book is also functioning as a kind of alternative history of the relationship between Russia and America for about a century. There were things I wanted to say not just about the personal relationships in the book, but about the relationships between the nations. I felt like the book just seems like a great opportunity to say them. And it was history that not a lot of people would have access to, because a lot of it had actually been whitewashed. It had been removed from the records, essentially of both countries."[19]

In the narratives considered in this chapter, American progressivism becomes intimately bound to Soviet and post-Soviet Russia—bound both ideologically and through the romantic and familial bonds of Soviet-born American Jews. Soviet-born American protagonists come to these stories through their personal family attachments, generating affective bonds that challenge simple demonizations. Literature as a medium seems to open to these affective dimensions that help demythologize simplistic historical narratives. These novels reapproach these narratives within a framework that historian Muriel Blaive has contrasted—as "life under Communism"—with the perspective of the Cold War: it "accentuates the dictatorial regime rather than the international conflict" and focuses on everyday practices rather than political rhetoric.[20]

The complex afterlife of communism appears as stories unearthed by descendants, from their family members or from secret Soviet Stalinist police files, as in *The Patriots*. Especially *The Patriots* effectively participates in creating gulag postmemory writing in English. This expands the domain of Jewish American postmemory writing and contributes yet another meaning of survival, considered in the previous chapter.

The afterlife of communism involves disinformation and denunciation, key features of the Soviet regime that nevertheless seem to translate easily to contemporary capitalist reality, whether in the oil business (Krasikov) or the neoliberal American academy (Gessen). Even though the writing of these novels occurred before the Trump era, that narrative logic has become characteristic of "fake news" in contemporary political contexts, as have questions about Russian entanglement in American politics.

Disinformation Literacy: Sana Krasikov's *The Patriots*

At over 500 pages, *The Patriots* tells a fragmented multigenerational story: Florence, whom we meet in New York City as a resolute Anzia Yezierska–like second-generation immigrant in the mid-1930s, chases a love interest into a brave new world; her Soviet-born engineer son, Julian, immigrates to the United States with his mother and his family in 1979; finally, her grandson Lenny, now in his midthirties, returns to Moscow in an attempt to make a post-Soviet fortune. Unlike other novels by Soviet-born writers, *The Patriots*'s oldest narrated moment is not from pre–World War II "Old World" as in some other narratives in the previous chapter. Rather, Krasikov's chronological starting point is 1930s Brooklyn.[21] It is only from there that the narrative centered on Florence takes readers to the Soviet Union and, after several decades, back to the United States. Then, in 2008, the story returns to post-Soviet Russia, this time following Julian and Lenny.

With its historical arc beginning in the United States and spanning eighty years and three generations, *The Patriots* provides a novel perspective on Soviet American family genealogies and communist itineraries. As Krasikov put it: "I have always been interested in writing something that was not from the point of view of someone who had grown up in Eastern Europe or in the Soviet mindset. But somebody who had to adopt it from coming from here. I wanted a book where somebody who is an American has to adapt and turn into a Soviet person, and then the ripple effect that has on your family and the decisions."[22] The historical panorama is vast and spans key moments in narrating lives and afterlives of communism in the U.S. context: the 1930s, the earlier decades of the Cold War, and the post-Soviet times. *The Patriots* complicates our common understanding of Soviet/Russian–American relationships in each of these eras.

The chapters largely alternate between Julian's first-person narration of his 2008 trip to Moscow and a third-person narration focused on his mother's gradual political downfall in Stalin's Soviet Union, and in this way they establish the axis of the afterlife of communism. Krasikov traces this afterlife on two interconnected levels. The first and most palpable is Julian's quest for his Jewish American mother's police file, now accessible from a state archive. Krasikov narrates the search for and discovery of this file, and even produces bits of its fictional documents for readers, which appear on the page in a small typewriter font throughout one of the chapters. Second, Krasikov makes disinformation the structuring framework of those parts of the narrative set in Soviet and post-Soviet Russia.

Disinformation, or *dezinformatsiya*, is a term that took off in Soviet Russia in the 1920s, where it denoted "incorrect or imaginary pictures of reality, on the basis of which the enemy would make decisions beneficial" to the party spreading disinformation.[23] It shapes both Florence's and Julian's plotlines, including the sometimes-formal level of narration. These communist and post-communist entanglements, which link the Soviet past to Julian's current business dealings, serve as the structuring principles of the novel. In addition, by focusing on Florence and her American and Jewish American comrades in Moscow, *The Patriots* points to disremembered narratives about American communism, the demonization of which also belongs to communism's post–Cold War afterlife.

The novel's three-page prologue sets the scene for Julian and sends us back to the Soviet Union of the 1950s. Like all the other forty-four chapters, the prologue features a stylized vintage postmark, a shorthand guideline orienting the readers as to the time and setting. Here it reads, "Saratov 1956." The postmark's five-pointed star with sickle and hammer provides another clear sign that we narratively enter the Soviet Union, continuing the theme begun on the book's sepia and blue-toned dust jacket, which depicts Moscow's emblematic Red Square a few decades earlier (see figure 6). The date locates us in the period just after the reign of Stalin, who died in 1953. Beneath the postmark, the prologue's opening sentence repeats the geographic coordinates as it introduces the main character: "On a Sunday in August, a boy and a one-armed man appeared on the platform of the Saratov train station."[24] The boy is Julian, accompanied by his children's home director while he awaits the arrival of his English-speaking prisoner mother "after all these years."[25] This initial image of current distance and past attachment establishes a driving force of the novel as it looks back at this Jewish American mother's story of arriving in the USSR as well as Julian's own story, set in post-Soviet Moscow, of discovering his mother's sentencing and imprisonment in a gulag.

Unlike many of the Soviet-born narratives discussed in previous chapters and, especially, in chapter 4, *The Patriots* centers on the parent generation rather than their immigrant children. In the character constellation of the novel, Julian is in fact a child of a gulag survivor, as the prologue makes clear. Such a design gives the readers access to a historical and political positionality rarely explored in this body of fiction. With Julian's late-Soviet adult backstory, readers witness what Jewishness and Jewish "nationality" mean in this historical context; namely, we witness Julian's humiliation when he is denied his doctorate in hydrodynamics in Moscow because of "restrictions," as a defense committee member unofficially informs him, "execrable quotas" based on Jewish nationality.[26] Krasikov poignantly captures Julian's imminent and overwhelming alienation from Moscow when in 1977 he was "flatly deserted by [his] illusions":[27] "None of it was any longer mine. The sight of *their* building made me sick. The sight of *their* statues, even *their* trees."[28] Soon after, he decides to leave this "cursed place."[29]

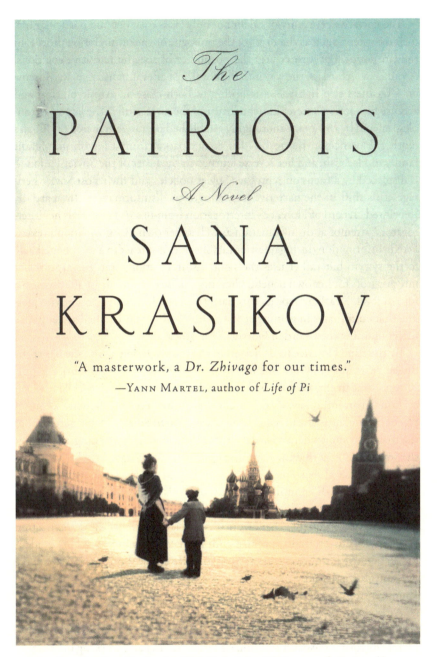

FIGURE 6 Sana Krasikov, *The Patriots* (New York: Spiegel & Grau, 2017). Designed by Debra Lil.

68 • Soviet-Born

The narrative centrality of Julian not only leads to a focus on particular historical content, such as the 1950s of the prologue or the immigration process in the late 1970s, but also creates the possibility of specific narrative solutions. Around two-thirds of the way into the novel, just after Julian arrives in Moscow on a business trip in 2008, attempting to both close an Arctic oil deal and acquire his mother's secret file, the thrust of the novel shifts. The largely chronological and by this point thoroughly established narrative centered on Julian's mother, Florence, in the 1930s—her emancipation from a Jewish immigrant family in Flatbush, and her reverse journey to the heart of the Soviet Union— is displaced by a focus on repressive Soviet policies and their post-Soviet heritage. This shift in the narrative logic hinges on disinformation. The partially "reprinted" record of Florence's interrogation from 1948/1949 reveals her interrogators' attempt at disinformation as well as her own disinformation literacy. Fed disinformation during questioning, she does not react in a way "beneficial" to the system but rather uses the same disinformation strategies against her interrogators for her own benefit. Creating a sense of communist afterlives on a formal level, Krasikov repeats this narrative logic in Julian's post-Soviet plotline that culminates in gaining access to his mother's declassified secret police file, containing the record of Florence's interrogation.

By the time Florence finds herself in the interrogation room, she has spent fifteen years in the USSR. She had moved to Moscow after romantically pursuing a Russian engineer she had met while working for the Soviet Trade Delegation. In an interview, Krasikov effectively characterizes Florence as out of place because she is ahead of her time in the United States: "it was natural that she would go somewhere where the future was already happening, which was the Soviet Union at that time."[30] Creating a woman protagonist, who was under stronger gendered social pressures, only strengthened that sense of her incommensurability with her milieu. Even though this social conditioning was key, Krasikov demonstrates how she constructed a character in a way that we may bond with her—a quality that on an affective level prevents the demonization of communism: "Actually, I didn't want to make her a kind of political ideologue, because it's not very interesting to write about. I don't think we make decisions for politically motivated reasons. I think we make them for entire, almost entirely personal reasons."[31]

After the initial relationship fails, the plot is propelled by another romantic engagement, this time with a fellow Jewish American communist: Leo Brink, Florence's future husband and Julian's father. Living and working in Moscow, she gradually entered a Kafkaesque world of Soviet bureaucracy and Stalinist policing. Her tale resembles that of many Americans, and especially Jewish Americans, in the prewar USSR. During the murky bureaucratic process of registering at an address, she loses her American passport and is issued documents as a Soviet citizen, thereby becoming one of thousands of stranded

Americans, as Krasikov's omniscient narrator usefully informs readers. Her husband has a short stint at Birobidzhan, then a recently created Jewish Autonomous Region. When for political reasons her work is discontinued at the state bank and she starts teaching politically correct American literature at a higher education institution, she has no choice but to become an informant for the NKVD, the Soviet Union's secret police. With the war's arrival in the Soviet Union, she evacuates to Kuibyshev and together with her husband works for the landmark Jewish Anti-Fascist Committee, later returning to Moscow.[32]

The prewar immigrant American Jewishness that we know from literature and history—with its "Old World" Eastern European attachments, religious ritual, and Yiddish language—is left behind in New York with her parents, with whom she is in contact only through letters to her brother. After hundreds of pages of almost no conspicuous Jewish references, Jewishness reappears when Florence's husband, Leo, attends an event (one that actually took place historically) with Golda Meir in a Moscow synagogue in 1948. Krasikov makes clear that, in the USSR, "Jewish American" entails the conflation of two separate identifications, two separate nationalities: one based on former American citizenship and visible only as the American nationality listed in a Soviet passport and in the form of one's familial ties in the United States; the other, implicated through a surname, suggesting that one is "not a real Muscovite" and, later, that one participates in Jewish "nationalist" activities, linked with a Jewish state.[33]

This collapsed understanding of "Jewish" and "American" resurfaces during Julian's reading of Florence's police file in 2008. Her two interrogators skew reality in order to persecute her due to the perceived impossibility of being a Soviet citizen and, at the same time, American and Jewish. The violent marathon interrogations, which last an entire seven months, persistently return to this supposed paradox. It is the undercurrent of the propaganda-filled accusations, as well as a more serious charge of espionage. The forced confessions feature the keywords "nationalism" and "nationalistic": "I was an accomplice to their slanderous nationalistic character";[34] "I was poisoned with bourgeois nationalism."[35] They gesture at the impossibility of Jewish identification in the Soviet Union. If interest in or contact with anything Jewish is perceived as contrary to the internationalism of the Soviet enterprise, an association with the Jewish Anti-Fascist Committee can gain the utmost negative connotations, implicating the association as an "accomplice" in non-normative and criminal behavior. In addition, the phrase "*bourgeois* nationalism" recalls the ways in which ethnic identification is just as foreign and dangerous to communist ideals as non-working-class backgrounds.[36]

From Julian's perspective sixty years later, the deposition record at times seems comical in its incongruity with the facts at hand. But the longer Julian— and readers of the novel—is immersed in the deposition, the clearer it becomes that this disinformation peddled by his mother's interrogators, is the only available version of lived reality, within the terms of which one is forced to negotiate. For Julian, the record is patently ridiculous: "Were I a film producer, I would instantly fling into the dustbin this shopworn script, stitched from stock phrases that even the lowliest hack in Hollywood would have avoided out of professional self-respect."[37] The deposition opens the world and language of disinformation, which has different rules and different stakes.

This incompatibility of language games—where words have different meanings depending on context, on the "rules" of the game being played—becomes especially conspicuous when languages other than Russian enter the scene— here, American English and Yiddish. A letter from Florence's brother, quoted to her in Russian translation, is a primary example: "I've passed your messages to the crew. The whole Mish-Pok thinks of you."[38] The translation into Russian appears potentially incriminating only because it is done without any cultural translation of the familiar and informal American English used, and without an understanding of a Yiddish word, *mishpokhe*, which merely means "family." The investigator's—or, as Julian says, the "inquisitor's"—interpretation of this line, when he talks about "the Mish-Pok espionage ring," illustrates manipulative disinformation overlapping with sheer incompetence.[39] While earlier Julian compared the deposition to a bad film script, here he associates this clash of language games with another type of cultural production, one that aims at hyperbolizing reality for comic effect: "It was like some cheap borscht-belt gag, a hopelessly corny joke about cultural misunderstanding between Gentiles and Jews. Only this was not the Catskills. It was the basement of the Lubyanka."[40]

Despite physical coercion, Florence refuses to confess, or act in a manner beneficial to the system (to return to our definition of "disinformation"). In a decisive moment that leads to the lifting of the heavier espionage accusation, Jewishness plays a major role. In a veritable jujitsu move, as it were, Florence herself creates disinformation and intimates that it can be the basis for one investigator denouncing the other. As Julian's uncle recollects, one of the men, "a real frothing anti-Semite investigator," called her a racial slur and wished she had been "in the hands of Gestapo."[41] Florence clung to this sentence, unorthodox within the Soviet ethos that was built on fighting the Nazis in the Great Patriotic War, then crisply expressed its denunciatory potential, parroting the investigators' own techniques: "How unpleasant it would be for you if your superiors heard you proudly modeling yourselves after the fascists."[42]

Disinformation and manipulation become routine for Florence, and as inherited knowledge—or gulag postmemory—they inform Julian's plotline in post-Soviet Russia and in this particular afterlife of communism. Florence's move of creating disinformation to protect oneself from disinformation appears twice more, creating a pattern in her response to the system, one that allows her to subvert it from within and survive. In these two other cases, however, her use of disinformation comes at a human cost. When, in an earlier chapter, her NKVD handler asks for specific information that might incriminate people around her, she invents stories for him to follow up on only so that she might buy time and try to escape the country, in the course of which she denounces her friend. Later, she uses the same strategy when she is in the gulag and the authorities summon her to serve as a translator in the interrogation of a captured American pilot. Hoping to stall for more time, to stay longer in better living quarters and not have to work in the woods, Florence manipulates both the gulag commandant and the pilot. Promising to inform the pilot's family of his capture and his fate in case (or rather, when) he perishes, she successfully extracts technical information about the American plane; in so doing, she—hoping that perhaps such intelligence will earn the commandant a promotion to Moscow—gains preferential treatment that might have saved her life. In retrospect sixty years later, Florence's brother bitterly concludes, "Those weren't her shining moments, Julian."[43] Krasikov suggests that Florence survived in this system despite its costs because she internalized it.

Because of insights gained from Florence's secret police dossier, Julian gains disinformation literacy that allows him to close his business deal in post-Soviet Russia. Disinformation becomes a literary device. The narration of this plotline follows the logic of disinformation, the mechanism of which we are now familiar with from Florence's story. The novel first immerses readers in disinformation created by a Russian businessman and portrayed as the valid narrative reality. Only retrospectively does Julian lay bare how it follows the same model of disinformation operating in his mother's plotline. Looking with him at his mother's secret file, we begin to understand the operational principle of the world around him, and, inspired by what he sees in the file, Julian emulates his mother's disinformation strategy, humiliates his post-Soviet business rival, and successfully acquires a joint-venture contract.

By placing Julian at the center of the narrative, relying on him to tell his own story in the first person and assemble the story of his mother, *The Patriots* creates gulag postmemory writing. Krasikov in fact gives us a quick primer on the canon of gulag literature. When Julian peruses his mother's Xeroxed file in a Moscow hotel room, he remembers the samizdat and other texts he read when he still lived in the USSR, often hastily passing them on to others. Krasikov name-drops Varlam Shalamov, Aleksandr Solzhenitsyn, and Evgenia Ginzburg, and even quotes extensively from Vasily Grossman's unfinished novel *Everything Flows*, which was suppressed in communist Russia, to illuminate "the unique political pathology of Russians."[44] The few chapters in which we return to Julian's childhood in the orphanage, as in the prologue, poignantly highlight these entanglements of family memory under communism. Their emblem is a list, discovered in the police file, of household items seized by the state during his mother's arrest in 1948. The long, detailed catalogue includes many items that belonged to him as a young boy.

A search for secret police files characterizes life writing by authors whose parents experienced police surveillance, yet Julian's fictional quest does not function as "a familial, generational duty to [his] parents' difficult existence, courage, and suffering."[45] Unlike in other examples of this literature, here the parent, Florence, is implicated in the system. It is true that the staged reproduction of excerpts from the file forms a record of "a complex oppressive state mechanism of surveillance, control, intimidation, coercion, and criminalization in the former Eastern European totalitarian societies."[46] But additionally, while clearly pointing to historical contingencies and specificities of the Stalinist regime, Krasikov, with her focus on disinformation, relativizes and generalizes the relevance of its mechanism. Julian's own post-Soviet story embodies the afterlife of communism in modern-day Russia. The afterlife of communism in modern-day Russia here takes the form of continuities between Soviet and post-Soviet repressive state apparatuses as he experiences them in the archive and, together with his son Lenny, in his business negotiations. It is not a truth about the past that the police files reveal, as is sometimes thought,[47] but rather the disinformation strategies in which we, too, as readers of Julian's story, become implicated.

The Capital of Denunciation: Keith Gessen's *A Terrible Country*

In *A Terrible Country*, Keith Gessen narrates a year in the life of a Soviet-born American, Andrew Kaplan, who travels to Moscow to spend a summer—or so it was meant to only be at first—taking care of his aging grandmother, Seva. In the exposition opening the novel, we promptly learn the basic setup of this autobiographically informed story.[48] The first two pages provide the key thematic parameters of the plotline: the (neo)liberal American academy, Slavic studies, aggressive and murky Russian capitalism under Putin, and its political opposition. Andrew—or rather, increasingly as the novel continues, Andrei—stays longer in Moscow than initially planned. In the span of the year he spends there, Andrei evolves from a penniless recent Russian literature PhD adjuncting online to a Columbia University "inaugural chair of Gulag studies"[49] with a comfortable salary and other benefits. *A Terrible Country* is a most "observant book about the country that has now been America's bedeviling foil for almost a century,"[50] as another Soviet-born writer in the United States suggested, but at its most perceptive, it actually reveals the imbrication of both systems. Namely, Andrei's American academic ascent relies on the idealization of his political dissent toward post-Soviet oligarchic capitalism. His contacts among local Marxists, who provide information about opposition to Vladimir Putin's regime, earn him a much-coveted scholarly publication in a prestigious journal, while his brief but internationally publicized arrest leads directly to the job offer from Columbia. Yet he would not have become the chair of gulag studies at an Ivy League university were it not for his prompt release from jail in Russia, which was only possible because he denounced the Marxist group of which he was a member. His success in the American neoliberal academy— which is itself proud of critically approaching the repressive Soviet state as its own "foil"—is therefore predicated on Andrei's conforming with the repressive post-Soviet state apparatus inherited from its Soviet predecessor.

A Terrible Country confronts the heritage of communist repressions, complementing Krasikov's *The Patriots* and also picks up some of the themes discussed in chapter 2, including third-generation Soviet-born narratives of World War II and the implication of one's grandparents in the postwar Stalinist regime. Gessen's novel is closest to Julia Alekseyeva's *Soviet Daughter*, with its transnational leftist genealogies and complex mixture of emancipatory heritage and the involvement of one's predecessors in Stalinism. Yet here these themes do not serve to tell a revisionary story of survival, despite the hopes of Gessen's protagonist. "This is great!" enthuses Andrei's mentor in Slavic studies. "You'll be on the ground. You can find something new and original. Or something old!"[51] Initially, Andrei is just as optimistic, musing, "I pictured myself sitting monastically in my room and with my grandmother's stories in hand adding a whole new dimension to my work."[52] The grandmother, however, suffers from dementia and only in random bouts of memory supplies her grandson with family stories, hardly what he was looking for: "Once in a while I tried to jog her memory about Soviet history—Stalinism, the purges, the war, the 'thaw'—but I never got anywhere. She didn't remember, and she didn't seem to want to try."[53] In contrast to third-generation Holocaust narratives, which often hinge on miraculously saved heirlooms and fragmented memories that still somehow cohere into a story, Gessen shows not only the unreliability of cultural memory but also the physiological impossibility of remembering. If nothing seems to work in this "terrible country," as grandmother Seva tags Russia, memory as such is also simply kaput.[54] *A Terrible Country* purposefully, then, fails to follow Andrei's initial idealized mnemonic impulse, not only in order to make a larger cultural comment on memory practices but also for reasons linked with the literary market. In 2004, Keith Gessen's sibling, the prominent journalist Masha Gessen, authored a nonfiction volume based on the life stories of both their grandmothers, including Rosalia "Ruzya" Solodovnik, to whom *A Terrible Country* is dedicated and who clearly served as the inspiration for the character of Baba Seva. Keith Gessen's novelistic form, including its auto-ironic neat plotlines, provides, however, the possibility to effectively comment on the paradoxes of memory work and its uses, in the academy and in politics.

Hoping for research inspiration from his Russian Jewish grandmother is only the beginning of Andrei's search for firsthand data from native informants. To amplify the crisis of memory, Keith Gessen pairs Baba Seva's almost complete memory void with her sense of a lack of collective belonging: a refrain that pierces through the text is Seva's complaint that "all my friends have died. All my relatives have died. Everybody is dead except me. What's the point?"[55] Practically speaking, Andrei too has virtually no one from among family and friends to offer oral histories that might aid him in his project.

This forgetting pertains also to Jewishness, which is present only as traces of antisemitic state policies in the past and articulations of everyday antisemitism in the present. The only remaining friend of Baba Seva, Emma Abramovna, who, unlike Seva, "managed to hang on at Moscow State despite the anti-Jewish campaign," is very difficult to reach and disappoints Andrei's grandmother by not inviting her to her *dacha* for the summer.[56] Any chance of mnemonic material from this elderly "intimidating person"—who "had escaped Hitler, had been exiled to Siberia as a Polish national, and had maintained good looks that had invited a great deal of unwanted male attention, including at one point from the NKVD"[57]—is thwarted when she announces she keeps her distance from Andrei's grandmother on purpose. Everyday antisemitism, on the other hand, provides no interesting material for an academic paper. It manifests in the Nazi salutes of skinheads in the center of Moscow, as well as ordinary acts of nastiness to Baba Seva from her neighbors. Gessen demonstrates Andrei's unpreparedness for Russia, as well as his grandmother's existential loneliness, with an incident involving elderly women in his grandmother's own courtyard: when Andrei engages in American-style politeness, attempting small talk about their plans for the summer so that he might find occasional company for his grandmother, they insinuate that "Seva *Efraimovna*" is "probably going to Israel" for vacation.[58]

Since family memory has failed and there are no consequential stories to be told, the focus falls on the context of this forestalled "act of transfer"[59]—in this case, the novel's narrator. As a result, the novel centrally reflects back on the position of the actual storyteller: a Soviet-born American academic and grandson, who tells his own story in the first person from the location of 2008 Moscow, and who—as becomes increasingly clear—is not "cut out for Russia."[60]

Andrei's academic background in Russian literature, a field traditionally linked to the Cold War paradigm of area studies, crucially shapes his actions in Moscow and the development of the plot. When area studies was established in the American academy after World War II, it followed a Cold War conceptual pattern "characterized by 'one hand clapping' due to an almost exclusive reliance on American and West European sources which often reduced Soviet and Communist actors to superficial caricature."[61] Owing its existence at least partly to the totalizing framework of "knowing the enemy," it posited a radical difference between the "Free World" and the communist bloc. However, since the transformations of 1989 and the collapse of the Soviet Union in 1991,

Afterlives of Communism • 75

post–Cold War historiography has instead "approached the struggle between the super-powers as a process of mutual escalation," both questioning easy binaries and historicizing its processes.[62]

Quite early in the novel, Gessen effectively communicates the stakes of an American academy still rather predicated on this older, binary concept of Russian studies, showing readers what a model Russian studies scholar looks like in this environment. Andrei's graduate school friend, Alex Fishman, is hugely successful at getting funding. His research focus combines an interest in the gulag with digital humanities: "People loved reading about the Soviet Gulag—it made them feel better about the U.S. of A."[63] Exploring Cold War totalitarian otherness, with the honorable desideratum "to bear witness to this suffering,"[64] he follows the logic of area studies, plays the academic game right, and lands first a postdoc at a prestigious university, then a full-time job. Nowhere visible here are the more recent historiographical trends advanced by scholars in Russian studies, involving, for instance, a global Russian or global post-socialist framework, or an exploration of the Global South as a playground of both the Soviet Union and the United States.[65] Moreover, Andrei's own academic focus, a marginal literary figure, earns criticism from his American mentor, who sees it as unlikely to help him on the crowded academic job market in Slavic studies post-2008 crisis—even though, from a cultural studies viewpoint, such a study from outside the canon or "looking at the pores of elite texts to tease out excluded itineraries" could lead to a counter-hegemonic contribution.[66]

For a good portion of the novel, Andrei—in his light, self-centered first-person narration—holds Fishman as a negative example of how to live a good (academic) life. Both may be Soviet-born Americans, yet Andrei believes he himself better represents an organic intellectual, engaged in his community and trying to make its disadvantages academically and socially meaningful (another cherished academic model). In this vein, Gessen convincingly paints Andrei's academic origin story, as he finally finds his place in the Slavic studies department:

> Whenever I saw a Russian class in the course listings I read the description and moved on; why study at college something that I could passively imbibe at home? But halfway through my first year . . . I walked over to the Slavic department. It was on the fourth floor of the gray foreign languages building, and unlike every other place on campus it was somehow homey. They had managed to Russify it. There was a big samovar in the corner, tea mugs everywhere, old Russian books in their Soviet editions like the ones we had at our house, and an ironic poster of Lenin. . . . I felt I had found, for the first time at that large and forbidding institution, a place where I could be at home.[67]

Gessen romanticizes this moment through the image of "home." However, it is not about nostalgia for the Russia of his childhood but rather something else: an affective attachment that seamlessly connects his family's home in the United States with his intellectual home in the Slavic department through the portable objects of memory retained by Soviet-born immigrants, whether intellectual (a "Soviet bookshelf"), political (Soviet state paraphernalia), or cultural (an emblematic Russian drink).

It is from this point of view—that of an organic, diasporic intellectual affectively engaged in his imagined collectivity—that Andrei attacks Fishman when they meet at a dinner party in Moscow. After Fishman systematically and indiscriminately derides contemporary Russia as "totalitarianism in a postmodern guise," Andrei protests: "You run down Russia so much! You complain about it and make jokes about it all the time. And yet you also profit from it. It's your job to study Russia and yet you seem to have nothing but contempt for it. . . . WHAT HAVE YOU DONE FOR RUSSIA?!"[68] Gessen pits a profiteering and implicitly unethical Fishman against an empathic Andrei who aims to "change the way people talked about Russia and thought about Russia" and, consequently, "Russia itself."[69] Ironically, this exchange sets off a crisis that results in the protagonist's ascent in the American academy. The pitched moment at the dinner party reveals to the other guests the extent of his failure to navigate the politics of American academia and consequently produces an invitation to a roundtable on the neoliberal academy, where he meets a Marxist group that becomes an object of his ethnography and the topic of a successful journal article.

If gulag studies reproduces an old area studies framework, then analyzing Russian socialists has a chance of representing "something new and original"— what Andrei's advisor told him to seek. On hearing that Andrei is in touch with such a group and might push his research in this direction, the advisor is explicitly enthusiastic: "The return of the repressed. The incorrigible Russian. Whatever. Yes. Do it."[70] For Andrei, the roundtable constitutes a veritable revelation, a "political awakening."[71] Readers of the novel get it all explained in detail: Andrei's evolution from son of conservative Soviet Union escapees to liberal college student, though never a socialist, perhaps even "an anti-socialist," to this particular moment when "everything . . . became clear" to him.[72] The key element for understanding his family's history in post-Soviet Russia is, as a roundtable discussant suggested, "the dictatorship of the market."[73] In an interview, Gessen suggests that Andrei's trajectory in Moscow over a few months parallels his own much longer trajectory toward a critique of capitalism, which materializes more directly in the documentary volume Gessen coedited on the Occupy movement.[74]

Andrei immerses himself in the Marxist group, which is named October: he attends their reading group, perusing Marx's *Capital*, dates one of its members, takes part in an anti-fascist protest, and finally "enlists" as a full member and receives training in subversive tactics and how to behave in case he is arrested. He also follows one of the group's leaders to his "mobile classrooms": an organic education framework he developed to tutor the underprivileged for free as a form of protest against the privatization of the university, which he dogmatically quit. Up to a point, Andrei's work for October, which includes translating texts into English for their planned international website, mirrors the work he puts into his academic article—both are cultural translations for new audiences. Andrei's interest in the Russian New Left in the "shell-shocked former Second World" might represent an alternative for Western Slavists, an opportunity to register oppositional entities beyond the Communist Party and the liberal opposition.[75]

In *A Terrible Country*, the afterlife of communism does not emerge only through the legacy of American area studies, a heritage of past political persecution, and the renewal of Marxist ideas of the New Left. Centrally, it also manifests itself at the police station after Andrei is arrested during an October-organized protest against an oil company. Gessen stages Andrei's denunciation of his comrades at this moment as an "everyday practice,"[76] since the state functionaries interviewing him just assume the existence of "popular collaboration," without "the exalted quality, the flavor of spiritual dedication," as was the case in the Soviet police state.[77] For his part, Andrei thinks he is merely having a friendly chat, with all the courteous niceties, about a Marxist political group. He misreads the situation as an intellectual debate, remaining oblivious to what his persuasive talking means in a repressive Russian context. His denunciation seems ordinary to the functionaries and remains naively unnoticed by Andrei himself, the Western Slavist.

Both the novel's closing and the academic capital of the protagonist hinge on this denunciation of his comrades. His arrest, read as a true test of academic/political engagement, becomes a cause célèbre that attracts the attention of Columbia University's president and leads to the creation of a gulag studies chair, with Andrei as its inaugural holder. Through his unknowing denunciation, he fails at knowing what an area studies academic should—"know your enemy"—but succeeds in the neoliberalized intellectual game of academic advancement.

In a circular manner, then, the closing of the novel both restates and challenges Andrei's self-presentation as given in the novel's opening and, more broadly, calls into question the position of the engaged intellectual from the West. On the first pages, the narrator strongly differentiates his leftist academic engagement from his brother Dima's murky business dealings in post-Soviet Russia, which forced him to flee to London. Echoing insights from migration studies, including the idea of decimal generations, he ascribes their dissimilar attitudes to the different ages they were at the time they immigrated: "I was six and Dima was sixteen, and that made all the difference. I became an American, whereas Dima remained essentially Russian."[78] His misreading of the interrogation room in Moscow as an intellectual debate or a college classroom confirms the contrast. Yet his unquestioning participation in the neoliberal university, which often uses the appropriately curated political engagement of its academics as a marketing strategy, is in principle not far off from Dima's love of capital.

Family Attachments

In *The Patriots* and in *A Terrible Country*, "afterlives of communism" does not refer to current demonizations of the personal Soviet past, as in the legislative vignette at the opening of this chapter, nor more generally conservatives' demonization of socialist politics in the United States. Rather, by setting their novels in an earlier Russia, during the first decade of the twenty-first century, Krasikov and Gessen point to Russian structures and institutions that very palpably constitute the afterlife of communism, be it in oligarchic capitalism or in state agencies, complicating the breakthrough narrative of transformation. In Gessen's novel, New Left politics in the United States is not demonized but rather challenged through a portrayal of twenty-first-century Russian socialists and their strategies. These authors do present the lives of their Soviet-born American protagonists as afterlives of communism, but they employ a very different framework than demonization.[79] By staging afterlives of communism through family memory and postmemory, Krasikov and Gessen create characters who seem familiar and who forge attachments through which readers become invested in them. Accessing their family memory is far from easy, and the results are emotionally and factually complicated. These afterlives mean dealing with previously inaccessible and currently imperfect knowledge: Florence's secret police file, with its cultural mistranslations and omissions, and Andrei's grandmother's dementia-addled memories. Gessen and Krasikov play with cultural and historical associations between Jewishness and radical politics, be it in the United States or Europe.[80] But the narrative manifestation of Jewishness and, with one exception, antisemitism occurs outside the narrative present, when we read about early twentieth-century Jewish immigrant neighborhoods in the United States, Orthodox Judaism, and institutionalized forms of state antisemitism. In this way, these narratives prepare us for the narratives set predominantly in late-Soviet times, discussed in the next chapter, where the focus on intimacies takes priority over the articulations of Jewishness.

The use of disinformation and denunciation as plot devices also produces readerly attachment. Set fully or partly in the twenty-first century, these stories implicate us, to hint at Michael Rothberg's term, in the ethical gray areas of agency by deploying modes of speaking and thinking that are markedly repressive and police state driven.[81] *The Patriots* makes readers the target of narrative disinformation; *A Terrible Country*, the witnesses of unwitting denunciation. How quickly, as the plot develops, do we understand with Julian the disinformation game his Russian business partner plays with him? And how long does it take us to see that during his interrogation, Andrei will end up a snitch?

It is not coincidental that *The Patriots*, foregrounding disinformation, uses omniscient narration, while *A Terrible Country* manipulates its readers with the first person. Krasikov understands that omniscience is contrary to what U.S. creative writing programs encourage.[82] These instead promote third-person narration linked to a particular and limited point of view, what literary scholar Paul Dawson calls "modernist impersonality."[83] In this context, an omniscient narrator appears both "technically obsolete" and "morally suspect."[84] But illustrating the all-encompassing and precisely "morally suspect" mechanism of disinformation aligns with omniscience, which only in select chapters in *The Patriots* is varied by Julian's first-person quest narrative.

By forging these attachments with their readers, the two texts put into perspective earlier, satirical novels by Soviet-born Jews in the United States, written in the first decade of the twenty-first century, about Eastern Europe after the "collapse of communism." Like comic relief in socialist states that anthropologist Sergei Oushakine calls "jokes of repression," this diasporic post-Soviet self-satire represented a "socially acceptable painkiller that modifie[d] the perception when the perception cannot be changed."[85] We might therefore call it jokes of "post-repression": what was satirized was the immediate aftermath of the end of the Cold War, aggressive capitalism, and its unchangeable global post-*Sovietness*. It was not just aesthetically appealing and "chic" but also constituted a way of coping with the detached American perception of the "communist bloc." Writing afterlives of communism as a part of family memory, creating affective transgenerational bonds, as in Krasikov and Gessen, comprises another strategy, another type of a "painkiller."

4

Soviet Intimacy

In Lara Vapnyar's short story "Puffed Rice and Meatballs," the protagonist's "American lover" flirtatiously and casually asks her to tell him about "the horrors of communism."[1] The narrator is at first puzzled: "Why would a man with whom she'd gone on only a few dates . . . be interested in something as intimate as her childhood?" Then she quickly clarifies: "He was simply asking for some entertainment—for an easy, amusing, and preferably sexy story about the exotic world to which his lover belonged."[2] Katya, the protagonist, caters to his needs and gives him a thematically appropriate and not-too-exotic guided tour of her first timid explorations of the other gender's genitals in preschool. It is a relatable experience, "horrific" strictly with regard to the disciplinary regulations of a late-socialist preschool, which add only a bit of foreign flair.

Here Katya may be a tour guide not only for her American lover but for American readers in general, as Vapnyar has elsewhere described herself as a writer.[3] The second part of the short story, however, reveals a narrative that remains concealed from her lover and that appears to be more defining for Katya's adolescence. In this bittersweet vignette from the 1980s, Vapnyar again refuses to illustrate any "horrors" of the late Soviet Union, unless being too late in line to get a rare snack—puffed rice, quite the delicacy in the midst of a shortage economy—may be considered one. This was a late-Soviet way of life: limited goods, the excitement sparked by clothing from *zagranitsa* (or the West, and a great deal of the everyday, near ceaseless experience of queuing in shops.[4] This ordinary story is not "touristic" enough to be shared with the lover. It is too mundane, neither exceptional nor attractive enough, and it does not quickly or easily convey the assumed radical and dramatic otherness of communism, which I explored in the previous chapter. Yet Vapnyar shares it with the readers as if to demonstrate that the actual lived experience of the Soviet Union in the 1980s *cannot* be told as "horrors," even if it was marked by panoptic control and traumatic repression.

This story comes from Vapnyar's second short story volume, *Broccoli and Other Tales of Food and Love*, which followed her debut collection, *There Are Jews in My House*. The title of the debut collection hinted at Jewishness as its theme, and indeed the titular story, a failed Holocaust rescue narrative with Russian antisemitism as its driving force, was in fact *horrific*.[5] But Vapnyar's second volume did not take up recognizably Jewish themes in such an explicit way (nor, for that matter, did any of her other later work). The focus notably shifted.

This virtual absence or at least sidelining of Jewishness in Vapnyar's later work, as well as in some other texts by women that create the memory of the late-Soviet moment, which they experienced before their emigration, stands in stark contrast to the texts included in the three previous chapters. The novels and short story discussed in chapter 1 showed diasporic renditions of post-Soviet space that ran counter to the spatial logic characteristic of the representation of Eastern Europe and, again, emphasized the unspoken normative underpinnings of American Jewishness. In chapter 2, on the postmemory of war and the Holocaust, Soviet-born writers entered into conversation with non-immigrant Jewish American authors, often creating a historical and memory counterweight to their narratives. Chapter 3, in turn, illustrated the memory of communism, creating connecting lines between Jewish leftist traditions. This chapter's writers, crafting Soviet memory in English, have placed it in a different relation to Jewishness. The virtual absence of Jewishness from Vapnyar's later texts—particularly the novel *The Scent of Pine*, but also several short stories—appears as a strategic choice responding to the critical reception of her early texts, which included reservations concerning their position under the rubric of American Jewishness: "After I was celebrated as a Jewish writer, I felt very complex contradictory feelings about this, because most of all, I felt guilty, I felt like an imposter. I did not know enough about Judaism, I didn't know a lot about Jewish culture, I didn't even know enough about Jewish American writers. While participating constantly in conferences and writing pieces about what it's like to be a Jewish American writer, I didn't feel fully as a Jewish American writer."[6] Still, Vapnyar emphasizes that her reservations involve the label "Jewish American writer," a specific and contextualized version of Jewishness serving as the rubric under which her texts are published and read. The form of Jewishness with which she actually identifies is an element that would only be misread, so—just in case—it could be subdued. It is less a comment on herself than on the context of the reception of her work: "I felt acutely Jewish when I was growing up in Russia, but I did not understand what it's like to feel Jewish here in the U.S., because it meant something different."[7]

Ellen Litman, whose novel *Mannequin Girl* I focus on in this chapter alongside Vapnyar's work, strikes a similar tone, highlighting the very different connotations of Jewish identification in the United States: "I had good friends, also Jewish, and we'd long ago learned what to expect: colleges we couldn't apply to, professions we couldn't pursue. We shared a certain sense of humor, a certain kind of sadness. We'd learned to recognize others like ourselves. 'Our people,' we called them. Here in America being Jewish meant something else entirely. I didn't quite know what it meant."[8] In Vapnyar's texts discussed here—and contrasting with her earlier stories as well as her intertextual links to other authors crafting late-Soviet memory—Jewishness becomes significant precisely in its relative absence. If read literally, it may pose a challenge for categorizing this literature. But it may also highlight how we need to complicate the category of Jewish American writing.

This "absence" functions as a way in which to mark difference from the identity narratives of American ethnicity and Jewishness. Late-Soviet memory as presented here is not predicated on narratives of religious persecution in the USSR, which—as we have seen in Bezmozgis's *The Free World*—were encouraged in the visa application process and underlay the Soviet Jewry movement.[9] Such solely lachrymose narratives would be a shortcut, sidelining the rich cultural lives of Soviet Jews. Scholars have recently elaborated how Soviet Jewishness found cultural expression in the USSR,[10] but this knowledge remains largely unavailable to the American mainstream. For fear of being misread, Vapnyar and Litman seem to shift what they perceive as the imposed logic of Jewishness—American Jewishness—to a focus on the regulation of gender, bodies, and intimacy in the Soviet Union at the time of their childhood and/or immigration.

The focus on late-Soviet regulations concerning gender, bodies, and intimacy and the emphasis on non-normativities within these regulations serve the articulation of otherness, of Jewishness.[11] It is not an attempt at building analogies but a strategic displacement to stay legible. In the context of contemporary feminist theorizing—which questions gender and sexual universalisms and is especially attentive to the particularities of non-Western locations—such a focus may be more effective than one that seeks to illuminate the idiosyncrasies of Soviet Jewishness. This holds especially for women, since the figure of the Soviet Jew was from the outset coded as quintessentially male, and thus this particular discourse was less available to them, as we already saw in Julia Alekseyeva's *Soviet Daughter* in chapter 2.[12]

Gender, body, and intimacy in the Soviet context have a great potential to articulate other kinds of otherness. Communist universalizing of Soviet citizens was a misnomer and a failure on many levels, with regard to both ethnicity and gender. Recent scholarship has extensively explored state socialist regulations of gender, sexuality, and bodies, not so much romanticizing its gender system but rather noting its "redeeming qualities."[13] Kristen Ghodsee, an anthropologist of Eastern Europe, has persuasively argued that "women had more fulfilling lives during the Communist era. And they owed this quality of life, in part, to the fact that these regimes saw women's emancipation as central to advanced 'scientific socialist' societies, as they saw themselves."[14] The system prevented the commodification and instrumentalization of sexuality that became the hallmark of the post-Soviet era, as we have seen, for instance, in Anya Ulinich's *Petropolis*, whose protagonist is a mail-order bride to the United States. While gender and sexuality regulations varied among Eastern Bloc countries, they all revolved around a top-down model of women's rights as workers, mothers, and leaders, and hence, for the purpose of a productive citizenry working toward the common cause, they focused on heterosexual marriage and sex rather than individual needs.

Evolving Soviet regulations of sexuality veered toward etacratic (those dictated by the Soviet regime) biopolitical priorities.[15] Progressive sexual regulations in the 1920s, including the decriminalization of homosexuality and the legalization of abortion, gave way to a Soviet model of virtue and chastity, leading again to the criminalization of male homosexuality in 1933–1934.[16] Sex education textbooks published shortly after World War II endeavored to uproot "capitalist vestiges of the past"[17] and stressed that "family and marriage were not a private matter in the Soviet Union."[18] They referred to the prewar pedagogue Anton Semyonovich Makarenko, who warned that knowledge and discourse about sexuality would divert young people from their revolutionary duties.[19] In the early 1960s, the tone of this newly intensified propaganda changed: it was no longer focused on the past but on the present, particularly the "negative" influences of Western culture entering the USSR in ever fiercer waves. The cure for this influx was to be found in educational policies, including the publication of such textbooks, in print runs of several thousand copies, covering (in the parlance of the time) the "hygiene" of sexual intercourse and married life.[20]

Part of the official party line was to disseminate warnings about the dangers of Western influence and the moral collapse it might effect: Soviet authorities had a very negative view of American rock-and-roll dances such as the twist, which had begun to become popular among young Soviets.[21] Just as in many other national contexts, male homosexuality was pathologized and persecuted, while female homosexuality was considered an illness requiring medical treatment. Consequently, the latter was less visible in the public sphere.[22] Sociologist Francesca Stella stresses that in the USSR, female homosexuality could only find its expression beyond the public sphere: "It was only within informal environments, such as dissident and subcultural circles and personal social networks."[23]

Much like sex, disabilities supposedly simply did not exist in the USSR. Anthropologist Sarah Phillips quotes a Russian state official in 1980 as claiming, "There are no invalids in the USSR!"[24] This opinion "encapsulated the politics of exclusion and social distancing that characterized disability policy under state socialism,"[25] and this politics of exclusion and isolation was largely based on a system of residential institutions for individuals with disabilities. The classification of disabilities in Russia and the Soviet Union developed from the system used for judging combat injuries and was based on evaluating individuals' "usefulness for society,"[26] including their ability to work. As a result, children (including the congenitally disabled), who were relatively low in this hierarchy of useful citizens, were not acknowledged by this system until the relatively late date of 1967, and a separate category for children with disabilities was not created until 1979.[27]

Narratives by Vapnyar, Ulinich, and Litman challenge the oft-repeated dictum "There is no sex in the USSR,"[28] known from the final days of the Soviet regime, but at the same time illustrate how some of these progressive measures conspicuously lacked two Western staples of women's and sexual liberation: sex education and the visibility and acceptance of same-sex relationships, themes especially present in Vapnyar's texts. While readers can relate to well-known topics like working women or mothers with state-provided childcare facilities, they see historical differences that illustrate the ambiguities of state socialist emancipation. The initial vignette from Vapnyar's short story, with its "exotic" preschool image, says it all: the Soviet-born protagonist talks about preschool as a natural part of her life, a state childcare facility available for all—a truly exotic idea in the United States, which previously relied almost entirely on stay-at-home moms and nowadays has exorbitant daycare fees. And indeed, Vapnyar and Litman characteristically set a good part of their novels in state-run communal childcare and educational spaces—a boarding school and a summer camp—which tacitly assume an emancipatory set of gender assumptions.

Vapnyar's and Litman's narratives are explicitly woven around body and gender normativity, abortion, same-sex desire, and sex education. As such, they appear just as relatable to the American reading public as they were to the American lover in Vapnyar's short story "Puffed Rice and Meatballs." As she noted in an interview: "Through sex we can see whatever is weird about the society in a distilled form. In general, it is so intense in people's life that whatever is going on, whatever it is we *are* in a society, it is even stronger and more noticeable with regard to sex. You can just write about sex in the Soviet Union; you don't need to write about politics or about anything else. If you just write about sex, you can show so much about culture."[29] That which is sexually possible—that is, socially and legally acceptable—becomes for Vapnyar a litmus test for the political organization of the state and the measure of a society. While Vapnyar highlights how the type of the state truly crystallizes in a livable sexuality, she also stresses just how much fun it is to write about sex—and, by extension, how much fun it is for the audience to read about it.[30] At the same time, it incurs no risk of being interpellated, to use philosopher Louis Althusser's term, into (American) Jewishness.

Because sexuality is socially organized or constructed, as second-wave feminist theorists have taught us, by examining social regulations on sexuality and intimacy we not only better understand its social conditioning but also, through this key instrument for biopolitical power and control of population, grasp the nature of the social organization as such. As anthropologist Alexei Yurchak has shown with respect to other domains of personal life in late socialism, stretching what was possible and creating new meanings in the everyday was not the opposite of ideologically controlled public life but its complementary and necessary other.[31] These stories do not explicitly relate the "horrors of communism," but the performance of a state ideology still significantly looms through them. As we will see, they also speak to other regulations of the late-Soviet body politic, such as those regarding Jewishness.

Writings by Lara Vapnyar and Ellen Litman, as well as Anya Ulinich (whose work I address briefly below), provide intimate knowledge of the late Soviet Union by foregrounding intimacy under state socialism rather than Jewishness. With their focus on regimes of intimacy, they also help us understand gendered scripts from other novels of migration featuring Soviet Jewish protagonists. In so doing, texts by these three authors serve as prequels to other American immigrant Soviet-born narratives that have unabashed women protagonists and women-dominated family structures, such as those by Julia Alekseyeva, Nadia Kalman, Sana Krasikov, and Maria Kuznetsova.[32] In the Soviet family model, women were supposed to work professionally (the primary duty of all Soviet citizens regardless of gender) but also have full responsibility for home life. No wonder, then, that the daughters of immigrant matriarchs see this model for what it is—a patriarchal arrangement—rebel against it, and consequently fail the test of domesticity, as Slavic studies scholar Karen Ryan has previously noted.[33]

While Lara Vapnyar, Anya Ulinich, and Ellen Litman belong to the Soviet-born literary cohort in the United States, they all immigrated in the 1990s as young adults. When Vapnyar compares herself to other Soviet-born writers, she notes their close birthdates, but also that they experienced immigration at a different stage in their lives: "I was more Russian and more adult. Even though we are almost the same age, when I read David Bezmozgis and Gary Shteyngart—and I love both of these amazing writers—I end up identifying with the parents, not the children, because I came here as an adult."[34] When pressed, she agrees that "Sovietness," too, could be a defining category. Vapnyar's autobiographically inspired fiction, as well as that of Ulinich and Litman, uses the perspective of a child to narrate memories of late-Soviet communism—in this, the works are similar to Gary Shteyngart's memoir *Little Failure*. Yet these women authors convey Soviet memory more specifically from the point of view of an adolescent girl or young woman, with an acute sensitivity for regulations concerning otherness, here articulated through women's intimacy.

The Warping of State Socialism:
Ellen Litman's *Mannequin Girl*

"It's just a boarding school . . . Like in *Jane Eyre*, except you go home on week-ends,"[35] says the well-read Anechka. In the novel *Mannequin Girl*, she is still a dissident when her seven-year-old daughter Kat is enrolled in a school for children with serious spinal "deformities"[36] located on the outskirts of Moscow. Ellen Litman's debut novel, published after her short story collection *Last Chicken in America* (2007), introduces readers to Katia Knopman as she attends first grade in 1980, and later narrates her years in grades seven and eight, right before the breakup of the USSR. Within the novel, this "special school"[37] shapes children to fit its vision of the ideal citizen: both literally (that is, physically), imposing itself on the bodies of students who do not fit mor-phological norms, and ideologically.

"Boarding institutes" (*doma-internaty*) were special education establish-ments for children up to the ages of sixteen to eighteen. Their system was based on specialized medical categorizations that, among other things, autho-rized separate facilities for children with mobility disabilities—as is the case in *Mannequin Girl*. The pressure on parents to place their child in such an insti-tution was strong because these institutions both showed that the state could meet the needs of all its citizens and guaranteed the separation of persons with disabilities from the rest of society, thereby supporting the image of a "healthy nation."[38] Memoirs and interviews reveal two different stories when it comes to these institutions—some maintained a decent standard of education, while others were more like prisons.[39]

The association of such places with Soviet correctional facilities is not acci-dental: boarding houses for children with disabilities were part of an extensive network of educational and reformative institutions established throughout the history of the USSR. Boarding schools for the children of laboring parents, for example, served as "'model teaching institutions' that would combine labor edu-cation and 'Communist education,' turning their graduates into well-balanced adults who could contribute fully to Soviet society."[40] In line with such phi-losophies, it was necessary for children with disabilities to undergo processes that would "correct" the flaws with their bodies so that they might later become model citizens.

Litman's novel thus addresses the formation of the universal Soviet citizen, but, importantly, she also reveals how this process assumes differences relating to gender and ethnicity. Regulations and restrictions are in this novel ubiquitous because Litman focuses on the special boarding school as a "total institution."[41] Following Erving Goffman's classic definition, "total" denotes here specific and all-encompassing regulations on the individual within a strictly defined place and time, and with a clear purpose.[42] Spatially, the location is restricted, "cut off from the wider society," and activities have a collective character, take place within a regulated and rhythmic temporality, and serve the "official aim of the institution."[43] While total institutions are "particularly distinctive" in democratic settings,[44] here in *Mannequin Girl* the boarding school, with its attempt at total control, functions rather like a miniature late-Soviet state. Through this institution's gradual transformation over the eight years Kat spends there, we witness its devolution in conjunction with the growth of an "underlife" at the school consisting of various non–centrally regulated activities—the same pattern evident in the devolution of the Soviet Union.[45] Moreover, if a total institution is based on a binary between its cadres and, in this case, its students,[46] the opening up of the school and the collapse of its total reach can be read through the presence of Kat's parents, who are later in the story hired as teachers. By narratively enlarging the focus of the novel to include them, Litman can address questions relating to reproduction.

The bodily transformation of the "students (patients)"[47] begins immediately upon entering the school: "Their hair is shorn . . . for some implausible reason that has to do with swimming."[48] It then continues through the centerpiece of the institute's medical treatment, orthopedic braces: "They allow these monstrous things to swallow their bodies, and when at last they rise, they're not the same."[49] In the beginning, seven-year-old Kat observes "deformed, freakish children,"[50] still as something of an outsider: "The girls look tiny. There's something odd in their appearance, something unyielding and stiff, and it takes Kat a moment to take in the contraptions they are in. Their heads are held up by white plastic collars; thin metal slats run alongside their necks; and beyond that, she can see the shape of something cumbersome, like armor, gripping them under their blue uniform jacket and pants."[51] Soon enough, Kat herself is called in to be fitted for such a brace. At this point, the book reaches the outer edges of metaphorization, as Kat feels the system physically oppressing her entire body: "A tall wooden construction resembling a gallows stands in the center of the room. They help her to this scaffolding. They strap her in. Hard wooden planks rest firm against her buttocks; a rubber harness is looped around her chin. The screws are tightened to the maximum, the harness cranked up so high she can't even glance at her feet. You must be absolutely still to get a perfect mold."[52] The "perfect mold" for a perfect citizen—the brace promising to create a real "mannequin girl." Significantly, Litman notes that the school is mostly attended by girls. This kind of treatment and bodily normativity is clearly gendered. In the naive voice of young Kat, the narrator muses that boys "must be less susceptible to scoliosis."[53]

The oppression experienced at the school and the panic it induces are most powerfully expressed in the first dozen pages of the novel, focused almost exclusively on seven-year-old Kat. Litman achieves a defamiliarizing effect through the narrator's naivete—the point of view of a child. A child "does not recognize [her] situation as the consequence of the political system, and not of a fatal givenness. The child cannot compare [her] own society with other political systems, and hence takes it as 'normal.'"[54] This point of view contributes to the implied parallels between the boarding school and the state, suggesting that "the child-like, naive point of view is one of the mechanisms used by the communist system for deception."[55]

Later on, with some sarcasm, the narrator notices that the critical attitude Kat and her parents have toward the institution is rather an exception: as one of the matrons suggests, the very opportunity to attend such a school should be seen as a privilege. And indeed, some parents managed to cheat the system by securing fake medical diagnoses that allowed their perfectly healthy offspring to be enrolled in this prestigious establishment. Because "where else can you find a boarding school like this, with a rigorous curriculum and swimming lessons three times a week? There are no boarding schools for healthy kids, not anywhere in Moscow."[56]

This control over the development of citizens' bodies goes hand in hand with the conditioning of their minds—ideological indoctrination that is especially evident in the catchphrases students are confronted with: "The school is your new family"[57] or "Loyalty to one's collective is more important than familial love."[58] While such phrases may be the performative residue of communist ideology, and thus characteristic for late socialism,[59] they also reflect the belief that congenital disabilities—which the school specializes in—can be effectively eliminated. Indeed, transformation is one of the principles of total institutions.[60] These slogans point to the supremacy of the environment and the collective over inherited genetics and nuclear family bonds in the production of Soviet citizens, which is consistent with the fundamental assumptions of Soviet biopolitics.[61] In the Soviet system, school was supposed to be "a new world," giving the students "a positive sense of their own identity as pupils, a feeling of corporate identity, and a grasp that the school differed from the rest of the world."[62]

Despite the idealization of the collective and the insistence upon the school as the new family unit, *Mannequin Girl* clearly shows the limits of camaraderie, which are defined by ethnic boundaries and the exclusion of Jewishness. "Are you foreign? . . . Are you from another country? You've got a weird name," Kat hears from other girls in her first-grade class.[63] Litman also provides rudimentary instruction on the location of late-Soviet Jewishness by including a scene in which Anechka answers Kat's question "What's a Jew?"—a question prompted by some girls whispering a racial slur when Kat walks by.[64] The episode is very similar to one in Lara Vapnyar's strongly autobiographical story "A Question for Vera," in which a classmate approaches the six-year-old protagonist with a denunciatory whisper: "I know something about you. . . . You are a Jewess."[65] Yet while Kat learns from her mother that Jews in the USSR share a "nationality" yet—contrary to other ethnic groups—lack their own republic, Vapnyar's protagonist, enclosed in the microcosmic world of her preschool, has only her doll Vera to comfort her and hear such quintessential questions: "What if Vera was right that there wasn't anything bad or special about being Jewish?"[66]

In *Mannequin Girl*, anti-Jewish attitudes are also institutionalized in the everyday life of the school. Officials place Kat in a permanent working group made up of only other Jewish girls, and they label her parents "not properly Russian."[67] During the celebration of the Day of Friendship Between Nations, Kat is forced to wear an ethnically marked costume—that of a person from the Caucasus—which leads others to perceive her as ethnically "other."[68] In 1988, when attitudes begin to shift as religiously tinged nationalism takes hold among the "old guard," antisemitism becomes more pronounced.[69]

The novel soon enough provides readers with more evidence of how this notion of citizenship is imposed on individuals. The abortion that Anechka has once Kat is enrolled at the boarding school is not only an expression of the freedom of choice available to her within the state regulations but also a decision made under direct pressure from the state via its approach to disability and the attendant medical treatment. "They just couldn't risk it," according to Kat's father. "Not with Kat's scoliosis in the picture."[70] The repressed discomfort with this decision later reemerges in the form of Anechka's increasing obsession with becoming pregnant, which unfortunately only leads to more miscarriages and—in a hyperbolic narrative tour de force—to extramarital affairs and attempted suicides. This manifest and apparently excessive focus on reproduction, at the expense of all other desires, culminating in a personal crisis, is a reaction to the stringent normativization of Soviet citizens' bodies and their offspring. At the same time, these are Anechka's desperate and unsuccessful attempts at recovering her sense of agency (after the immediate and reflexive decision to have an abortion for fear of congenital disabilities). On a smaller scale, Anechka's attempt at reclaiming control over her body includes going to a dressmaker for a fitting after recovering from the procedure. There, *zagranitsa* clothing catalogues set the tone for the bodily ideal, but the dress must still be sown from the available "domestic" fabric.[71]

In the parts of the novel set in the late 1980s, when Kat is a teenager and the world of her school has become the norm for her, Litman alludes to the twilight of the USSR by making references to Chernobyl, perestroika, and Mikhail Gorbachev. These parts delve less into intimacy in late-Soviet socialism, though the school context is useful in once more illustrating the conflicts between the old guard and the new within the ruling Communist Party, both of which are represented in the novel by groups of teachers. We see hints of the coming end of the Soviet Union when Kat's parents become dissidents and are hired as teachers, supervising a drama club that allows the performance of works that would previously never have passed state censors. The club serves as the under-life of this total institution. It is the antithesis of the norms regarding collective life that lie at the heart of the school: "Here they can be themselves, they can be individuals and intellectuals. No one in the school is like them. The rest of the students are land-bound, practical, more than content to act en masse."[72]

As the political system devolves, Kat matures and her brace is removed. The adolescent point of view adopted by the narrator becomes more reliable, more aware of the political situation. Kat reaches an age where she begins to probe other, more adult areas of Soviet intimacy. Her observations of "sex manuals" at a friend's house offer glimpses of Soviet-style sex education: "They seemed crude, these drawings, purposefully unflattering, as if meant to discourage you from having sex."[73] Total institutions evoke negative associations, maybe even "the horrors of communism" for those in "the free world." But in Litman's novel the narrator is ambivalent toward the boarding school, as becomes clear late in the book: "This year—her last year—she doesn't mind the school at all. The schedule that used to feel oppressive, the jumble of classes and medical procedures, now seemed soothing, well controlled."[74] Perhaps this sentiment reflects the Soviet educational ideal: a school different from any in the rest of the known world, "on a higher level—a metaphysical level, one might almost say."[75] Yet even at that point, when Kat takes off her brace and looks at her reflection in a window pane, she does not feel beautiful.

Mannequin Girl is a narrative shaped by specific regulations at a late-Soviet special boarding school: its politicized faculty, ideological emphasis on the new collective over the nuclear family, and racialized ethnic hierarchies, including Jewishness. Yet many of the bodily technologies employed there to shape future citizens resonate more broadly with regard to body normativity. The total institution centered on a specific disability only crystallizes these norms. This resonance, however, extends well beyond this specific context and underlines how the "access to our own bodies and our own pleasures are also co-opted and pathologised through the interventions of education, medical and social care professionals."[76]

Sexual Education in Russia:
Lara Vapnyar's *The Scent of Pine*

Lara Vapnyar's 2003 short story "Love Lessons, Monday, 9 A.M." picks up very close to where Ellen Litman's *Mannequin Girl* left off: "The Ministry of

Education now required every school to introduce sex education in the tenth grade, and . . . [the principal] had to pick two sex-education teachers. I had good reason to worry."[77] In this story, which concludes her debut volume, Vapnyar provides a glimpse of a high school in the early 1990s from the point of view of a university student who is working as a math teacher. She is randomly assigned to teach sex education but, like Vapnyar herself when she was a young high school teacher, is less experienced than her women students.[78]

This story originated as an assigned "non-fiction piece about sexual education in Russia" for the *New Yorker*, then morphed into Vapnyar's second novel, *The Scent of Pine*.[79] In the context of English-language narratives concerning late-socialist intimacies, it functions as a companion piece to Litman's book. Vapnyar's protagonist is a university student working as a camp counselor during her vacation. The late-Soviet summer camp in the Russian woods functions as a microcosm, just as Litman's special boarding school had, though with quite different aims and regulations. Yet because of the structure of the novel—a retrospective tale related by an immigrant in the United States to her American-born colleague turned lover—the story also picks up a theme explored by the other short story in the volume, "Puffed Rice and Meatballs": that of translating the knowledge of communism.

Lara Vapnyar's *The Scent of Pine* is set in the United States and takes place in the early 2000s. Lena, a middle-aged Soviet-born migrant from Boston, is an adjunct professor who meets Ben, another professor, at a conference on the "aesthetics of oppression." Following the conference, they spend a romantic weekend at Ben's *dacha*, or vacation cottage, which becomes an opportunity for Lena to go into retrospective narrative mode, which in turn becomes a thematic extension of her lecture about sexual education in the USSR. Beginning as they drive together to the *dacha*, Lena tells him stories from the late USSR. In effect, the novel stages a debate about how best to transnationally relate stories of the Cold War: should they focus on the conventions of totalitarian oppression, as is the case with the academic conference the novel's characters take part in, or rather—as in the stories Lena tells—should they proceed more informally, allowing us to wonder about various spheres of influence and agency? The distance between these perspectives emerges clearly in the following quote, in which the narrator compares Lena and Ben during the conference: "He was talking about graphic novels set in oppressive societies, the speaker had a soft, pleasant voice, a calm and confident manner. Not a trace of an accent. He had no business talking about prison states. What could he possibly know? There were notes of warm amusement in his tone that suggested that he had understood whatever there was to understand about it. She had lived in America for thirteen years, and she didn't understand it at all. Where did this arrogance come from?"[80] En route to Ben's *dacha* in the state of Maine, Lena acts out the role of "native informant" in retelling stories from her youth, subtly challenging her companion's confident, knowledgeable arrogance. Her stories, though set in a very different time and place, sound on many levels familiar.

Contravening the official Cold War cultural narrative, Lena's stories of attending summer camps address Soviet era sexual chastity but go beyond the typical "oppressive" image of the communist state.[81] The summer camp, with its overt regulation of sexuality, represents a center of production of regulative sexual discourse. One of the fundamental demands made of youths is for them to keep their "hands over blankets,"[82] with numerous variations on this rule heard throughout the retelling. In the words of the main camp supervisor, "Masturbation is very bad for boys . . . bad and dangerous."[83] What is at stake here is the production of model citizens, something threatened by masturbation, which supposedly causes a number of unfortunate issues: "Memory loss. Impotence. Early death. Poor grades."[84] Due to this lack of sex education, which typically serves as a vehicle for state-delimited intimacy, classic works of Western literature become the basic practical and educational texts used by the students hired as camp instructors. This includes cultural texts created before firmly regimented rules for the regulation of sexuality were introduced in the nineteenth century, such as the fifteenth-century *Canterbury Tales* by Geoffrey Chaucer or the film *Last Tango in Paris* and other movies produced since the 1960s. This is the context for the characters' fascination with the sexually charged lambada, homoerotic experiments, and obsession with dating, which the camp instructors organize according to a carefully detailed schedule.

For Ben, the 1980s in Soviet Russia seem to resemble life in the United States before the sexual revolution. Indeed, according to sociologist Igor Kon, the sexual revolution did not begin in Russia until the 1980s.[85] The intensification of Soviet-style moral discourse and the increased emphasis on the differences between genders, moving away from the much more equality-focused discourse of the early 1980s, arose from a demographic crisis. In response to this crisis, schools introduced sex-ed classes called "The Ethics and Psychology of Family Life," which in fact was a traditionalist program of "gender socialisation."[86] Anya Ulinich's graphic memoir *Lena Finkle's Magic Barrel* provides a useful complementary narrative regarding this development. Across nine pages, Ulinich satirically draws five lessons from "The Glorious People's Sex Education of Lena Finkle,"[87] from early hints at where babies come from, through sexual harassment as a young child in Moscow's high rises, and up to the language of sexual prohibitions—reminiscent of those in Vapnyar's novel—pronounced by her mother against "onanism . . . a terrible affliction" when she was twelve.[88] Another lesson entitled "Useful Tips" depicts the obligatory sex education classes in ninth grade, "this new advancement in the late-Soviet civilization,"[89] which Vapnyar illustrated from the point of view of an instructor in "Love Lessons, Monday, 9 A.M." Here, in Ulinich's graphic novel (figure 7), the class

FIGURE 7 Anya Ulinich, *Lena Finkle's Magic Barrel* (New York: Penguin, 2014), 28.

instructor, a former emergency room nurse, "is clearly more at ease with dis-embodied limbs than with living bodies."[90] But even if the sex-ed classes are indeed an "advancement" with regard to body-skeptical prohibitory language and the path they offer toward Sovietness, they seem perfunctory. Ulinich's fifth lesson, "Everything you ever wanted to know . . ." in the times of pere-stroika, is an unfiltered wave of information about all the things, including sex, best "gleaned just by walking down a subway underpass."[91] Meanwhile, Ulinich's "the freedom of the press" vignette points to the larger phenomenon of not only the sexual revolution of the 1980s but also the apparent explosion of sex and violence in the ensuing post-Soviet years.[92]

Vapnyar similarly remembers the contrast between, on the one hand, the early 1980s, when she was growing up and "there were no books on sex, no mag-azine pieces. None of the TV shows or movies ever mentioned the physical side of love," and on the other hand, the early 1990s: "The burgeoning yellow press was filled with stories of incest, bestiality, necrophilia and rape, rape, rape, rape. My friends and I were consumed by dreams of pure romantic love, and simultaneously drowning in all that violent sexual imagery. We felt even more hapless and clueless than when we were kids."[93] Yet when comparing the Amer-ican sex-ed classes that her fifteen-year-old daughter had in the United States in the mid-2010s, she hesitates to make any quick assessment: "I can't tell which one is more oppressive."[94] Namely because "the pressure for contemporary American teenagers is to know everything, to understand everything, and too much information also creates fear."[95]

The sense of uncertainty and ambivalence concerning any comparison of the two worlds grows with the parallels between the setting of the main narrative in *The Scent of Pine*—that is, the "present" in which Lena relates these things to Ben—and the setting of the retrospective narrative nested within it. It brings us back to the diasporic spaces described in chapter 1 that use setting to com-plicate the hierarchical perception of the former USSR and the United States. The summer camp Lena remembers for Ben took place in the woods, a three-hour drive from Moscow. The novel itself is also set in idyllic nature: though far from Russia, Ben's *dacha* sits in the forests of Maine. The titular "scent of pine" underscores this metageographical link and encourages readers to under-stand Lena's stories accordingly. Vapnyar juxtaposes the two settings even earlier, when Lena arrives at the conference location of Saratoga Springs and feels it could be a Russian town: "There was nothing specifically American about this place. This could be anywhere. Western Europe. Eastern Europe. Russia. Lena had a fleeting thought that her summer camp memories had actu-ally transported her to Russia."[96] In Saratoga Springs, Lena feels uneasy, but it is the universal discomfort of a migrant intensified by the academic setting: "As if everyone was engaging in some sort of chemical reaction, from which she was excluded. Lena was suddenly seized by an acute feeling of being a stranger in America."[97] For readers, the exclusive resort town of Saratoga Springs in northern New York State may call to mind the Seligman affair of 1877, one of the most widely reported cases of antisemitic discrimination in U.S. history,[98] but for Vapnyar this setting does not carry these associations.[99] While in Litman's novel routine antisemitism intensified as the plot progressed through the 1980s, in *The Scent of Pine* the Jewishness of the protagonist is barely even marked. In contrast to *Mannequin Girl*, the retrospective narrative within contains only hints of Soviet antisemitism: a friend with a non-Russian-sounding name, Grisha Klein, was not admitted to a university.[100]

Lena's localized vignettes of everyday intimacies in the 1980s reveal to readers how it might be possible to move beyond "horrors" and "oppression" when talking about the Soviet Union and, more broadly, the "Eastern Bloc." And yet, at the same time, by the story's end Lena shows that she is an unreliable narrator. In an improbable series of coincidences, in Ben's *dacha* she finds an autobiographical comic strip book by another participant of the summer camp where she had worked that seems to give an alternative account. In this way, the novel leaves readers questioning their ability to connect to the former "Second World."

Queering Peripheries: Lara Vapnyar's "Lydia's Grove"

"We did not know anything and they know too much," is Lara Vapnyar's quick comparison of sex ed in the late Soviet Union and in the contemporary United States. Vapnyar's short story "Lydia's Grove," from the volume *There Are Jews in My House*, stages this un-knowledge—specifically with regard to same-sex relationships—from the point of view of a young child. Until more recently, Soviet-born Jewish writing in English has not featured many queer presences.[101] At the same time, queerness has recently become a defining programmatic characteristic of inclusive writerly and activist groups within the post-Soviet diaspora. A combining of non-heteronormativity and womanhood, including trans women as well as non-binary gender identification, is seen, for example, in two recently established collectives. The Cheburashka Collective brings together "women and non-binary writers from the Russian diaspora," as they write about themselves on Twitter, now known as X.[102] The Kolektiv Goluboy Vagon, meanwhile, defines itself as "Queer & Trans, Gender-Marginalized, Post-Soviet Jewish Immigrant-Settlers."[103] Creative enterprise, including writing, is one aspect of their progressive activities. In this case, gender/sexuality becomes a key coordinate intersecting with (post-)Sovietness and Jewishness—a configuration that is crucial to Soviet-born writers' narratives of state-regulated intimacy.

Just like the protagonists in the works of Litman, Vapnyar, and Ulinich, members draw on experiences from their late-Soviet childhoods, and the names of these collectives make such connections explicit, calling to mind memories of Russian animated children's films such as *Gena the Crocodile*, which features the character Cheburashka, and children's songs such as "Goluboy vagon."[104] Anna Fishzon has shown how animated films from the Brezhnev era can be read as cultural texts that disorient our sense of time.[105] And so references made to these animated films on the one hand recall Russian childhoods, while on the other direct our attention toward representations that undermine the collective norms of the Soviet age of stagnation. In this context, Vapnyar's "Lydia's Grove" serves as a kind of Soviet backstory for these newer initiatives countering gender and sexual normativity. Even if not told from an explicitly queer point of view, the story includes a perspective from within a late-Soviet childhood that has been theorized as queer in relation to the normative Western notions of Cold War time.[106]

"Lydia's Grove" is set in 1980s Moscow and narrated by eight-year-old Lara, who tells the story of the literary partnership between her mother and Lydia Petrovna Rousseau. Across several winter months, every weekend Lara and her mother take long trips by bus and metro to Lydia's apartment on the peripheries of Moscow—that is, to the titular Lydia's grove. Lydia and Lara's mother are coauthors of books for children, published under the shared pen name Veller-Rousseau, combining the names and identities of both authors. Lara's mother is close to Lydia, bound by a relationship that remains unnamed—is impossible to be named—by Lara. The bond between the two women slowly unravels as a new friend of Lydia's, Emma, appears on the scene and then moves in with her. The narrator, using Lara's perspective, notices the multilayered aspect of this relationship, wondering to herself, "Friends sometimes stayed at our house, too, but never for such a long time."[107]

The virtual absence of a Jewish theme in "Lydia's Grove" contrasts with the titular story from the same volume, poignantly titled *There Are Jews in My House*, which focuses explicitly on Russian antisemitism during World War II. As in her *Scent of Pine*, Jewishness is virtually invisible in the short story "Lydia's Grove," suggested only implicitly through Lara's mother's surname. Together with Lydia's non-Russian surname, it becomes yet another slight marker of otherness, yet one that historically cannot be underestimated.[108]

This story serves as a model example of the classic narrative involving the homosexual/homosocial continuum among women as described by Eve Kosofsky Sedgwick, in which female friendships with erotic elements are narrated from the naive and unreliable perspective of a child.[109] This sort of epistemological uncertainty regarding relationships between women correlates with the transformative way time and place are presented in "Lydia's Grove." Lydia's home is out of date and ill-fitting with the topography of Moscow as imagined in the story, which aligns with the way queer spaces are theorized. The apartment is carefully presented in ways that make it seem odd: situated far from the city center, clearly set apart from "where we lived," as if in some "fairytale."[110] The old-fashioned yet elegant furnishings, dark carved wood upholstered in satin, contrast sharply with the typical "Moscow apartments."[111] At the same time, the story utilizes familiar tropes of unproductive bodies floating about aesthetic delights, tropes that are characteristic of queer fantasies, especially those from the turn of the twentieth century. Lydia herself embodies a wholly elegant aesthete, at nights "wearing dark pants and soft white blouses, often with a big opal brooch."[112] Emma, Lydia's younger friend, is a stereotypical representation of womanly apathy from the early twentieth century. Dressed in kimonos or flowery pajamas, she wanders around the apartment with neverending migraines, hugging a pet dog: she is beautiful, yet useless. Meals consumed in "Lydia's Grove" do not serve the needs of nutrition but are a source of exotic, sensual delight: for Lara, these are dishes with "unknown subtle flavors,"[113] bought in delicatessens rather than cooked at home because Lydia considers cooking too ordinary and a waste of time.

Vapnyar moves beyond the dominant Russian or more broadly Soviet era socialist gender templates based on productivity, according to which working mothers are dutifully bound to serve their men.[114] Working mothers embody a gender stereotype that is "etacratic": they are figures with the ability to be both demographically and economically productive for the benefit of the state. The Soviet regime actively promoted motherhood in ways that allowed women to work professionally: daycare centers were developed, encouraging women to have children.[115] The female characters in "Lydia's Grove" create a network of dependencies supporting and at the same time surpassing state-sanctioned templates. Lara's mother makes superficial efforts to be the ideal working mother; Lydia, by cooperating with her, helps create a doubly productive motherhood. The romantic relationships between women demonstrate an aspect of intimacy that creates a network of supportive interdependence, going beyond state-prescribed models that ignore individual, corporeal, and sexual pleasures (and the right to choose them).[116] While the unspoken partnership between Lara's mother and Lydia adheres to the state-sanctioned ideal, the relations between Lydia and Emma directly represent "bourgeois"[117] flaws that have no place in the workaday, party-approved collective.

By setting the story in a stylized private home—a heterotopia in the standard Russian gender framework—on the outskirts of Moscow, Vapnyar does not create a model narration that treats queer presence as something untimely and inappropriate, on the borders of nonexistence, as it might at first appear, but rather refers to the idealized gender patterns of late-Soviet socialism. Oral histories reveal that late-Soviet lesbian circles often met in private homes.[118] In that context, Vapnyar's short story is an attempt to extract an anachronistically

Translating Citizenship

Litman's and Vapnyar's stories advance a specific way of presenting ambivalent memories of gender structures from late-Soviet state socialism that to various extents displace the narratives of Jewishness. State socialist etacratic and thus limited emancipatory principles prompted Francesca Stella to suggests that using the phrase "sexual citizenship" in reference to a regime that medicalized and penalized non-heteronormative sexualities would not be "entirely adequate."[119] But how do we account for the ambivalence in, for instance, the late-Soviet regime of sexuality and intimacy that this chapter illustrated? Another phrase, in sociologist Ken Plummer's conception, is broader and encompasses a whole spectrum of possible choices and control over "our most intimate desires, pleasures and ways of being in the world"[120] involving not only sexualities but also questions of the body, "experiencing gender,"[121] and representation. To the three commonly theorized dimensions of citizenship—legal frameworks, political representation, and social welfare—Plummer adds a fourth, "linked to our most intimate desires, pleasures and ways of being in the world."[122] What he calls *intimate* citizenship relates to "the control (or not) over one's body, feelings, relationships; access (or not) to representations, relationships, public spaces, etc.; and socially grounded choices (or not) about identities, gender experiences, erotic experiences."[123] While sexuality is a key component here, intimacy itself is broader, encompassing various aspects of gendered embodiment and, for example, regulations concerning disability. As a result, it encapsulates complex regulations, personal choices, and states of existence, marked with the culturally defined genders of late-Soviet era modernity. Intimate citizenship is an especially useful framework when thinking about the Soviet Union's "communist horrors" (as expected by American readers) and the perceived absence of "sexual citizenship."

The sweeping notion of intimate citizenship helps us understand the range of body narratives in the 1980s as written by Vapnyar, Litman, and Ulinich. Their stories relating to the sexual revolution of the tail end of the twentieth century, the political changes affecting special schools, and the interstices of state control where romantic relationships between women could exist suggest that this broader perspective may be necessary to comprehend the many interdependent aspects of bodily presence in the world. Since the 1970s and especially the 1980s, aspects of intimate citizenship have influenced the way Russia and the Soviet Union are presented in American historiography.[124] Revisionist works from these decades obviously did not reference Plummer's categorization, but with their then-innovative interest in the possibility of grassroots processes in the USSR and broadly understood social processes affecting women, they were already touching on Plummer's yet unarticulated concept.[125] Historian Małgorzata Fidelis emphasizes that this historiographical trend in the United States only developed fully in the post–Cold War period, after the breakup of the communist system. The picture emerging from new analyses shows "individuals and groups which were not powerless against the system, and whose activities in fact facilitated the formation of ruling structures or noticeably changed these structures."[126]

This emphasis on individual agency influences more than academic historiography. Decades of writing history in this way have accustomed American readers to a specific presentation of the history of the Soviet Union, one that includes scattered stories, firmly fixed in geographical settings, that question the standard, binary ways of understanding the Cold War world, as presented by totalitarian theories popular after World War II. This approach to historical narratives works much like the narrative templates that emerged from second-wave feminism and efforts to promote queer rights and increase queer visibility: these frequently autobiographical narratives familiarized audiences with literature thematically relying on intimate citizenship. And literary forms—through voice, point of view, setting, use of language, and other devices discussed above—are especially well equipped to illustrate this opposite of powerlessness vis-à-vis the state. Soviet-born women authors, by writing about late socialism and perestroika, use these discursive connections known from the U.S. publishing market—both those relating to the history of the (former) Soviet Union and those concerning notions of intimate citizenship familiar from feminist and queer works. These narratives by Litman and Vapnyar, relying heavily on aspects of intimate citizenship, spur us to venture beyond the "horrors of communism" in grasping the former state socialist region. Their predominant displacing of Jewishness in favor of the regulations of intimacy resonates with the well-researched "interarticulations," to use anthropologist Matti Bunzl's term, of Jewish sexual and racial difference in modernity. These narratives of disobedient intimacy make us think about the tradition of a "dialectic that interarticulated the modern production of sexual species with the anti-Semitic racialization of the Jew."[127] Intimacy becomes here a narrative vehicle to articulate other regulations on the body politic, especially ethnic otherness and Jewishness, a way to circumvent the realm of American Jewishness.

5

Keyword: Migration

In the mid-2010s, the global refugee resettlement crisis resonated strongly in post-Soviet North America, many of whose members had endured the refugee experience. In early 2017, just after the announcement of the highly criticized executive order known as "the Trump travel ban," social media exploded with gestures of empathy and solidarity with citizens of the seven countries who were barred from entering the United States, including Syrian refugees.[1] Former Soviet Jewish refugees posted photos from their arrival in North America, organized a Facebook group, and created a "Soviet Jewish Refugee Solidarity Sign-On Letter" that would eventually be signed by over 1,000 people, including several Soviet-born writers and artists.[2] Julia Ioffe, then a staff writer for *The Atlantic*, who had herself arrived from the USSR as a child in the late 1980s, summarized the sentiment underlying such actions: "And to most people watching the refugee crisis unfold, the refugees detained and turned back at airports across the country are likely abstractions, too. . . . I look at them and I see us, sitting in that strangely lit room with the Immigration and Naturalization Service officers who processed us and to whom, I'm sure, we were an abstraction. . . . But I think about that room and the refugee cards they filled out, cards we still have to this day, and what would have happened if we too had been turned back."[3] Ioffe's identification with these refugees crosses both time and traditionally understood identity markers. Refugee status and, more broadly, migration become the lines of connection.[4] Another factor that emerges is the shared experience of a forced migration triggered by a repressive political regime,

Such political emotions point at a dynamic that does not completely fit what Caroline Rody has termed "interethnic imagination" in the context of literary dialogues between American Jews and other ethnic minority population groups—Native Americans, Asian Americans, and African Americans.[5] For Rody, these "interethnic" dialogues transcended ethnic identification. Yet one can argue that the keyword "interethnic" itself affirmed an ethnic imaginary and aimed at thinking how these dialogues are made possible through minoritarian positioning that is imagined as shared. Nor is it a new take on affinities with a particular minoritarian group, along the language of rights or imagined citizenship models.[6] Ioffe's statements go beyond identity or social positioning particularities and point to the mechanisms and limitations of human movement. Its determinants are bureaucratic "processing," invasive environments of "strangely lit rooms," often at the borders, dehumanizing paperwork and procedures, turning persons into "abstractions." While she does not acknowledge the value of whiteness of Jewish Soviet refugees of the (post–)Cold War era in determining legality and borders, she emphasizes rigid and violent state mechanisms rather than malleable individual and group identity.

As such, Ioffe's op-ed resonates with the texts of prominent writer, literary scholar, and critic Viet Thanh Nguyen that advocate for replacing the concept of the immigrant with that of the refugee, arguing that it is emblematic for today's world. Literary scholar Yogita Goyal explains how for Nguyen, the category of the immigrant is "less controversial, less demanding, and less threatening than the refugee."[7] Goyal concludes that "what we understand as immigrant literature all too often remains beholden to the burden of ethnic representation and only reaffirms celebratory narratives about the nation's progress."[8] While the idea of the immigrant is predicated on—and therefore affirms—the nation-state, the vulnerable, stateless refugee is more radical, challenging the framework of the nation-state, the idea of borders, and the concept of legality.[9] For Nguyen, this figure of forced migration registers the crisis of the present and holds explanatory potential for the future: "the refugee is the iconic figure of the contemporary era."[10] It is, then, not who one is, but what term, with its particular history of use, we employ to illuminate the major stakes of the current migration situation.

In relation to literature, writer Bharati Mukherjee continues to use the term "immigrant," but gives it a new spin, referring to the writing of the new millennium. In contrast to earlier (midcentury) immigrant literature, which operated largely within the framework of assimilation, twenty-first-century American literature of migration, which she calls "The Literature of New Arrival," turns toward the country of origin.[11] Thus, for Mukherjee, "The newly arrived immigrant-artist is likely to be less a petitioner for inclusion in America as had been the European immigrants of Philip Roth's grandparents' generation, and more an edgy critic."[12] Recent "arrival" points toward a positionality from a distance, perspective that is not keen on bending toward an assumed and cherished mainstream, but rather a position from which to discern power hierarchies. The turn toward the "country of origin," narrating its lived history from the perspective of the migrant, may also effectively reflect the geopolitical conditioning that spurned the population movement.[13] Mukherjee thus registers a literary historical shift over the second half of the twentieth century, a shift concomitant with a terminological evolution: the change from "petitioner for inclusion" to "edgy critic" mirroring the transition from an older "immigrant literature," with its assimilationist narrative of progress, to a "literature of migration" that registers transnational mobility.

I am invoking recent critical voices on contemporary literature of migration generally to situate more broadly works by Soviet-born Jewish authors. The theorizing of migrant writing takes place only rarely within Jewish studies, and when it does, it is often in a dialogue with migrant writing from other geographic or cultural contexts.[14] Thinking about "interethnic imagination" or interethnic dialogues, for example, assumes there are representative characteristics inherent to particular ethnicities and the literatures linked to them, even if set in comparison. Often such a comparative impulse arises from the ethnic positioning of identity-based groups perceived as adjacent or entering into localized interactions, whether real or imaginary.[15] However, Nguyen, Goyal, and Mukherjee highlight not the particularities of migrant writing by specific ethnic groups but rather their shared condition produced by population movement, displacement, and the concomitant legal regulations. Characters in Soviet-born writing in the United States have different migrant itineraries: some are temporary migrants, as in Anya Ulinich's *Petropolis*, while others are refugees or the children of refugees, as in David Bezmozgis's *The Free World*. Many works have protagonists whose entire families arrived from abroad, and readers can infer their refugee pasts (Boris Fishman's *A Replacement Life*, Julia Alekseyeva's *Soviet Daughter*, Yelena Akhtiorskaya's *Panic in a Suitcase*, Nadia Kalman's *The Cosmopolitans*). Nguyen's insistence on refugee stories and refugee writing allows us to cast off the exceptionalism that often attends Soviet Jewish stories in the United States, though they may be read as exceptions if the reference point is the uniquely large number of temporary migrants (as suggested by literary scholar Claudia Sadowski-Smith in the context of ethnically nonspecific post-Soviet migrants) or if they are narrated as linked—via ethnic particularities—with the stories of the post–World War II refugee wave. But Nguyen and Goyal give us instead a framework to see refugees as a part of a global logic operating in the last decades of the Cold War, with the arrival to the United States of refugees from Southeast Asia.

Previous chapters used *Soviet and post-Soviet* migration as an unchallenged variable to reveal differences with the well-sedimented narratives of nonimmigrant American Jewishness. In contrast, this chapter centers *migration* and explores its potential for telling Jewish stories in contemporary North America. In particular, I illustrate how gender and sexuality play a key part in narratives of migration. Approached critically as a pivot in stories by Soviet-born writers, together they reveal how these stories strive to create Jewish meanings beyond essential ethnic identity and, ultimately, beyond diasporic post-Sovietness as well.

Nearly a decade separates Nadia Kalman's *Cosmopolitans* (2010) from two other works discussed in this chapter, David Bezmozgis's "Immigrant City" (2019) and Gary Shteyngart's *Lake Success* (2018), and the texts are discernibly located in different cultural moments, which is also amplified by the Canadian setting of Toronto in Bezmozgis's story. Yet, throughout this decade, the topic of migration (including forced migration) has only gained momentum, not least because of current global political discourse. As these writers suggest, migration and the literature of migration—rather than simply the assimilatory "immigrant literature"—can serve as a tool to critically approach ethnicity. The literary texts discussed in this chapter interrogate gendered Jewish American (literary) genealogies and re-center migration while imagining more expansive possibilities for thinking about Jewish American writing.

Queered Genealogy beyond Jewishness: Nadia Kalman's *The Cosmopolitans*

Nadia Kalman's novel *The Cosmopolitans* begins with a clipped sentence: "None of them were fans of tradition." It refers to the Molochniks, a Russian Jewish family with three daughters, now living in Stamford, Connecticut, who stand at the center of the novel. Providing an updated take on Sholem Aleichem's *Tevye's Daughters* (1894), as well as Anton Chekhov's contemporaneous Russian classic *Three Sisters* (1901), Kalman traces throughout the novel the daughters' romantic engagements with various men and women. Yet already in this opening sentence Kalman undermines any direct connection to Aleichem's work, as well as to *Fiddler on the Roof*, which is based on his stories and more widely known to the American public. Kalman follows this opening with a more nuanced characterization: "Tradition is for great-grandparents, and not even for theirs, who traded their shtetls for the Universal Struggle."[16] Tradition, however understood, belongs to a different, much older generation, one that experienced tsarist Russia—in other words, the generation of which Aleichem's and Chekhov's characters were members. But the narrator distances the Molochniks even further from this generation—"for great-grandparents, and not even for theirs"— pointing out that they are not even blood relatives to these "fans of tradition."

The Cosmopolitans may begin with a reference to a Yiddish classic, but it immediately becomes clear that Kalman does not want her work to be seen as descended from that literary work. With her glib reference to the first song in *Fiddler on the Roof*, she may here trivialize Aleichem and instrumentally use him to make a broader point about the assumed genealogy of late twentieth-century Soviet Jewish immigrants, ideas that contributed to the popularity of turn-of-the-century shtetl images after the 1960s.[17] According to performance scholar and museum curator Barbara Kirshenblatt-Gimblett, the original 1964 *Fiddler on the Roof* nostalgically revived the shtetl life, which also served the purpose of reflecting on its annihilation.[18] In this way, it participated in Holocaust memorialization, which, as historian Peter Novick influentially argued, by the turn of the twenty-first century had become "virtually the only common denominator of American-Jewish identity."[19] On a different level, the American reception of Aleichem—notably, his inclusion in Irving Howe's canonical 1977 *Jewish-American Stories*—facilitated the invention of a Jewish American writing tradition founded on its "prehistory" in Yiddish.[20] Some have also read this centering of Yiddish Eastern Europe in political terms as a "Cold War discursive project of Jewish identification."[21]

Kalman's subversiveness toward received notions of Jewishness deriving from prewar Eastern Europe intensifies in one of the chapters narrated by Milla, when she, her husband, and her parents go to see *Fiddler on the Roof*—one of the few cultural texts that created the dominant image of Eastern Europe in the United States.[22] In an even more critical direct reference to the popularized image of the ahistorical shtetl,[23] Milla's mother, Stalina, remarks sarcastically in her imperfect English, "[T]his Fiddler is big education for me." She then explains further: "For example I know why American ladies say when we arrive, 'Look, is shower,' 'Look, is toilet.' Why are they telling me with such big smiles? Are they engineers who built the toilet? No, they think this is first toilet we ever see. They think we came out of shtetl fighting over if horse was a mule. . . . They see little Jews in little towns with cows."[24] The tendency to Orientalize Eastern European Jews reaches back to the turn of the twentieth century, both in Western Europe and the United States.[25] Even while the shtetl stands at the center of Jewish American genealogy, others can use it to marginalize contemporary Eastern European immigrants. Eastern Europe is often Orientalized, or, in other words, rendered as radically other and belonging to different times or even a different temporal order: it is timeless and unchanging, with no civilizational development, no technological modernization.[26] According to this logic, even today Eastern European Jews come as if from one eternal shtetl under many names, becoming nothing more than a type. Ironically, this antimodern timelessness is completely foreign to Stalina, a biologist married to an engineer. Her resistance toward the myth of the shtetl is additionally underscored by her first name, an ambivalent tribute to Joseph Stalin and, consequently, the modernizing and nationalizing drive of the Soviet Union under his rule. However discrepant the histories of Soviet and American Jews may be, the pivotal difference was not civilizational or economic, but systemically political: the Molochniks immigrated to the United States, in Stalina's words, because of "freedom, not pantyhose."[27]

By challenging the way Tevye's story popularly functions in the United States, Stalina dissociates herself from his lineage. The debunking of stereotypes often crops up in immigrant fiction, but here it gains fresh momentum through the participation of nonimmigrant and privileged American Jews. Milla Molochnik's in-laws, Jean and Bobby Strauss, are liberal Upper West Side Jews, who in fact purchase the tickets to *Fiddler on the Roof* for Milla's family. The Strausses propagate this canonical past of American Jewishness, but in the end, they do not attend the show themselves, and it seems to remain for them an ethnographic curiosity. The genealogy they assert is far removed from the shtetl, embodied instead by the original eighteenth-century family Torah from the large industrial city of Łódź; Milla carries it during her marriage ceremony. In addition, Jean cannot stress enough how their Jewish particularities did not prevent them from gaining recognition in the United States: they are the descendants of the first Jewish presidential cabinet member, under Theodore Roosevelt. Even if Jean gave charity to help free Soviet Jews—who, for her, represent a parallel post-shtetl universe—she never expected her genealogical line to merge with that of Milla, "this pale and unfashionable sub-European."[28] As a result, both Soviet-born and American Jews distance themselves from the ostensible pivot of American Jewishness.

Kalman introduces these inter-Jewish misrecognitions to point to the difficulties in community building based on the abstract idea of (Ashkenazi) Jewishness—or Ashkenormativity—without other identity coordinates, such as being a first- or 1.5-generation immigrant.[29] On the level of the family, this tendency culminates in Milla's breakup with her husband, while the marriage that succeeds in the novel is, tellingly, between characters who share the experience of migration: Milla's sister, Yana, and Pratik Rehman.[30] Pratik is a Bangladeshi exchange student who fell for Yana, a feminist teacher, while living with the Molochniks. Introducing a South Asian into the constellation of characters, Kalman opens an alternative narrative of potential relationship between migrants, which for literary scholar Werner Sollors "function[s] as an American lingua franca."[31]

Kalman gestures at this expansion beyond Soviet-born Jewishness, as well as beyond Jewishness more broadly, in the novel's title, which draws on the Soviet usage of the term *cosmopolitan*. As Lev, the uncle of the Molochnik sisters, remembers, the Soviet notion of cosmopolitanism as internationalism meant that "once, the Bolsheviks said that all nations would be equal and welcome in the Soviet Union. Jews—and what greater proof of their effete Cosmopolitanism may be?—believed them."[32] But Stalina's father learned that "cosmopolitan" soon became a well-known antisemitic slur, code for a Jew, a *luftmensch*, supposedly foreign to the Soviet national cause. In this not-so-subtle way, the title hints at the Molochniks' ethnicity. But taken less literally, it may indicate a critical attitude that arises from interethnic constellations. With a worldview that embraces Orientalization—as in the racism directed toward the Rehmans, for example—the Molochniks are far from unprejudiced. Cosmopolitanism here may not function in its older guise as a utopian or idealizing vision, but rather as critical cosmopolitanism. In literary scholar Rebecca Walkowitz's definition, it is "not universalist 'planetary humanism,' but rather an aversion to heroic tones of appropriation and progress, and a suspicion of epistemological privilege, views from above or from the center that assume a consistent distinction between who is seeing and what is seen."[33] This is a nonuniversalist stance, sensitive to various hierarchies and differences.

The formal aspects of the novel mirror the nonuniversalism in its content: the text consists of a few dozen short, usually one- or two-page chapters, each told by one of thirteen narrators. Such a composition not only de-universalizes the point of view but also ruffles temporal progression. The flow of narrated time may progress, but not at a steady pace, and with only a few explicit indicators of how much time has passed since the previous "vignette." Like the conspicuous form of narration, the Molochniks' steadily evolving genealogical trees, drawn at the beginning of each of the novel's eight parts, work against the comprehension of a single, persistent story.

The first such chart seems merely practical: a quick glimpse into who is who. But even here it differs from the typical graphic genealogical convention of mirroring "the social recognition of biological ties."[34] These charts do not begin with and descend from a single heterosexual couple—a convention that usually identifies such a couple as the clear origin of the family—which indicates that not only vertical biological relations are here at stake. Whereas the tree conventionally represents the parents, Osip and Stalina, as well as their daughters, Milla, Yana, and Katya, it places the girls' paternal uncle, Lev, in a separate box next to Osip's. Conventional diagrams, as anthropologist Mary Bouquet remarks, conceal their maker's agency behind straightforward design, but Kalman's graphs instead expose their constructedness and their power to "differentiate and create identities."[35] Accordingly, in the second diagram (figure 8) Katya's box becomes disconnected and moved to the side, which—as we learn in the following pages—indicates her geographical distance, as she has moved to California. On the other hand, the addition of an unconnected box for "Pratik Rehman" next to Yana's signals his arrival from Bangladesh and the couple's imminent romance. Moreover, the genealogical trees include an almost personified "Russian Soul" (figure 9), manifesting in the story as Stalina's internal monologues in Russian and signaled by her handkerchief. It is enclosed in a unique rhomboid box and connected with an arrow to Stalina in the first seven diagrams, only to attach itself to a minor character—Leonid Chalkin, one of the daughters' suitors—in the last graph.

Keyword: Migration • 107

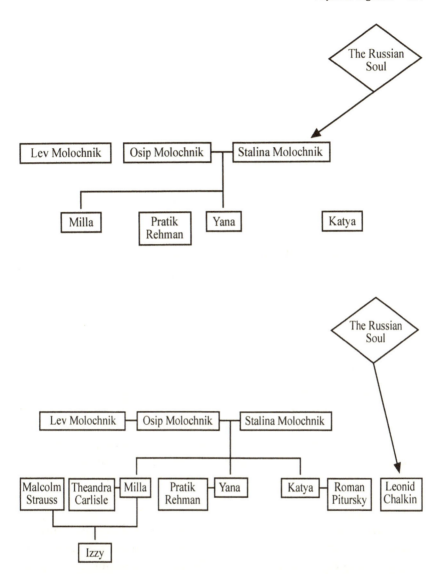

FIGURES 8 (TOP) AND 9 (BOTTOM) Nadia Kalman, *The Cosmopolitans* (Livingston, Alabama: Livingston Press, 2010), 37, 237.

The genealogical trees included in the novel function as dynamic summaries of the preceding chapters or foreshadow forthcoming events, and as such they upend conventional ways of narrating origins and showcase the queering of genealogy effected within the novel's plot. Modifications to the graphs grow more traditional with marriages (that of Milla and Yana) and births (that of Milla and Malcolm's son Izzy). Yet the sixth relationship graph represents Milla and Malcolm's breakup by disconnecting their boxes; the eighth (figure 9), among others, illustrates Milla's new same-sex romantic engagement with Theandra Carlisle. Just as marriage is a mere construct, as Yana pronounces early in the novel, so are the idealized genealogical trees.[36] This critique appears most visibly in Milla's storyline, which starts off conventionally: Milla marries Malcolm, a Jewish boy from a good family, and gives birth to a child. When they encounter problems in their marriage, Malcolm suggests countering with "sexual adventurousness" and plans a foursome with his music partner, Jelani, and Jelani's girlfriend, Theandra.[37] Surprising both men—but not readers, who know about Milla's earlier same-sex relationship with a coworker—Milla and Theandra start making love without them, and the men are left merely watching. Ironically, then, Malcolm, who was supposed to "help her un-acquire" lesbianism, unknowingly pushes her into a nonnormative love scenario.[38] Whereas a same-sex relationship might be thought to disrupt the genealogical diagram at the start of this chapter, the unchanged position of Katya's box in it illustrates how conventional genealogical trees might hide such realities. As we later learn, Katya is the product of her mother's pragmatic love affair with a communist official back in the Soviet Union—a scheme to obtain passports.

By including Soviet-born and nonimmigrant American Jews, a Bangladeshi, and an African American among her narrators, Kalman offers us a multiplicity of perspectives. As a result, she can address multiple coordinates determining how Jewishness functions in the United States today: she examines the currency of American classics such as *Fiddler on the Roof*, explores diasporic Soviet-born Jewishness, and foregrounds migration. Importantly, this multiplicity of narrative voices influences the flow of time in the novel and signals its queered, unstable genealogy, which emerges through the genealogical trees in the text. Even if the queer relationship feels underwritten, it points toward a less normative version of Jewishness that foregrounds women and migrants.

Kalman's provocative denouncement of "tradition" and a specific American Jewish cultural genealogy speaks to these various dimensions. It serves as a starting point for queering the genealogy of Soviet Jews. "Queering" here denotes challenging received notions—specifically, the tacit assumptions about how Eastern European Jewishness functions in popular narratives. For her purposes, Kalman satirically and coarsely depicts these assumptions, with the aim, however, of destabilizing them and making them more usable for contemporary immigrants and women. Kalman not only debunks this pan–Eastern European genealogical tree of American Jewishness but also, through graphic elements in the book, plays with the very concepts of genealogy and inheritance: how they function and how stable they are.

Influenced by Victorian novels, "with their complicated genealogical systems," as well as by Alison Bechdel's queer comics and the Hernandez brothers' women-centering Latinx graphic oeuvre, *The Cosmopolitans* creates a world in which genealogy and tradition are far from ethnically coherent heteropatriarchy.[39] We associate genealogical trees with heterosexual families in specific monogamous constellations that endure forever and reproduce ethnic heritage, but Kalman provides diagrammatic genealogical trees for the Molochniks, which evolve over the course of the novel's eight parts to show separations, new romantic relations—not necessarily heteronormative—and other people-of-color characters. Such diagrams, with their challenging of genealogy, call into question the genealogy of tradition in the context of Jewish American writing, whose histories portray it as insular and overly determined by the "fathers" of this literature.

Kalman's critical approach to cultural narratives of Jewishness *queers* genealogy, where "queering" refers not only to the introduction of queer presences but also, more generally and structurally, to the displacement of both the convention of the genealogical tree and the dominant, often tacit and uncritically embraced, shtetl-based genealogy of American Jewishness. Beyond certain elements of the plot, this displacing of genealogy occurs through the graphic play with genealogical diagrams and the nonlinear, multivocal narration. At the same time, in reference to the larger picture, Kalman disenchants the idealized vision of prewar Jewish Eastern Europe as the basis of American Jewishness from the perspective of Soviet-born immigrants. She challenges the notion that this romanticized past might serve as the axis of a shared identity for Soviet-born Jewish immigrants and nonimmigrant American Jews. Moreover, rather than develop an exclusively Jewish story line, she introduces other ethnicities and people of color, creating a network of uneasy intermigrant dependences.

The Limits of Intermigrant Solidarities: David Bezmozgis's "Immigrant City"

In his short story "Immigrant City," David Bezmozgis disenchants the migrant solidarity idea that the initial vignette by Julia Ioffe in the opening of this chapter and select plotlines in Nadia Kalman's novel put forth.[40] This story functions as a critique of unqualified solidarity with refugees, and it illustrates how Soviet-born migrants engage in ethnicizing and, in this case, racializing, modes of thought. The critique is especially poignant because of the condensed form it takes—a story that transpires in a single afternoon, encapsulated in the exchanges between two protagonists linked by their refugee experience. Gender plays a key role in debunking the solidarity myth because the story portrays women as the bearers of ethnoreligious difference.

Immersing the readers in the perspective of a 1.5-generation Soviet-born immigrant, Bezmozgis characterizes the trigger for this extended intermigrant

110 • Soviet-Born

encounter as straightforward and practical. The narrator mangles the door of his car in a fender bender and travels to a distant part of the city to purchase a replacement door from a private seller. Because care work is always tricky, he must embark on this public transportation adventure with his clingy, preschool-age daughter, Nora. Their journey takes them across Toronto, the eponymous immigrant city, to the outskirts where one finds "few representatives of white privilege"[41] but many high-rise housing projects, the light outlines of which frame the cover of the volume that includes this story. By the end of the short story, Nora and her father are on their way home with the door, but also with other items—a hijab and a Somali refugee memoir—that succinctly dramatize the limits of intermigrant solidarities.

Yet, before these limits become apparent, the story first relishes in its migrant logic, as it were, which Bezmozgis suggests inspires the narrator to not get the door fixed by a mechanic but rather "manage" it outside the official system—to improvise Soviet style. In his first-person narration, he speaks more of his history of displacement than of any other identity marker: previously "an immigrant child with all the heartache and superiority that conferred," he contrasts greatly with his wife, "born in America and raised in mindless California abundance."[42] The narrator's "immigrant childhood"[43] resurfaces with his arrival in Rexdale, an immigrant neighborhood close to Toronto's Pearson Airport, and extends to the local topography, pace of life, and, initially, the other protagonists we encounter: Mohamed, the Somali man selling the used car door, and his own young daughter, who share with the narrator a "fraternal understanding."[44]

The empathic bond between them leads to the climax of the story. Mohamed has googled the narrator, discovered he is a writer—in particular, an immigrant writer—borrowed his novel from the library, and now asks him to take on an assignment: rewriting the memoirs of his uncle, a former Somali minister of justice who was tortured after the government takeover, or, in short, a "national hero."[45] The man directly identifies his uncle with an elderly character in the narrator's novel: "I took your book from the library. At the story of the old Jew dying, I wept. I thought that Jew is my uncle."[46] Bezmozgis invokes here his own novel *The Free World*, discussed above in chapter 2, in which the Krasnansky patriarch dies in Rome en route to North America waiting for his refugee application to be processed. Thus, the purchase of a car door becomes an exchange of memories and a writerly transaction. Even though Bezmozgis's narrator makes no promise at all to take the gig, he nonetheless pulls readers into the overbearing transtemporal solidarity of the oppressed, a "genuine spiritual communion"[47] similar to that expressed by Julia Ioffe in *The Atlantic*: "We carried the door together out of the apartment, it was heavier than I'd expected, but I thought of the Syrians, the Iraqis, the Afghans, the Eritreans, the Sudanese, as well as my father, my grandfather and all my persecuted forebears."[48]

Yet Bezmozgis does not idealize or trivialize this gradually layered solidarity. Despite his own refugee prehistory as a Soviet escapee, which we can infer, the narrator projects a sense of "refugeeness" on the Somalis he visits: he others them as "incapacitated objects of rescue,"[49] defamiliarizes their living space, and creates fear around this racialized otherness in a "priority neighborhood."[50] Upon leaving his daughter for a moment with Mohamed's wife and kids as he goes to another apartment, where only men are allowed, to pick up the car door, he wonders, "If I am dismembered upstairs, what will happen to Nora? Or what if upstairs is only a ruse?"[51] Rather than romanticized solidarity, for the narrator the chaotic situation engenders racial othering akin to the stigmatization of the Roma and Sinti in the former Soviet bloc—or "Gypsies," as the narrator dubs them—who were said to kidnap white children. Similarly, the apartment upstairs becomes an uninviting space, with the main room almost empty of furniture, but full of men sleeping on the blankets covering the floor, and an "old man" sitting in a chair, Mohamed's uncle. In a scene imagined in the story as an otherworldly spiritual ritual, the elderly uncle, blind and mute, gently touches the palms of the kneeling narrator. A moment later, the narrator encounters antisemitism from one of the younger men.

Ethnic difference comes to the surface in reference to writing. To Mohamed's request concerning his uncle's memoir, Bezmozgis's narrator reacts categorically with: "I know nothing about Somalis."[52] The statement reflects a hesitation surrounding not only unfamiliarity with the subject matter but also literary categories, which are so often ethnically defined and marketed accordingly, as biologistic record of a population.[53] Bezmozgis's narrator dramatically illustrates the challenges of transmigrant writing.

Ultimately, however, the disquieting ethnoreligious difference is meaningfully assigned to women and girls in the story. The narrator had already, upon entering the neighborhood, characteristically noticed "Somali women in traditional dress" and girls in hijabs,[54] the headscarf that constitutes a controversial marker of ethnoreligious difference in Western liberal democracies and recently caused a major controversy in Quebec.[55] Later, his daughter, terrified at being left alone with strangers, is given a blue hijab, here an element of difference that can be playfully incorporated by a small girl as merely a pretty gift. This gendered object, pinned on a feminine body, conveys the conflicting experience of this intermigrant transaction.

The narrator's perception of Somali girls and women, as well as the narrative use of his own daughter in this gendered setting, drives home the limits of intermigrant solidarity. In her influential definition of gender, the historian Joan Wallach Scott underscores that gender is a "primary way of signifying relationships of power."[56] Bezmozgis's story functions similarly: the primary gendered object, the hijab generally and the hijab the unwanted gift for his daughter, signify or stand for the potential of identification between refugees and for the ethnicized and racialized difference. The few fragments that focus on women bear a disproportional significance, as if it was only possible to articulate a certain discomfort and distance through the racialized gender difference.

Capitalizing on Migration: Gary Shteyngart's *Lake Success*

In the many reviews and interviews with its author, the novel *Lake Success* appears mostly as a "Trump era" literary work. It centers on Barry Cohen, a fabulously wealthy hedge fund manager who one evening has enough of his cushy life and absconds on a Greyhound bus. Like the novel itself, its glamorous video ad featuring Shteyngart and Ben Stiller satirizes the hard life of the wealthiest Americans.[57] As Shteyngart explained when interviewed by the *Financial Times*, such a stylistic presentation serves the deconstruction of Barry's (Jewish) white masculinity.[58] Cohen's stark heterosexism is an important ingredient of the immense privilege he enjoys. It pops up throughout the book, but especially surfaces in relation to Barry's much younger second-generation Indian American wife, Seema, carefully selected to fit his private portfolio: "Unlike white wives, she could wear many grams of gold around her neck, the miraculous hue of her skin catching its glow."[59] The rationale for his calculated matrimonial transaction and, more generally, his approach to women is clear: "One of the many things on his marriage checklist was to marry a woman too ambitious to ever become fat."[60] But Barry is not the only protagonist whose story we read about in the novel.

While Barry travels from New York to Baltimore, Richmond, Raleigh, Atlanta, El Paso, and then Phoenix and finally San Diego—travel that functions as a pretext to illustrate the true nature of an America on the verge of electing Donald Trump—Seema stays at home, finds intimacy with a Guatemalan Jewish American writer who is also her neighbor, and struggles to arrange care for her and Barry's autistic toddler. The dual structure of the novel gives ample space for exploring ethnicity and migration in a configuration that updates the discussion of privileged nonimmigrant American Jewishness from Kalman's *The Cosmopolitans*. This update may result in an effective critique of ethnicity (and its literary marketability), however only with limited gender inclusiveness.

The two storylines are as separate and, at the same time, codependent as the divisions in a scene that Shteyngart imagines as the origin of this non-love story between the stock trader Barry and Yale Law School graduate Seema: "The roof garden was divided into roughly two demographics: capital on one side, and cultural capital on the other. It wasn't quite as split as a Hasidic wedding, gender-wise, but it was close enough, and Barry worked up the gumption to leave some of his Wall Street bros behind and wade into the more dangerous territory of feminine culture-meisters."[61] In a riff on Barry's ethnoreligious positioning, Shteyngart compares the party guests, split along occupational and therefore—given the nature of these fields—gender lines, to the participants in an Orthodox religious event known for its codified gender separation. The Wall Street circle is an exclusive men's club with a rigid and ritualized gender hierarchy and gender normativity. Seema, although not a "culture-meister" herself (she is merely invited by one), belongs to the sphere of the feminine to be conquered by Barry, who is on the lookout for "the right *young* woman with *young* perfect eggs."[62]

If *Lake Success* was indeed a novel "very much of our times," it was because Barry represents a mix of financial, class, and racial privilege and aggressive misogyny.[63] Seema serves as a much-needed foil to the unlikable, boorish Barry, whose general outlook and attitude might be summarized as "toxic masculinity," a phrase that enjoyed wide currency during Trump's presidency.[64] While one might satisfyingly "hate-read" the parts of the novel centered on Barry, the chapters on Seema provide a detox, so to speak.[65] As one critic put it, "the most remarkable passages of *Lake Success* take place when the novel shifts back to Manhattan."[66] *Lake Success*'s female main character seems also a reminder of the novel Shteyngart abandoned after negative feedback from an editor.[67] This never-published work was touted as an "international thriller": "the story of a young woman who works in finance, travels the world and searches for her brother, who has mysteriously disappeared."[68] Yet Shteyngart thought that it was hard to satirize a woman financier because, according to his research, they are too competent.[69] We can speculate that it might also not hit the right note, culturally speaking.

Lake Success is Gary Shteyngart's first novel that does not feature a Soviet-born Jewish immigrant (even if the next one, *Our Country Friends* focuses on one again[70]). And, in another first for him, it has a woman—Seema—as a fully fledged protagonist. Contrary to his previous novels, and especially *The Russian Debutante's Handbook* and *Absurdistan*, the woman character here is not "a figuration of the alluring but taboo shiksa" emblematically known from Philip Roth's *Portnoy's Complaint*.[71] Shteyngart has been compared to Roth in his iconoclasm, and particularly with regard to the "vivid sexual content" in his novels.[72] In his interviews, he himself explicitly expresses his affinity with this author.[73] While his depictions of the love interests in *The Russian Debutante's Handbook* and *Absurdistan* certainly take after Roth's one-dimensional representations of young women in *Portnoy's Complaint*, Seema escapes this fate.[74] Chapters in the novel alternate between those focused on Barry's trans-American journey and Seema's life in New York City. This dual structure, and especially the chapters centered on Seema, dissects not only the gender dynamic of privileged Manhattanites of various ethnicities but also, with the inclusion of an "ethnic writer" in the cast of characters, the idea of the ethnic writer as an established and lucrative profession. The autobiographical Soviet-born immigrant may not be present here, but Shteyngart creates an immigrant writer whose style mirrors his own writing "with an accent."[75] Ethnic writing and "giving voice" to marginalized characters serves as an attempt to target a specific, more progressive audience, as well as an academic audience, who tend to then produce monographs.

The alternating chapters focusing on Seema, her lover Luis Goodman, and her parents zero in on migration. The novel may not include a Soviet-born Jewish immigrant character, but immigrant Luis provides an occasion to discuss the pitfalls of Jewish ethnic thinking and writing. For Luis, who flirts openly with Seema, their immigrant backgrounds clearly differentiate them from Barry: "He's not an immigrant like us."[76] But in these scenes, Shteyngart endeavors to portray them as what some might call the "good immigrants." While Barry emphasizes that a majority of portfolio managers are first- and second-generation immigrants, Luis takes pains to identify as a representative of model minority: "But we are different kinds of immigrants. We are not the traditional arrived-by-steamer-with-three-suitcases or scampered-over-the-Rio Grande kind of immigrants. Our parents came here with college degrees."[77] Luis parrots here the immigration discourse favored by multi-million-dollar condominium owners who wish to be radically distinct from the turn-of-the-century "masses" fleeing economic hardship in Eastern and Southern Europe, or from Mexican immigrants, who are coded as illegal. Luis puts forth the educated and law-abiding immigrant as a model of citizenship. This notion of the model immigrant—educated and striving for success—calls to mind the assimilation narrative of migration. As Viet Thanh Nguyen suggests, this narrative is ethically suspect and inappropriate as a model for thinking about migration when forced migration and refugees are the test case of national boundaries and the boundaries of citizenship. On the other hand, the assimilation narrative maintains and strengthens existing limits on citizenship, including the idea of a "perpetual foreigner": the novel's characters—even the supposedly sympathetic Luis—consistently misread Seema, born in Ohio, as an immigrant.[78]

Mirroring the ubiquitous push in the United States toward ethnic identification and self-identification, *Lake Success*'s characters almost automatically fall into categories according to ethnic belonging. This applies equally to the main characters and the supporting cast of nannies, neighbors, coworkers, and friends. Such cataloguing propels the formulation of unambiguous, essentialist ethnic definitions. It also parallels the current tendency of specifying preferred pronouns, a practice increasingly considered not extraordinary but standard. In a similar way, if everybody is interpellated into an ethnicity, everybody has one, constituting a challenge to normative whiteness as the *lack* of ethnicity.

Shteyngart also explores "the question of identity"[79] and interrogates the mechanisms of ethnic identification. During their first dinner with the neighbors, which ends with Barry storming out of the apartment, he exclaims at the Jewish Luis Goodman, "You are not even Latino."[80] Later Barry thinks of Luis as a "*faux* Guatemalan."[81] These designations suggest that, in popular discourse, Jewishness displaces Latinx pan-ethnicity or any specific national belonging, even though academics have extensively explored such questions.[82] Indeed, for liberal universities—as well as publishing markets—the ability to claim multiple identities or identifications creates more opportunities. As a writer, Luis cherishes his multipositionality: "I do have some admirers in university departments, Latino studies, Jewish studies, multicultural studies. My peg fits a few holes."[83] Although *Lake Success* has no Soviet-born characters, its questions about ethnicity relate equally to the categories applied to Soviet-born Jewish authors, especially at the beginning of the literary wave, when critics and academics endeavored to make sense of this emerging literature under such rubrics as "a new paradigm for Jewish multiculturalism."[84]

These considerations of a gendered reading public, the portrayal of a woman protagonist, and a writer's ethnic positioning matter because Shteyngart himself addresses questions of audience in interviews and carefully curates his social media presence. In *Lake Success*, such awareness of the bookselling market peeps through when Barry looks up what he calls Luis's "Amazon ranking," a quantifiable value of "1,123,340," which Barry corroborates personally: "after reading one page of his novel, Barry could see how the ranking came to be."[85] Shteyngart jokes that the cover of his novel was tested for its marketing potential in multiple focus groups so that it might appeal to as many travelers as possible "at Heathrow terminal 2."[86] The garish cover (figure 10) consists of the title and author's name in a three-dimensional font of bold red and yellow on a white background, surrounded by red, yellow, and blue variations on a symbol that has become eponymous with large-scale book business: Amazon's smiling arrow.[87] Six such bendy arrows grace the cover; though they curve in the opposite direction as Amazon's, they nonetheless create that association.

Shteyngart creates multiple interdependencies between writing and finance: Luis is a financially comfortable author producing ethnic literature; Barry is a wannabe writer with a college minor in creative writing, a fan of Hemingway and Fitzgerald whose collapsing hedge fund empire is spun out of financial fictions. With their literary proclivities, the two characters represent different moments of what the literary scholar Mark McGurl has called the "program era" of American fiction.[88] Luis's books give voice to his native Guatemala: "You should stick to your beautiful portraits of Central America. Write about the voiceless," Seema encourages.[89] Shteyngart echoes here the notion of "finding one's voice," a literary trend popularized within academia and the publishing industry, and characteristic of the "high cultural pluralism" of the 1960s

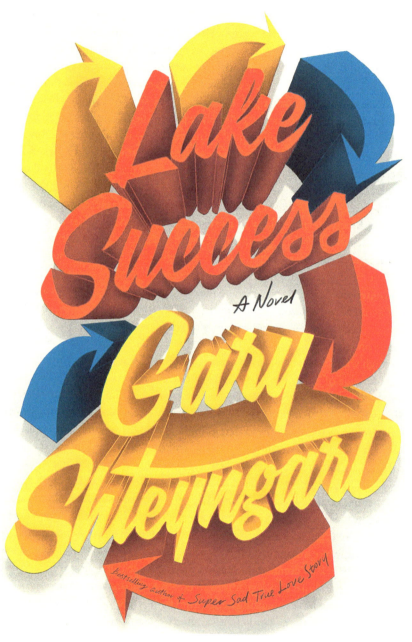

FIGURE 10 Gary Shteyngart, *Lake Success* (New York: Random House, 2018). Designed by Rodrigo Corral.

onward.[90] In the case of "ethnically marked," women, or queer authors, finding one's voice was not a subjective turn but rather a move "in defiance of the silencing forces of social oppression and cultural standardization."[91] Indeed, Barry portrays these novels as a provocation to white America: "There were dozens of acronyms of local political parties and organized gangs and tons of Spanish terms and words that had been left untranslated for no good reason other than taunt Barry's whiteness."[92] Barry no doubt feels burdened by not just the foreign words but also the, to his mind, excess of form. The turn toward "a textual performance of vocal authenticity" undermines the long-held ideal of narrative impersonality or "minimalism," embodied by his favorite author, Ernest Hemingway.[93]

Luis's literary works are a stable brand that fits a market niche. He acknowledges that his books are "all the same," with elements of "American colonialism, crimes against the indigenous, yada yada yada."[94] Yet, to stay relevant he needs to repeatedly deliver his product: these are separate books, but with an indistinct and predictable concept, encapsulated in "yada yada yada." His Amazon score suggests that he is not the best-selling author but—as confirmed by his "modest" Upper West Side condominium—has become well-off by providing a consistent, in-demand literary product. His readings at universities are generously remunerated, to the point that the affluent financier and writer manqué Barry gasps at the payment of $20,000 for giving a short reading to academics and "a single Latino janitor."[95] In light of these commercial opportunities for an "ethnic writer," Barry feels fundamentally disadvantaged, inherently incapable of delivering a marketable product: "All I know is I never had any advantages. . . . I wasn't even lucky enough to be born to immigrant parents."[96] Barry may romanticize the immigrant background only within this narrow context, but it remains a more-or-less verbatim rendition of the conservative idea of reverse racism: autobiographical potential for narrating migrant stories is a natural capital.

Gary Shteyngart's *Lake Success*, with its global financial flows theme paired with the circulation of literature among audiences, dialogues with literary scholar Caren Irr's characterization of the twenty-first-century migrant novel as digital. Playing on and extending James Clifford's imbrication of roots and routes, Irr imagines a "router" as the new figure of transnational writing or, as she calls it, the geopolitical novel: "The new migration fiction positions the narrator as a router, filtering and processing an overwhelming sensory global system."[97] Situating the narrative in relation to the medium avoids the possibility of literature of migration "perpetually reconstituting the private works of the migrant's trauma," which "reproduces elite nationalism and precludes a more contestatory and pragmatic focus on interethnic coexistence in the present."[98] These are not straightforward genealogies of ethnic filiation but complex worlds of multidirectional memory and the uneven global flow of capital.

Pairing the paradigmatic financier, Barry, and the model migrant/ethnic writer, Luis, Shteyngart comments on the literary capital of migration and ethnicity. On the literary market, these are fused, amplifying each other. Nonimmigrant Jewishness is a foil against which Luis, an immigrant Guatemalan Jew, defines himself. Seema as a character underscores the cultural capital of narrating migration, through which we can observe rivalries of Barry and Luis. She herself provides a comment on the marketability of gendered ethnic difference. The novel may not include a Soviet-born Jewish protagonist, but it foregrounds speaking from the position of a Jewish migrant writer, additionally amplified by his Global South provenience.

Toward New Coordinates of Jewish American Fiction

David Bezmozgis's 2014 essay "The End of Jewish American Literature, Again" testifies to how literary lineage is produced and how genealogical figures have an important function in the making and theorizing of literary connections: "If my work or my story can be considered anomalous it is only that [Irving] Howe didn't account for it. He, like many others, didn't, and probably couldn't, have anticipated that there would come another immigration from Eastern Europe in numbers sufficient enough to engender its own literature—really just a new branch sprouting from the old tree. The fact is that I have more in common with the writers Howe included in his anthology than with most of my contemporaries."[99] Only if we take Howe's account as canonical does Bezmozgis's oeuvre appear atypical. A gesture undermining Howe's 1978 diagnosis of the imminent end of Jewish American writing has become a rather standard critical move to illustrate the vividness and variety of contemporary Jewish writing in the United States. Rather than question the reasoning that allows Howe to naturalize a progression in Jewish American writing from the Yiddish past to the transcending of parochial immigrant writing, Bezmozgis only adds to this supposedly self-explanatory image.

"A new branch sprouting from the old tree" is not only a metaphor of vitality. It also represents how Bezmozgis's writing fits into the established story or preconceived genealogy of this literature, even if he achieves this belonging by declaring himself the odd one. Portraying the history of a literature as genealogy has significant consequences. The concept of successive "generations" functions, in the cultural critic Sigrid Weigel's words, "as a symbolic form, that is, as a cultural pattern for constructing history."[100] Weigel sees genealogical narrative as "naturalizing"; it is not only the story that appears as obvious and inevitable, but also gender relations, due to the dominance of fathers.[101] And this genealogy is at its core skeptical toward the role of women and non-normative gender positions and sexualities.

Because genealogy as a mode of thinking strives to smooth out any narrative, enclosing it into easily graspable, conflicting, and thus differentiable units of descent, it also tends toward easily graspable ethnic identifications.[102] Consequently, the dominant literary genealogy of Jewish American authors is problematic not only because it is undertheorized and functions as a supposed expression and straightforward mirror of factual and natural population development, a "biologized transcription of culture."[103] But as such, it also produces a narrow norm of American Jewishness and, among other things, results in exclusions—for example, Jean Strauss's use of "sub-European" to refer to a recent Soviet-born immigrant in Kalman's *The Cosmopolitans*.[104] What seems to be a simple family structure becomes a normative organizing principle of narrating communities into being.[105]

The literary works considered in this chapter suggest how we might conceive of narratives of Jewish American writing as something other than sedimented, genealogical, or vertical stories of descent. These works may initially seem to just follow the logic of interethnic fiction, but finally go beyond it. In Caroline Rody's words, "What drives ethnic fiction today is not only the 'vertical' axis of memory and return, traditionally dominant in ethnic literatures, but increasingly, the spatial, 'horizontal' axis of encounter."[106] Rody's emphasis on horizontality reproduces Werner Sollors's classic description of the two modes of ethnic literature: descent (single ethnic, genealogical) and consent (engaging multiple ethnicities and their literary traditions).[107] Yet Kalman, Bezmozgis, and Shteyngart go beyond *ethnicity* not only as a category of identification but as a mode of thinking. They are after not universalism but rather the placing of ethnicity—here, American Jewishness—in crisis. Kalman accomplishes this by riffing on the dignified standard Yiddish literary genealogy and by challenging genealogical narratives, with their stable structures of family and sexuality. Bezmozgis attempts to think along intermigrant or even inter-refugee lines, even if the narrator's automatized way of ethnicizing and racializing inevitably resurfaces, cleaves firmly on women, and seems to prevent the work from becoming truly transmigrant—that is, from telling a story of other migrants without shared descent. Finally, Shteyngart, by creating a Jewish Guatemalan author—and not a Soviet-born one—explores the pitfalls of "ethnic literature" and literature of migration, including its predictable shape and its capital on the literary market. The migrant women's figure serves as a foil for ethnicized imaginary. Here interethnic plot lines are only a starting point for stories in which ethnicity is a suspect category, even if it inevitably appears as a point of reference that is strongly articulated though gender.

The fiction discussed in this chapter are meta-stories, writerly stories, stories about telling stories that think about going beyond ethnic particularism. Several of the writers I have interviewed—namely, Bezmozgis, Lara Vapnyar, and Boris Fishman—also spoke of writing about what they intimately know, yet with the ambition of their writing being universal. Ulinich, Fishman, and Vapnyar each addressed the challenges of publishing within narrowly defined ethnic categories and the perils of transethnic writing—that is, creating characters across ethnic or racial lines.[108] These interviews resonate with the literary scholar Jonathan Freedman's idea that "questioning of the particularities"— that is, ethnic particularities—will imply "a move toward a truly integrative vision on the model of a real diaspora studies, Atlantic studies, or area of regional studies that would include religious, ethnic, national, and global differences in a larger, globalized, and thoroughly comparative framework."[109] While ethnicity constitutes here only one category of difference, migration results in the emergence of fundamental inequalities, is symptom of global flows, and provides an analytical framework in which to see literary production. Thus the Soviet-born writers discussed here use migrant narratives to explore and question the established, gendered genealogies of Jewish American particularity and the category of ethnicity itself to help us gain comparative literacy.

Conclusion

Jewish American Literature
as a Site of Critique

Throughout its five chapters, this book argues that Soviet-born Jewish writing in North America provides a site of critique of "Jewish American literature," and expands its cultural relevance and portability. At the same time, the texts under scrutiny here at times question the idea of Jewishness as an organizing category and even perform an ethical critique of the privileged position of Jewish whiteness. Apart from being instrumental in the critique of the field, Soviet-born writing—with its self-reflexivity as well as intertextuality—promises to extend the critical potential of "Jewish American" for literary study more generally. How can it be used not to consolidate hierarchies but rather perform their critique? What historical and current power relations does the rubric "Jewish American" make visible? This by no means relinquishes its significance; it merely reframes the issue in a way that is relevant universally.

The positionality of Soviet-born writers cuts across various coordinates that have been significant for canonical thinking about Jewish American writing, as well as those that are relevant to a larger field of writing in North America. Through their relation to the peculiarly imposed construct of "Soviet Jewish" identity in American discourse, this writing helps expose the Cold War logic that coincided with and fueled the "rise" of Jewish American literature.[1] As a result, these writers maybe in a sense grasped as a "new branch of the old tree," as David Bezmozgis identified his own writing within the Russian-speaking Jewish immigrant body of texts. At the same time, such a patently nature-bound metaphor draws attention to itself and invites

121

questioning as to the cultural continuity between early twentieth-century Jewish immigrant writers and late twentieth-century Soviet and post-Soviet authors with migration experience, as well as the stakes that the field may have in such a continuity. To put it differently, these authors point anew to migration as a key determinant of Jewish American writing, but at the same time foreground how different the late-capitalist migration regimes were and how the early/midcentury category of "immigrant"—together with the ideological construct of the "nation of immigrants"—unravels and loses its critical power.[2] Through its migrant positioning, this writing links to the "New Jewish Diaspora," as Victoria Aarons and others characterized the rise of Jewish writing of migration the Americas.[3] However, more broadly, its protagonists— with a relatively privileged religion-based refugee status during the Cold War and then often the "new immigrant whiteness" of the post–Cold War era, help point to larger cultural issues of racialized migration logic: the limits of citizenry and legality.[4]

If this sounds like a cultural theory primer, that is probably because it is one, to an extent. It reflects my own theoretical engagements and stakes. But more broadly, it reflects the potentiality within Soviet-born writing.[5] Namely, with their self-referentiality and intertextuality, these texts supply a theorization of the field itself. Soviet-born writing functions as an effective site of such critique of the Jewish American literary complex.

Critique is not an academic exercise or a Twitter/X-friendly polemical stance that seeks to outradicalize itself. It is rather an intellectual act in reaction to a crisis or, to speak with philosopher Judith Butler, "a practice in which we pose the question of the limits of our most sure ways of knowing."[6] Butler explains its stakes as follows:

> One does not drive to the limits for a thrill experience, or because limits are dangerous and sexy, or because it brings us into a titillating proximity with evil. One asks about the limits of ways of knowing because one has already run up against a crisis within the epistemological field in which one lives. The categories by which social life are ordered produce a certain incoherence or entire realms of unspeakability. And it is from this condition, the tear in the fabric of our epistemological web, that the practice of critique emerges, with the awareness that no discourse is adequate here or that our reigning discourses have produced an impasse.[7]

Thus understood, critique implies an engagement from within ("field in which one lives") as well as, with the emphasis on "social life," a significance that goes beyond the academy. The need for critique gestures at the need to reconfigure the categories and terms used to effectively communicate what the stakes are and repair "the tear in the fabric of our epistemological web."

Conclusion • 123

This emphasis on critique—which holds a promise of relevance, that is, universal relevance within a "social life"—puts in a new light the debates on "the new resistance to include Jewish American writers in a multicultural context" and the meaning of the category "ethnic," as in "ethnic studies" or an "ethnic writer."[8] It may be an old song from the 2000s, but these arguments still occur in popular outlets and general discussions. At the beginning of the millennium, literary scholar Andrew Furman characteristically discussed and criticized the "exclusion" of Jewish American writers as based on a *socioeconomic* factor" of the Jewish American demographic, belonging to the "white mainstream."[9] He advocated for its inclusion "in the multicultural mix because they have their own distinct voice or portfolio peculiar to their *sociocultural* experience outside the mainstream."[10] There are multiple points and categories used in the formulation above that may be read as perpetuating relative insularity and potentially preventing the possibility of productive emancipatory dialogue with other literatures in the United States or in North America. Already two decades ago, the framework based on a "distinct voice" or a "multicultural mix" was under scrutiny from, among others, Asian American, feminist, and queer scholars.[11] While it is key to think of literature across identifications and group affiliations to build what I would like to call comparative literacy, we must also formulate "inclusion"—or any other form of reciprocal relation—on theoretically solid grounds so that it is not counter-effective and does not in fact paradoxically create self-exclusions and re-create relative insularity. Expansive thinking about Jewish American writing means taking notice of and using theory from other fields: a dialogue in framing has a *chance* to lead to a dialogue in literary knowledge. The footnotes in this and in the subsequent paragraphs demonstrate that such a critically inclined work on literary production is well under way, developing the constructive impetus behind longing for dialogues in sophisticated ways.

This book traces these displacements and disruptions, looking for chances that open up the field to dialogues with other fields in which I live as a scholar. Accordingly, chapter 1 focused on the post-Soviet space as a lived experience rather than as a site of memory. As such, it may serve as a distant prequel for the current geopolitical crisis and the Russo-Ukrainian War, as the currently ongoing military invasion begun in 2014 is increasingly known.[12] Moreover, with its geographical reach outside Eastern Europe and its attention to people of color in that space, it connects with the current impetus of decolonial theory, both in Slavic studies and in Jewish studies. Chapter 2 points to yet another way to contextualize Holocaust memory and go beyond long-known narratives that stabilize its precise meaning as a set of canonized and expected stories, and may exceptionalize it. It foregrounds stories about Jewish soldiers in the Red Army as well as stories about the Holocaust in the East, thus extending the meaning of survival. Even if it does not address Western postcoloniality, but rather the communist and post-communist contexts, it participates in the thrust created by expanding the conversation about multidirectional memory, reaching into the post-Soviet space and illustrating other interdependent and localized dynamics of Holocaust memory. The last part of chapter 2, and then also chapter 3, recovers the memory of the Jewish Left in both Europe and the United States, and showcases another narrative that has been marginalized for historical political reasons: communist postmemory in English, which includes gulag postmemory. While recent popular culture has become engrossed in gendered narratives of Jewish Orthodoxy, exploring its gray areas and emancipatory limits, there have also been some representations of Soviet-born Jewish women characters, such as in *Broad City*.[13] One of the protagonist's queerness in *Broad City*, for example, effectively and influentially reconfigures women's Jewishness and gender/sexuality beyond the heteronormative framework. This reconfiguration has its genealogy in secular late-Soviet narratives about intimacy, which chapter 4 explores. Finally, chapter 5 not only looks critically at intra-Jewish hierarchies but also explores the limitations of the ethnic as a writerly and literary category. In doing this, it most fully attempts to realize a critique of Jewish American literary insularity and posit a way broader dialogues may happen. Such a comparative literacy links with other attempts in the field to go beyond ethnic particularism and question the crisis narrative of Jewish continuity.[14]

This self-reflexivity, especially toward the ethnic rubric, manifests also in the intertextual references to canonical Jewish American literary works by men. These figures do not appear in a celebratory way. Rather, the texts stage tensions with what they construe as these authors' normative understanding of Jewishness, one predicated on an early twentieth-century Ashkenazi descent as well as a cis-hetero-male-centric genealogy. These mentions gesture at a combination of anxiety about *wanting* to belong to this canon and a frustration with the rigidity of the definitions of Jewishness and the exclusions that underpin it. While "Jewish American" imagines itself through an inherited history of persecution, it does not prevent itself from constructing hierarchies, centers and margins, blind spots and silences. Recently scholars have highlighted the dominant position of Ashkenazi culture in relation to Sephardic or Mizrahi strands, but as Soviet-born writers demonstrate, even Ashkenazi literary tradition is not unitary; it has its own unspoken hegemonies. Early in the introduction, I discussed Philip Roth, who appears as a figure in Anya Ulinich's graphic novel, a work that itself remains in an intertextual relation with Bernard Malamud's *Magic Barrel*. Also, Jonathan Safran Foer, a literary celebrity in the early twenty-first century, and Sholem Aleichem, a quintessential Russian Jewish writer from a century earlier, make appearances throughout the chapters (in one of the novels and one of the short stories discussed).

Conclusion • 125

There is so much writing, literary and nonliterary, happening *in* this fiction. Fiction, as it appears here, is carved out in between all of these other modes of textual production, negotiated between them, which draws attention to its affordances as a form and also to its agency—what it can and what it cannot do in the world. The self-referential bent of these texts permeates the chapters (an indication of the high level of reflexivity this writing performs). It appears clearly in chapter 2, focused on the memory of war and the Holocaust. There the writing (and drawing) of fiction is an act juxtaposed with bureaucratic discourses. Fiction features as a form that can put into focus the uses and misuses of memory and, through voice, perspective, and plot construction, create a condensed, as if heightened, reality of how textual production of memory takes place. Chapter 3, too, dealing with archival records and their uses as well as academic writing, focalizes fiction writers and fiction as a medium. A poet is a prominent figure in chapter 1; writers and a professor producing academic knowledge appear again in chapter 4. On a different level, self-referentiality also shapes chapter 5, both with the nonnormative genealogical diagrams and with the comments of writers on how writing (especially "ethnic writing") is produced and marketed today.

Revealing these hierarchies and hegemonies is the work of critique that Soviet-born writing helps accomplish, generating its potential to be read in relation with other literatures outside "Jewish American literature." As I have discussed throughout the book, in some texts Jewishness seems to be absented or articulated through other categories of difference; in others, canonical narratives are made more capacious. Genealogies are undone or "queered." "Jewish" takes on meanings that are connective and willing to speak to experiences beyond ethnic particularities. Accordingly, the writers whose works populate the chapters have expressed irritation with their pigeonholing as "ethnic writers," be it in literary marketing or criticism. Soviet-born writing appears more radical than suggesting an "interethnic" framework, which only consolidates distinct categories along its delimited boundaries. In Boris Fishman's words: "I do not want to be a Soviet American writer, I do not want to be a Soviet Jewish American writer. Frankly, I do not want to be an American writer. I just want to be a *writer*. A writer who uses his experiences and community to write something of universal relevance, and I want to be evaluated artistically on those grounds."[15]

Around the time I was starting to think about this project, Lori Harrison-Kahan and Josh Lambert, in their introduction to the special issue of *MELUS* titled "The Future of Jewish American Literary Studies," offered alternatives to expand the category of Jewishness while drawing attention to the calcification of the established canon. As Harrison-Kahan and Lambert suggest, drawing attention to contemporary diasporic identities (including "Russian immigrant writers") as well as women's and queer narratives constitutes an important step in the project to give this literature universal meaning in an American context.[16] Employing such cultural studies categories puts this literature into a methodologically recognizable conversation with other texts written in the United States.

Over a decade after Harrison-Kahan and Lambert persuasively advocated for the expansion of the canon and the simultaneous attentiveness to its calcification, multiple works (discussed already in the introduction) have contributed to this agenda. Today, the stress seems to have shifted from broad "expansion" to works that portray themselves as critical takes on race, colonialism, gender, sexuality, ability, or sometimes class. Exposing norms is key to the study of Jewish American writing, with its stress on the decolonial, including Palestinian American writing.[17] This mirrors the larger trend within the Association for Jewish Studies and larger funded research projects, where the previous few years saw a heightened attention to Jews of color.[18] The establishment of the Gender and Sexuality Division of the Association for Jewish Studies in 2019 and the introduction of Disability Studies as a pilot division in 2022 signal the relevance of critical cultural studies categories to the field. The conference in 2022 also witnessed a discussion on "queering Jewish studies," as well as its "transing"—reflection on the presences of trans Jews in the canon and the archives.[19] This is not to romanticize how "radical" the field is but instead to point out existing dialogues with perspectives that are critical and self-reflexive and perceive this critique as an opportunity for relevance rather than a risk to continuity and existence.

Labels can generate recognition and profit. Their affordances are sensitive to time and place. With the many ways of performing Jewishness, what is the use of that category for "Jewish American literature" if it can hardly be consolidated or essentialized (if indeed anyone still wants to do that?) It may be worth asking about the ability of the label "Jewish American" to circumscribe a field that seems to escape its boundaries, and about how attempts at reestablishing these boundaries constitute a never-ending normative nuisance or, conversely, a sign of the term's openness and capaciousness.

Soviet-born writing is just one of many possible sites that invite such questions, so it is not privileged in this respect. At the same time, through its textualized Soviet experience, it centers several lines of inquiry that show up throughout the twentieth century. As new works and new writers arrive on the scene, they hold the promise of providing further sites of critique that will engage, expand, and question the label "Jewish American" in literature and beyond.

Notes

Introduction

1 Cf. Benjamin Schreier, *The Rise and Fall of Jewish American Literature: Ethnic Studies and the Challenge of Identity* (Philadelphia: University of Pennsylvania Press, 2020), 54f. For "Jews becoming white," see the classic formulation in Karen Brodkin Sacks, *How Jews Became White Folks and What That Says about Race in America* (New Brunswick, NJ: Rutgers University Press, 1998). Cf. Ruth R. Wisse, "Jewish American Renaissance," in *The Cambridge Companion of Jewish American Literature*, eds. Michael P. Kramer and Hana Wirth-Nasher (New York: Cambridge University Press, 2006), 190–211.

2 Some of the critics I invoke below have been in methodological conflict, which is polemically expressed in their work. Also, destabilizing the canon from one critical angle often results in less engagement with or blind spots toward other aspects. But this trial-and-error process is necessary and cumulatively has a productive metacritical effect on the field, which expands multidirectionally. Often the dominant intervention concerns not only the textual material but also the position of the critic themselves, which I see in my own thinking about Soviet-born writing as well.

3 The other Jewish writers on the list were Jonathan Safran Foer, Nicole Krauss, and Rivka Galchen; see The Editors, "20 under 40," *New Yorker*, June 9, 2010, https://www.newyorker.com/magazine/2010/06/14/20-under-40.

4 Cf. Anna Katsnelson, "Introduction to the New Wave of Russian Jewish American Culture," *East European Jewish Affairs* 46, no. 3 (2016): 241–244.

5 One prominent example is Ruth Madievsky whose novel *All-Night Pharmacy* won the National Jewish Book Award (the Goldberg Prize for Debut Fiction) in 2024; see Ruth Madievsky, *All-Night Pharmacy* (New York: Catapult, 2023).

6 See, e.g., Jennifer Creese, "Negotiating and Performing 'Jewish Australian' Identity in South-East Queensland's Jewish Community: Creolization, National Identity and Power," *Journal of International Migration and Integration* 21, no. 4 (2020): 1279–1294. Creese traces the use of the term, originally spelled "Ashke-normativity," to a blog post: Jonathan Katz, "Learning to Undo Ashke-normativity: a Jew in the

128 • Notes to Pages 2–4

Motherland," *New Voices,* October 22, 2014, https://newvoices.org/2014/10/22/learning-to-undo-ashke-normativity-a-jew-in-themotherland/.

7 Dalia Kandiyoti, "What Is the 'Jewish' in 'Jewish American Literature'?" *Studies in American Jewish Literature* 31, no. 1 (2012): 50.

8 Schreier, *The Rise and Fall.*

9 Kandiyoti herself has questioned the internal coherence, tacit exclusions, and troubling intersections of "American Jewishness" with her focus on Sephardi literature in her *The Converso's Return.* Dean Franco, meanwhile, has interrogated potentially competing positionalities in *The Border and the Line*, while Sarah Phillips Casteel has similarly explored intersectional thinking—namely, between Jewish and Caribbean identities—in her *Calypso Jews.* Casteel's focus on both the Caribbean and Canadian contexts puts not only the "Jewish" of "Jewish American" under scrutiny, but also the "American." Finally, a generally comparative—though not so much intersectional—focus shapes Jonathan Freedman's *Klezmer America*, in which he seeks out connectivities and normative overlaps in "ethnic" formations. Several of these literary critics contributed to the 2014 *Cambridge Handbook of Jewish American Literature*, which as a whole provides a great variety of entry points into this critique of "Jewish American." Hana Wirth-Nasher, ed., *The Cambridge History of Jewish American Literature*, (Cambridge: Cambridge University Press, 2015).

10 Lori Harrison-Kahan and Josh Lambert, "Guest Editors' Introduction Finding Home: The Future of Jewish American Literary Studies," *MELUS* 37, no. 2 (2012): 11. While Josh Lambert's *Literary Mafia* has examined literary institutions, including publishers, to show how the canon has been constituted, Benjamin Schreier's *The Impossible Jew* as well as *The Rise and Fall of Jewish American Literature* has shed light on the Jewish American academic-literary critical complex, unearthing the normative identity logic behind it. Josh Lambert, *The Literary Mafia: Jews, Publishing, and Postwar American Literature* (New Haven, CT: Yale University Press, 2022); Benjamin Schreier, *The Impossible Jew: Identity and the Reconstruction of Jewish American Literary History* (New York: New York University Press, 2015); and Schreier, *The Rise and Fall.*

11 Anya Ulinich, *Lena Finkle's Magic Barrel: A Graphic Novel* (New York: Penguin, 2014), 182.

12 Ulinich, *Lena Finkle's Magic Barrel*, 183.

13 This intertextuality resonates with the graphic novel's title, a clear, gendered riff on a canonical Jewish American story collection, Bernard Malamud's *The Magic Barrel* (1958), and the eponymous short story. Malamud's original Leo Finkel (an Orthodox rabbi engaging the services of a matchmaker) transforms into Ulinich's Lena (a secular immigrant and divorcée in search of love).

14 Until recently, the centering of Roth, Malamud, and Saul Bellow (with Cynthia Ozick also making an appearance) has been a staple of guides and anthologies of Jewish American literature in the postwar period. I discuss a critical shift from this canonical shorthand later in the introduction. Cf., e.g., Wisse, "Jewish American Renaissance."

15 See Shaul Kelner, "Where Is the Next Soviet Jewry Movement? How Identity Education Forgot the Lessons that Jewish Activism Taught," in *Beyond Jewish Identity: Rethinking Concepts and Imagining Alternatives*, ed. Jon A. Levisohn and Ari Y. Kelman (Brookline, MA: Academic Studies Press, 2019), 193–215. See also Gal Beckerman, *When They Come for Us, We'll Be Gone: The Epic Struggle to Save*

Soviet Jewry (Boston: Houghton Mifflin Harcourt, 2010). These interpretations and hegemonic cultural memory of the movement are currently reapproached: a recent special section "The Soviet Jewry Movement, Revisited" in *Jewish Currents* is characteristic here. See Tova Benjamin, "Introduction: The Soviet Jewry Movement, Revisited," *Jewish Currents*, May 23, 2022, https://jewishcurrents.org/introduction-the-soviet-jewry-movement-revisited. Other texts in this issue of *Jewish Currents* address Soviet-born experience through nonfiction, fiction, conversation, and poetry; see The Soviet Issue, *Jewish Currents*, accessed September 3, 2023, https://jewishcurrents.org/issue/winter-spring-2022. See especially Julia Alekseyeva, Tova Benjamin, Oksana Mironova, and Sasha Senderovich, "We Need New Stories of Post-Soviet Jews: A Letter from the Issue Committee," *Jewish Currents*, March 28, 2022, https://jewishcurrents.org/we-need-new-stories-of-post-soviet-jews.

16 Zvi Gitelman, ed., *The New Jewish Diaspora: Russian-Speaking Immigrants in the United States, Israel, and Germany* (New Brunswick, NJ: Rutgers University Press, 2016), 24.

17 Mark Tolts, "Demography of the Contemporary Russian-Speaking Jewish Diaspora," in *The New Jewish Diaspora*, ed. Zvi Gitelman (New Brunswick, NJ: Rutgers University Press, 2016), 23–40. Cf. Annelise Orleck, *The Soviet Jewish Americans*, The New Americans Series (Westport, CT: Greenwood Publishing Group, 1999), 2. "Prior to 2000, the number of immigrants from the 15 countries that were part of the former Soviet Union is not shown by individual country. From 2000 on, the Census Bureau reports data on Armenia, Belarus, Kazakhstan, Latvia, Lithuania, Moldova, Russia, Ukraine, and Uzbekistan, but not for the other six former Soviet Union republics." Migration Policy Institute, "U.S. Immigration Trends," accessed September 3, 2023, https://www.migrationpolicy.org/programs/data-hub/us-immigration-trends#source.

18 Pew Research Center, *Jewish Americans in 2020*, May 11, 2021, https://www.pewresearch.org/religion/wp-content/uploads/sites/7/2021/05/PF_05.11.21_Jewish.Americans.pdf. According to the survey, Soviet-born Jews constitute 4 percent of Jewish Americans, or ca. 230,000 (173); the "former Soviet Union" remains a separate analytical category in the survey. For the estimate of the percentage living on the East Coast, see Jonathan Sarna, "Toward a Comprehensive Policy Planning for Russian-Speaking Jews in North America," 2013, http://www.brandeis.edu/hornstein/sarna/contemporaryjewishlife/russian-speakingjewscomeofage-jppi.pdf.

19 For a more specific narrative of Jewish American literature and father figures, see Schreier, *The Rise and Fall*, 78ff.

20 What is at stake here are competing gender readings of Roth's texts, as Debra Schostak elucidates (cf. *Cambridge Companion*). Lena's character speaks in line with readings of certain Roth texts emphasizing that however he may be negotiating the "masculinist myth," he still critically approaches sexual and gender normativities, as Debra Shostak argues in "Return to the Breast: The Body, the Masculine Subject, and Philip Roth," *Twentieth Century Literature* 45, no. 3 (Autumn 1999): 326. Roth in Ulinich, on the other hand, leans toward less ambivalent gendered readings of his texts—namely, as misogynistic. For more on Roth in Ulinich, cf. Victoria Aarons, "Reinventing Philip Roth in the Fiction of Others," *Revue Française d'Études Américaines* 1 (2021): 62–74. The Ulinich passage resonates with the controversies around Blake Bailey's biography of Roth, in which Roth

apparently tried to control his image so as not to appear misogynist; following Bailey's accusations of sexual misconduct, the publisher W. W. Norton distanced itself from the author; see Alexandra Alter and Rachel Abrams, "Sexual Assault Allegations against Biographer Halt Shipping of His Roth Book," *New York Times*, May 17, 2021, https://www.nytimes.com/2021/04/21/books/philip-roth-blake-bailey.html. For a review underscoring the uncritical treatment of Roth's misogyny in the biography, see Laura Marsh, "Philip Roth's Revenge Fantasy," *New Republic*, March 22, 2021, https://newrepublic.com/article/161640/philip-roths-revenge-fantasy-review-blake-bailey.

21 Accordingly, expansive gender and queer critique of the field has drawn attention to its masculinist logic and foregrounded women-centered ways of telling its story. Significantly, Zohar Weiman-Kalman's *Queer Expectations* privileges a literary network of queer women poets, contesting fatherly genealogies of literature; in *Women Writing Jewish Modernity*, Allison Schachter likewise programmatically stages a conversation between women writers. Tahneer Oksman's work foregrounds Jewish women's work in graphic novels. See Zohar Weiman-Kelman, *Queer Expectations: A Genealogy of Jewish Women's Poetry* (Albany, NY: SUNY Press, 2018); Allison Schachter, *Women Writing Jewish Modernity, 1919–1939* (Evanston, IL: Northwestern University Press, 2021); and Tahneer Oskman, *How Come the Boys Got to Keep Their Noses: Women and Jewish American Identity in Contemporary Graphic Memoirs* (New York: Columbia University Press, 2016).

22 Claudia Sadowski-Smith, *The New Immigrant Whiteness: Race, Neoliberalism, and Post-Soviet Migration to the United States* (New York: New York University Press, 2018).

23 This book focuses on published fiction in English, even though this literary wave encompasses more than just fiction writers. Ilya Kaminsky is its most prominent representative in poetry, while the Cheburashka Collective, a group of multi-genre women and non-binary writers (Luisa Muradyan, Julia Kolchinsky Dasbach, Ruth Madievsky, and Olga Zilberbourg, among others) has been active on Twitter/X and other online spaces. A plethora of online events during the COVID-19 pandemic and the Russian invasion of Ukraine gave space to other Soviet-born nonfiction writers, while yet others created their own online cultural and literary magazines (*Punctured Lines: Post-Soviet Literature in and outside the Former Soviet Union*, accessed September 3, 2023, https://puncturedlines.wordpress.com/; *Pocket Samovar*, accessed September 3, 2023, https://www.pocketsamovar.com/). All the writers considered here write in English, which is largely characteristic of "Russian American" writers born in the 1970s and 1980s in general. For earlier as well as contemporary writing in Russian in the United States, see Margarit Tadevosyan and Maxim Shrayer, "Russian American Literature," in *Greenwood Encyclopedia of Multiethnic American Literature*, vol. 3, ed. Emmanuel S. Nelson (Westport, CT: Greenwood Publishing Group, 2005), 1940–1951.

24 On the tacitly assumed centrality of Eastern European Jewish or Ashkenazi culture in the United States, see Kandiyoti, "What Is the 'Jewish.'"

25 My discussion of an evil twin, understood as a constellation sharing many characteristics with its double but, through their slight displacement, revealing its underlying aporia, is influenced by Susan Stryker, "Transgender Studies: Queer Theory's Evil Twin," *GLQ: A Journal of Lesbian and Gay Studies* 10, no. 2 (2004): 212–215.

26 Hayden White, *Metahistory: The Historical Imagination in Nineteenth-Century Europe* (Johns Hopkins University Press, 2014), 12.

Notes to Pages 5–6 • 131

27 Konrad H. Jarausch, Christian F. Ostermann, and Andreas Etges, "Rethinking, Representing, and Remembering the Cold War: Some Cultural Perspectives," in *The Cold War* (Oldenburg, Germany: De Gruyter, 2017).

28 I do not wish to re-center Jewishness as an *ethnic* category per se to make it relevant to study of American writing, a suggestion that has already been made, and subsequently criticized, by others. The gender-critical and migration-critical narratives within Soviet-born texts are, rather, an occasion for comparative literacy, for reading them, even if only implicitly, in conversation with other literatures also shaped by the logic of migration—a logic that goes beyond identity coordinates that often too closely circumscribe what is "ethnic" in the United States or in "Jewish American." Cf. Andrew Furman, *Contemporary Jewish American Writers and the Multicultural Dilemma: Return of the Exiled* (Syracuse, NY: Syracuse University Press, 2000); Lambert and Kahan, "Guest Editors' Introduction"; Schreier, *The Rise and Fall.*

29 Kristen Ghodsee, *Second World, Second Sex: Socialist Women's Activism and Global Solidarity during the Cold War* (Durham, NC: Duke University Press, 2019).

30 With reference to migration, Jewish American literary study has probed a dialogue with Asian American writing; see, e.g., Jonathan Freedman, *Klezmer America: Jewishness, Ethnicity, Modernity* (New York: Columbia University Press, 2009); Cathy Schlund-Vials, *Modeling Citizenship. Jewish and Asian American Writing* (Philadelphia: Temple University Press, 2011); and Sadowski-Smith, *The New Immigrant Whiteness.* Outside of Jewish studies, but still involving Soviet-born writers, a transethnic perspective under the rubric "geopolitical novel" shapes Caren Irr's *Toward the Geopolitical Novel: U.S. Fiction in the Twenty-First Century* (New York: Columbia University Press, 2013); see also Diana Kielar, "'We Need New Names': Conditions of Belonging in the Contemporary US Immigrant Novel" (PhD diss., Brandeis University, 2021).

31 Cf. Michael Rothberg, *Multidirectional Memory: Remembering the Holocaust in the Age of Decolonization* (Stanford, CA: Stanford University Press, 2009).

32 Schreier, *The Rise and Fall,* 175. "DIY Jewishness" resonates with the category "Just Jewish" that was used in sociological studies of children of Soviet immigrants to the United States, which accentuates that "while there is notable religious engagement and activity, this is not the dominant understanding of Jewishness nor of Jewish practice among Russian-speaking Jewish immigrants." Jay (Koby) Oppenheim, "Group Distinctiveness and Ethnic Identity among 1.5 and Second-Generation Russian-speaking Jewish Immigrants in Germany and the U.S." (PhD diss., City University of New York, 2016), 31.

33 Adam Rovner, "So Easily Assimilated: The New Immigrant Chic," *AJS Review* 30, no. 2 (2006): 317.

34 Adrian Wanner, "Moving beyond the Russian-American Ghetto: The Fiction of Keith Gessen and Michael Idov," *Russian Review* 73 (2014): 281–296. See also Adrian Wanner, *Out of Russia: Fictions of a New Translingual Diaspora* (Evanston, IL: Northwestern University Press, 2011); Yelena Furman, "Telling Their Hybrid Stories: Three Recent Works of Russian-American Fiction," *The Slavic and East European Journal* 59, no. 1 (Spring 2015): 116–124; and Min Hyoung Song, *The Children of 1965: On Writing, and Not Writing, as an Asian American* (Durham, NC: Duke University Press, 2013). The following works have used a diasporic or transnational lens: Anna Katsnelson, "Transnationalism in Contemporary

132 • Notes to Pages 6–8

Post-Soviet North American Literature," *Twentieth Century Literature* 65, no. 1–2 (2019): 145–166; and Margarita Levantovskaya, "Homes without a Homeland: Finding Diasporic Intimacy in Contemporary Russian-Jewish-American Fiction," *Comparative Literature* 69, no. 4 (2017): 394–412. Taking inspiration from the research of Jonathan Sarna, one could also refer to the category of "Russian-speaking Jewish authors in the USA"; see Jonathan Sarna, "Toward a Comprehensive Policy Planning."

35 See Karen Ryan, "Failures of Domesticity in Contemporary Russian-American Literature: Vapnyar, Krasikov, Ulinich, and Reyn," *TranscUlturAl: A Journal of Translation and Cultural Studies* 1, no. 4 (2011): 63–75. Gary Shteyngart's work especially has been discussed more broadly within global writing or as a variation on the "geopolitical novel"; see Irr, *Toward the Geopolitical Novel*.

36 Schachter, *Women Writing Jewish Modernity*, 167.

37 Schachter, *Women Writing Jewish Modernity*, 167.

38 Cf. Vladimir (Ze'ev) Khanin, "The Diaspora of Russian-Speaking Jews: Political Attitudes and Political Influence," *Osteuropa* 9–11 (2019): 107–115.

39 Jeff Diamant, "How Younger U.S. Jews Are Similar to—and Different from—Older U.S. Jews," June 8, 2021, https://www.pewresearch.org/fact-tank/2021/06/08/how-younger-u-s-jews-are-similar-to-and-different-from-older-u-s-jews/.

40 On such a reading of Benjamin, see David Suchoff, "New Historicism and Containment: Toward a Post-Cold War Cultural Theory," *Arizona Quarterly: A Journal of American Literature, Culture, and Theory* 48, no. 1 (Spring 1992): 154.

41 Cf. Sergii Gurbych, *Mother Tongue, Other Tongue: Soviet-Born Jewish Writers in Their New Language Environment* (Heidelberg, Germany: Winter Verlag, 2021); and Sasha Senderovich, "Russian Jewish American Lit Goes Boom!" *Tablet*, June 17, 2014, https://www.tabletmag.com/sections/arts-letters/articles/russian-jewish-am-lit.

42 I myself have termed this writing "post-Soviet" before, with reference to earlier theoretical work considering it not as a temporal designation but as a quality of being conditioned by the Soviet past; see David Chioni Moore, "Is the Post- in Postcolonial the Post- in Post-Soviet? Toward a Global Postcolonial Critique," *PMLA* 116, no. 1 (2011): 111–128; Jennifer Suchland, "Is Postsocialism Transnational?" *Signs: Journal of Women in Culture and Society* 26, no. 4 (2011): 837–862; Madina Tlostanova, "Can the Post-Soviet Think? On Coloniality of Knowledge, External Imperial and Double Colonial Difference," *Intersections. East European Journal of Society and Politics* 1, no. 2 (2015): 38–58; and Aleksander Etkind, *Warped Mourning: Stories of the Undead in the Land of the Unburied* (Stanford, CA: Stanford University Press, 2013). This includes the particular status of Jews in the USSR—that is, as an oxymoronic "discriminated elite"; see Larisa Remennick, *Russian Jews on Three Continents: Identity, Integration, and Conflict* (London: Routledge, 2012). At the same time, the term hoped to locate this literature within the politics of the Cold War and the larger horizon of U.S. imperialism. Recently, the "post-Soviet" rubric has been more broadly adopted, including in scholarly writing and as part of the self-identifications of younger collectives.

43 See Martin Müller, "In Search of the Global East: Thinking Between North and South," *Geopolitics* 25, no. 3 (2020): 734–755. That said, I strategically use "post-Soviet" in this book to refer to the territory of the former Soviet Union as well as its cultural and political legacies.

44 A host of popular publications have stressed the threat of a "new Cold War" following the February 2022 full-scale invasion; see Ian Bremmer, "The New Cold

War Could Soon Heat Up: Why Russia and the West Might Escalate the Fight Over Ukraine," *Foreign Affairs*, May 5, 2022, https://www.foreignaffairs.com/articles/russia-fsu/2022-05-05/new-cold-war-could-soon-heat; Jaro Bilocerkowycz, "A New Cold War Emerging as Russia Launches Full-scale Invasion of Ukraine," *The Conversation*, February 25, 2022, https://theconversation.com/a-new-cold-war-emerging-as-russia-launches-full-scale-invasion-of-ukraine-175872.

45 A portion of these Soviet Jewish immigrants came to the United States and Canada as political refugees before the end of the Soviet Union thanks to the "parole power" of the attorney general and later on the basis of the 1980 Refugee Act. See Zvi Gitelman, "Exiting from the Soviet Union: Emigrés or Refugees?" *Michigan Journal of International Law* 43 (1982): 43–61. On the links between the Soviet Jewry movement and this immigration, see Kelner, "Where Is the Next Soviet Jewry Movement?"; Beckerman, *When They Come for Us*; Gitelman, *The New Jewish Diaspora*.

46 The genealogy of this literary wave may resemble to some extent the cohorts of Asian American writers who immigrated as young refugees—Min Song's "children of 1965," or Cathy Schlund-Vials's "subjects of 1975"; see Cathy Schlund-Vials, "The Subjects of 1975: Delineating the Necessity of Critical Refugee Studies," *MELUS: Multi-Ethnic Literature of the United States* 41, no. 3 (2016): 199–203. While I will discuss, at some points in this study, a certain logic of migration broadly shared by both Asian American and Soviet-born Jewish writers, the latter's privileged (Soviet Jewish immigrant) whiteness is critically different. For a reading stressing the similarities and differences between post-Soviet (not just Jewish) migration and that of other ethnic groups—though she does not focus explicitly on the literary context—see Sadowski-Smith, *The New Immigrant Whiteness*.

47 For the institutional support of this wave of writing, especially linked to *The New Yorker*, see Josh Lambert, "Since 2000," in *The Cambridge History of Jewish American Literature*, ed. Hana Wirth-Nasher (Cambridge: Cambridge University Press, 2015), 624–641.

48 Cf. Jarausch, Ostermann, and Etges, "Rethinking, Representing, and Remembering."

49 Suchoff, "New Historicism and Containment," 139–142.

50 On the terminological shift, see Schreier, *The Rise and Fall*, 56.

51 Brian Goodman, "American Jewish Writers and the Cold War: The Dissident Generation," in *The Bloomsbury Handbook to Cold War Literary Cultures*, ed. Greg Barnhisel (London: Bloomsbury, 2022), 113–130.

52 Schreier, *The Rise and Fall*, 87, 119.

53 Goodman, "American Jewish Writers and the Cold War."

54 Sasha Senderovich, "Scenes of Encounter: The 'Soviet Jew' in Fiction by Russian Jewish Writers in America," *Prooftexts* 35, no. 1 (2015), 115.

55 See Kelner, "Where Is the Next Soviet Jewry Movement?"

56 Penny Von Eschen, *Paradoxes of Nostalgia: Cold War Triumphalism and Global Disorder since 1989* (Durham, NC: Duke University Press, 2022), 6.

57 In suggesting that Soviet-born migrants are the afterlife of the Cold War, I am inspired by Saydiya Hartman's formulation in the prologue to *Lose Your Mother: A Journey along the Atlantic Slave Route* (New York: Macmillan, 2008), 6. I by no means seek to equate these disparate histories, but I do see parallels in the mechanisms governing how past political and economic systems affect individuals today.

134 • Notes to Pages 10–16

58 See Etkind, *Warped Mourning*.
59 Hanna Gosk, "Tożsamościotwórcze aspekty polonistycznych studiów postzależnościowych," *Teksty Drugie: teoria literatury, krytyka, interpretacja*, no. 3 (2012): 51–62.
60 Claudia Sadowski-Smith and Ioana Luca, "Introduction: Postsocialist Literatures in the United States," *Twentieth Century Literature* 65, no.1–2 (2019): 1–22.
61 Often "socialism" is used instead of "communism" to underline the lived experience of the political system and stress commonalities between this system and socialist political modes globally, beyond the "Eastern bloc," with "state-socialist" pointing to political organization of the states within the Soviet orbit; cf. Magdalena Grabowska, "Revolution(s), Socialist Legacies, and Transnational Silences in the Trajectories of Polish Feminism," *Signs* 37, no. 2 (January 2012): 385–411. I am using "communist" here to mirror the Cold War logic of bipolarity and the (imagined) radical political difference demonized according to that logic. Elsewhere in this book, I employ "socialist" and "state-socialist." These may be interchangeable on an ontological level, and so are often used interchangeably (cf., e.g., Ghodsee, *Second World, Second Sex*), but they show divergent discursive investments.
62 Marianne Hirsch, *The Generation of Postmemory: Writing and Visual Culture After the Holocaust* (New York: Columbia University Press, 2012), 6.
63 Hirsch, *The Generation of Postmemory*, 5
64 See Ann Rigney, "Remembering Hope: Transnational Activism beyond the Traumatic," *Memory Studies* 11, no. 3 (2018): 368–380.
65 The dates given in parentheses indicate the first editions and sometimes throughout the book they differ from the editions cited and included in the bibliography.

Chapter 1   Diasporic Spaces

1 For a popular account, see David Sax, "Rise of the New Yiddishists," *Vanity Fair*, April 8, 2009, https://www.vanityfair.com/culture/2009/04/yiddishists200904.
2 Anya Ulinich, "The Nurse and the Novelist," September 8, 2008, https://pen.org/fiction-short-story/nurse-and-novelist.
3 Michael Hoberman, *A Hundred Acres of America: The Geography of Jewish Literary History* (New Brunswick, NJ: Rutgers, 2019), 121ff; cf. Benjamin Schreier, *The Rise and Fall of Jewish American Literature: Ethnic Studies and the Challenge of Identity* (Philadelphia: University of Pennsylvania Press, 2020).
4 Ulinich, "The Nurse and the Novelist."
5 Cf. Marek Kucia, "The Europeanization of Holocaust Memory and Eastern Europe," *East European Politics & Societies* 30, no. 1 (2016): 97–119, esp. 113–114. If we follow the parallels between the novelist in the short story and Foer, Ulinich changes the setting of Foer's novel from Ukraine to Belarus. Yet for these two locations, the argument proposed here still holds. For a complementary critical perspective on how Eastern Europe is used in nonimmigrant Jewish American literary texts, including those by Foer and Dara Horn, see Josh Lambert, "Since 2000," in *The Cambridge History of Jewish American Literature*, Hana Wirth-Nasher, ed. (Cambridge: Cambridge University Press, 2015), 624–641.
6 Ulinich, "The Nurse and the Novelist."

Notes to Pages 16–18 • 135

7 Ulinich, "The Nurse and the Novelist." On "material witness," see, e.g., Oren Baruch Stier, *Committed to Memory: Cultural Mediations of the Holocaust* (Amherst: University of Massachusetts Press, 2003), 115ff.

8 I recognize the function and aesthetic value of these works of literature, but at the same time I want to draw attention to what kind of power relations they seem to reify. What I call here "flattening of the local context" is especially visible in the protocols of constructing Holocaust museums; see, for example, Marianne Hirsch and Leo Spitzer, "Incongruous Images: 'Before, During and After': The Holocaust," *History and Theory* 48, no. 4 (2009): 9–25. On East-Central European conditioning of the Holocaust in its multiple articulations, see John-Paul Himka, and Joanna Beata Michlic, eds., *Bringing the Dark Past to Light: The Reception of the Holocaust in Postcommunist Europe* (Lincoln: University of Nebraska Press, 2013).

9 Martin W. Lewis and Kären E. Wigen, *The Myth of Continents: A Critique of Metageography* (Los Angeles: University of California Press, 1997).

10 For a useful grasp of magical realism, see Michael Valdez Moses, "Magical Realism at World's End," *Literary Imagination: The Review of the Association of Literary Scholars and Critics* 3, no. 1 (2001): 105–133. Moses's cultural approach sees it as "sentimental compensatory fictions that allow, indeed encourage, their readers to indulge in a nostalgic longing for and an imaginary return to a world that is past, or passing away" (106). This point is especially valid when magical realism supports hegemonic metageography.

11 Nicole Krauss, *The History of Love: A Novel* (New York: W. W. Norton & Company, 2006); also see my "Narratives of Generationality in 21st-Century North American Jewish Literature: Krauss, Bezmozgis, Kalman," *Eastern European Jewish Affairs* 46, no. 3 (2016): 285–310.

12 Hoberman, *A Hundred Acres of America*, 123, 121.

13 Hoberman, *A Hundred Acres of America*, 123.

14 Sarah Phillips Casteel, "Landscapes: American and the Americas," in *The Cambridge History of Jewish American Literature*, ed. Hana Wirth-Nasher (Cambridge: Cambridge University Press, 2016), 416.

15 Casteel, "Landscapes," 416.

16 Casteel, "Landscapes," 413.

17 Michael P. Kramer, "Acts of Assimilation: The Invention of Jewish American Literary History," *Jewish Quarterly Review* 103, no. 4 (2013): 557; see also Irving Howe, introduction in *Jewish American Stories*, ed. Irving Howe (New York: Penguin, 1997), 1–17.

18 Cf. Jeffrey Shandler, *Shtetl: A Vernacular Intellectual History*, vol. 5 (New Brunswick: Rutgers University Press, 2014); Steven J. Zipperstein, *Imagining Russian Jewry: Memory, History, Identity* (Seattle: University of Washington Press, 1999); Matthew Frye Jacobson, *Special Sorrows: The Diasporic Imagination of Irish, Polish, and Jewish Immigrants in the United States* (Cambridge, MA: Harvard University Press, 1995).

19 Casteel, "Landscapes," 427.

20 Madina Tlostanova, "Why the Post-Socialist Cannot Speak," in *Postcoloniality-Decoloniality-Black Critique: Joints and Fissures*, ed. Sabine Broeck and Carsten Junker (Frankfurt, Germany: Campus Verlag, 2014), 169.

21 David Chioni Moore, "Is the Post- in Postcolonial the Post- in Post-Soviet? Toward a Global Postcolonial Critique," *PMLA* 116, no. 1 (2001): 111–128. For a

136 • Notes to Pages 18–19

critical view of Chioni's text along these lines, see Madina Tlostanova, "Postcolonial Theory, the Decolonial Option, and Post-Socialist Writing," in *Postcolonial Europe? Essays on Post-Communist Literatures and Cultures*, ed. Dobrota Pucherová and Róbert Gáfrik (Leiden, Netherlands: Brill, 2015), 28–29. About the need to deconstruct the "post-Soviet," see Alexei Penzin, "Post-Soviet Singularity and Codes of Cultural Translation," June 17, 2009, http://www.lcca.lv/e-texts/17.

22 Tlostanova, "Why the Post-Socialist Cannot Speak," 169. Because of these larger global asymmetries, some scholars reworking postcolonial frameworks in reference to post-socialist Europe and post-Soviet space call the field post-dependence studies. This quote may have a different ring to it now, after Russia's 2022 invasion of Ukraine. However, it should not be read by any means as a justification of Russia's imperial ambitions but, again, as a testament to power asymmetries on various levels.

23 For the 1985 formulation about "a *strategic* use of positivist essentialism in a scrupulously visible political interest," see Gayatri Chakravorty Spivak, "Subaltern Studies: Deconstructing Historiography," in *The Spivak Reader*, ed. Donna Landry and Gerald MacLean (London: Routledge, 1996), 214.

24 Susan A. Glenn, *The Jewish Cold War: Anxiety and Identity in the Aftermath of the Holocaust* (Ann Arbor: Michigan Publishing, University of Michigan Library, 2014), https://hdl.handle.net/2027/spo.13469761.0024.001.

25 On this "different strand," see Alan M. Wald, *The New York Intellectuals: The Rise and Decline of the Anti-Stalinist Left from the 1930s to the 1980s* (Chapel Hill: University of North Carolina Press, 1987), as well as his trilogy on American writers on the Left, especially Alan M. Wald, *Exiles from a Future Time: The Forging of the Mid-Twentieth-Century Literary Left* (Chapel Hill: University of North Carolina Press, 2002). Recent exploration of the poet Zukofsky and Marxism can be found in Mark Steven, *Red Modernism: American Poetry and the Spirit of Communism* (Johns Hopkins University Press, 2017).

26 Daniel Soyer, "Back to the Future: American Jews Visit the Soviet Union in the 1920s and 1930s," *Jewish Social Studies* 6, no. 3 (Spring–Summer 2000), 135.

27 Soyer, "Back to the Future," 125.

28 Recently, scholars have explored the connection between Jewish American writers and dissident writing in communist countries, but I would suggest that their positioning pushes them toward a different kind of agenda and does not include migration as a constituent moment, which it is for the Soviet-born writing discussed here; cf. Brian K. Goodman, "Philip Roth's Other Europe: Counter-Realism and the Late Cold War," *American Literary History* 27, no. 4 (2015): 717–740. Recent acclaimed literary narratives, even if they take place in or otherwise address postwar communist Europe, rather tend to perpetuate its radical difference; see, e.g., Molly Antopol, *The UnAmericans* (W. W. Norton & Company, 2014).

29 Jonathan D. Sarna, "Toward a Comprehensive Policy Planning for Russian-Speaking Jews in North America," 2013, http://www.brandeis.edu/hornstein /sarna/contemporaryjewishlife/russian-speakingjewscomeofage-jppi.pdf. See also Yasha Klots, "The Ultimate City: New York in Russian Immigrant Narratives," *The Slavic and East European Journal* 55, no. 1 (2011): 38–57.

30 Yalta as the setting for Bezmozgis's *The Betrayers* is an example here and could also hint at a growing diversity of locations in this fiction. Another novel set in post-Soviet space but unapologetically mediated through mainstream American

Notes to Pages 19–20 • 137

cultural and geopolitical sensibilities is Gary Shteyngart's *Absurdistan* (2006); see Robert Saunders, *Popular Geopolitics and Nation Branding in the Post-Soviet Realm* (New York: Routledge, 2016), 178ff.

31 Lara Vapnyar's *The Scent of Pine* (2014), discussed in chapter 3, can be also read as creating a link through landscape—specifically, the woods—between rural Russia and New England, while Sana Krasikov's *The Patriots* and Keith Gessen's *Terrible Country*, also discussed in chapter 3, question the post–Cold War divide based on political proclivities and the performance of leftism.

32 The negotiation of spatial networks can be achieved in literature in several other ways, although they are not the focus here. First, fiction that straddles both spaces—Anya Ulinich's *Lena Finkle's Magic Barrel*, Irina Reyn's *Mother Country*, Maria Kuznetsova's *Something Unbelievable*—may include plotlines that mirror one another in various ways, creating parallels within the text. Second, links can be made not directly, through spatial coordinates, but through intertextuality, as, for example, in Irina Reyn's *What Happened to Anna K.*; for an argument that "similar to postcolonial and other diasporic writers, Russian American writers' intertextual use is inextricably linked with a negotiation of cultural identities," see Yelena Furman, "Hybridizing the Canon: Russian-American Writers in Dialogue with Russian Literature," *Canadian Slavonic Papers* 58, no. 3 (2016): 205. Anya Ulinich, *Lena Finkle's Magic Barrel: A Graphic Novel* (New York: Penguin, 2014); Maria Kuznetsova, *Something Unbelievable* (New York: Random House, 2021); Irina Reyn, *Mother Country* (New York: Thomas Dunne Books, 2019); and Irina Reyn, *What Happened to Anna K.* (New York: Touchstone Books, 2008). Another way would be designing a larger network of locations, one that includes Western and Central Europe, as in Michael Idov's *Ground Up* or Gary Shteyngart's *Russian Debutantes Handbook*; however, these works are notably not interested in challenging the existing metageographical scheme. Another novel set in the United States and the post-Soviet space but unapologetically mediated through mainstream American cultural and geopolitical sensibilities (and satirizing them) is Gary Shteyngart's *Absurdistan* (2006); see Saunders, *Popular Geopolitics*, 178ff; Michael Idov, *Ground Up* (New York: Farrar, Straus and Giroux, 2008); Gary Shteyngart, *A Russian Debutante's Handbook* (New York: Riverhead Books, 2002); and Gary Shteyngart, *Absurdistan* (New York: Random House, 2006).

33 To be sure, these novels engage different regional spaces and use different formal means to serve what I identify as a similar function—namely, rewriting the dominant mode of imagining space in recent mainstream Jewish American fiction. Because they are engaged in regional traditions of both American and post-Soviet space, this kind of analysis requires considerable contextualization on both sides.

34 Adrian Wanner, *Out of Russia: Fictions of a New Translingual Diaspora* (Evanston, IL: Northwestern University Press, 2011), 168.

35 In addition to Phoenix, parts of the novel are set in urban centers of more prominence in the Jewish American literary imaginary—namely, Chicago and New York City (mostly Brooklyn). My claim here is that the initial American setting of the novel is crucial for Sasha's self-perception as a migrant. The character's relocation to Chicago and New York City is predicated on the support system among fellow Russian immigrants and on her genealogical ties to her father, who lives in New York.

138 • Notes to Pages 20–24

36 Cf. Stephen Tatum, "Postfrontier Horizons," *MFS Modern Fiction Studies* 50, no. 2 (2004): 460–468.

37 The author's interview with Anya Ulinich, February 15, 2021.

38 The author's interview with Anya Ulinich, February 15, 2021.

39 Mark Bassin, "Inventing Siberia: Visions of the Russian East in the Early Nineteenth Century," *American Historical Review* 96, no. 3 (1991): 763–794, esp. 770–777. Bassin explicitly states that his reading of Siberia is influenced by the American critique of the American frontier. Such anti-imperial approaches seem to provide the most progressive perspective on the Russian North-East, as well as a starting point for ethnographic research. For an approach to Siberia as a "contact zone" generally more in tune with most progressive strands in New Western Studies, see Eva-Maria Stolberg, "The Siberian Frontier Between 'White Mission' and 'Yellow Peril,' 1890s–1920s," *Nationalities Papers* 32, no. 1 (2004): 165–181. However, this kind of approach does not correspond to Ulinich's metageographical style.

40 Bassin, "Inventing Siberia," 766.

41 Anya Ulinich, *Petropolis* (London: Penguin Books, 2008), 56.

42 Ulinich, *Petropolis*, 41.

43 Ulinich, *Petropolis*, 59.

44 Alan Wood, *Russia's Frozen Frontier: A History of Siberia* (London: Bloomsbury Academic, 2010).

45 Ulinich, *Petropolis*, 49.

46 Ulinich, *Petropolis*, 62.

47 Ulinich, *Petropolis*, 42.

48 Ulinich, *Petropolis*, 69.

49 Dean J. Franco, *The Border and the Line: Race and Literature in Los Angeles* (Stanford, CA: Stanford University Press, 2019), 13.

50 The author's interview with Anya Ulinich, February 15, 2021.

51 I am borrowing this phrase from Carrie Tirado Bramen, who talks about forging such a link between regions within the United States; see her *The Uses of Variety: Modern Americanism and the Quest for National Distinctiveness* (Cambridge, MA: Harvard University Press, 2001), 134ff.

52 Ulinich, *Petropolis*, 109.

53 Ulinich, *Petropolis*, 117.

54 Ulinich, *Petropolis*, 117.

55 Ulinich, *Petropolis*, 109.

56 Ulinich, *Petropolis*, 134.

57 Ulinich has a localized corrective, as it were, to this kind of parallelism: Sasha later, when transferring in Moscow, points out that "black" in the Russian metropolis now denotes origins in Caucasus; see Ulinich, *Petropolis*, 280.

58 The author's interview with Anya Ulinich, February 15, 2021.

59 Cf. Monica Popescu, *At Penpoint: African Literatures, Postcolonial Studies, and the Cold War* (Durham, NC: Duke University Press, 2020); and Kristen Ghodsee, *Second World, Second Sex: Socialist Women's Activism and Global Solidarity during the Cold War* (Durham, NC: Duke University Press, 2019).

60 The author's interview with Anya Ulinich, February 15, 2021.

61 Ulinich, *Petropolis*, 109.

62 For "failure of domesticity" as a defining feature of femininities in the subgenre, see Karen Ryan, "Failures of Domesticity in Contemporary Russian-American

Literature: Vapnyar, Krasikov, Ulinich, and Reyn," *TranscUlturAl: A Journal of Translation and Cultural Studies* 1, no. 4 (2011): 63–75.

63 On gender imbalance in the nineteenth-century Southwest, see Elizabeth Jameson, "Bringing It All Back Home: Rethinking the History of Women and the Nineteenth-Century West," in *A Companion to the American West*, ed. William Daverell (Oxford, UK: Blackwell, 2004). On the earlier "importing" of brides to Siberia, see Wood, *Russia's Frozen Frontier*, 233. On Western space as "gendered male," see Krista Comer, *Landscapes of the New West: Gender and Geography in Contemporary Women's Writing* (Chapel Hill: University of North Caroline Press, 1999), 27.

64 Annelise Orleck, *The Soviet Jewish Americans*, The New Americans Series (Westport, CT: Greenwood Publishing Group, 1999), 91.

65 Orleck, *The Soviet Jewish Americans*, 92–96; Yelena Akhtiorskaya and Alexey Yurenev, "Welcome to Брайтон Бич, Brooklyn," *New York Times*, December 14, 2018, https://www.nytimes.com/2018/12/14/nyregion/brighton-beach-photo-essay.html; *From Selfie to Groupie*, accessed March 7, 2021, http://www.selfietogroupie.com/.

66 Akhtiorskaya and Yurenev, "Welcome to Брайтон Бич, Brooklyn."

67 Orleck, *The Soviet Jewish Americans*, 93.

68 Yelena Akhtiorskaya, *Panic in a Suitcase* (New York: Riverhead Books, 2014), 171.

69 Cf. Trinity College English Department, "Yelena Akhtiorskaya at Trinity College," May 22, 2017, https://www.youtube.com/watch?v=RuUlM9hMGuk.

70 Charles Sabatos, "Panic in a Suitcase," *East European Jewish Affairs* 46, no. 3 (2016): 370.

71 Akhtiorskaya, *Panic in a Suitcase*, 95.

72 Akhtiorskaya, *Panic in a Suitcase*, 95.

73 Akhtiorskaya, *Panic in a Suitcase*, 17.

74 Cf. Larry Wolff, *Inventing Eastern Europe: The Map of Civilization on the Mind of the Enlightenment* (Stanford, CA: Stanford University Press, 1994); Maria Todorova, *Imagining the Balkans*, updated ed. (Oxford: Oxford University Press, 2009).

75 Akhtiorskaya and Yurenev, "Welcome to Брайтон Бич, Brooklyn."

76 Akhtiorskaya, *Panic in a Suitcase*, 9.

77 The author's interview with Yelena Akhtiorskaya, May 16, 2021.

78 Akhtiorskaya, *Panic in a Suitcase*, 144.

79 Akhtiorskaya, *Panic in a Suitcase*, 144.

80 See "Panic in a Suitcase," GoodReads, accessed March 8, 2021, https://www.goodreads.com/book/show/18693848-panic-in-a-suitcase.

81 The author's interview with Yelena Akhtiorskaya, May 16, 2021.

82 Akhtiorskaya, *Panic in a Suitcase*, 169.

83 Akhtiorskaya, *Panic in a Suitcase*, 183.

84 See Jonathan Freedman, *Klezmer America: Jewishness, Ethnicity, Modernity* (New York: Columbia University Press, 2009).

85 See Caren Irr, *Toward the Geopolitical Novel: U.S. Fiction in the Twenty-First Century* (New York: Columbia University Press, 2013).

86 Bharati Mukherjee, "Immigrant Writing: Changing the Contours of a National Literature," *American Literary History* 23, no. 3 (2011): 680–696.

87 Cf. Efraim Sicher, "Odessa Time, Odessa Space: Rethinking Cultural Space in a Cosmopolitan City," *Jewish Culture and History* 16, no. 3 (2015): 221–241.

140 • Notes to Pages 29-33

88 Akhtiorskaya, *Panic in a Suitcase*, 171.

89 Akhtiorskaya, *Panic in a Suitcase*, 211.

90 The author's interview with Yelena Akhtiorskaya, May 16, 2021.

91 Cf. Reyn, *Mother Country*; Sana Krasikov, "The Muddle," *New Yorker*, August 15, 2022, https://www.newyorker.com/magazine/2022/08/15/the-muddle.

92 "Return journey" is Victoria Aarons and Alan L. Berger's term; see Victoria Aarons and Alan L. Berger, *Third-Generation Holocaust Representation: Trauma, History, and Memory* (Evanston, IL: Northwestern University Press, 2017). For the understanding of the space of Eastern Europe in post-Holocaust fiction, see Michael Hoberman, *A Hundred Acres of America*.

93 The photo is indeed of Brighton Beach. It is a part of Emine Ziyatdinova's master's degree portfolio on Brighton Beach, shot around 2012. For the portfolio, see David Gonzalez, "In Brighton Beach, a Bittersweet Place," *Lens* (blog), November 23, 2012, https://lens.blogs.nytimes.com/2012/11/23/brighton-beach-bittersweet/. As Akhtiorskaya notes in an interview with the author, she did not have any control over the cover and her first reaction was lukewarm, but it has "grown" on her: "I did not want anything schlocky, anything caricature-like, like; 'Brighton Beach' or 'the immigrant.' I just did not understand why this particular lady because I think for them [the publisher] she was probably evocative, like something exotic." The author's interview with Yelena Akhtiorskaya, May 16, 2021.

94 Ulinich, *Petropolis*, 280.

95 Ulinich, *Petropolis*, 121.

96 The author's interview with Anya Ulinich, February 15, 2021.

97 Akhtiorskaya and Yurenev, "Welcome to Брайтон Бич, Brooklyn."

98 Akhtiorskaya, *Panic in a Suitcase*, 24.

99 Cf. Elizabeth DeLoughrey, "Heavy Waters: Waste and Atlantic Modernity," *PMLA* 125, no. 3 (2010): 703–712.

100 The demythologization of the "Russian poet" in this novel is discussed in detail in Adrian Wanner, "'There Is No Such City': The Myth of Odessa in Post-Soviet Immigrant Literature." *Twentieth Century Literature* 65, no. 1–2 (2019): 121–144; Baruch Beckerman writes about this first chapter in terms of Virginia Woolf's and James Joyce's poet-on-the-beach literary models. Baruch Beckerman, "Poetics of Place and the Transformation of the Russian Jewish American Self in Lara Vapnyar's *The Scent of Pine* and Yelena Akhtiorskaya's *Panic in a Suitcase*," *East European Jewish Affairs* 46, no. 3 (2016): 250. My argument here goes in a different direction. For a more detailed discussion of Frida's return to the Nasmertovs' *dacha* and of the novel in terms of the poetics of place, see Beckerman's essay. Characteristically, Beckerman calls Frida's traveling to Odessa "not homecoming born of nostalgia but a movement forward." Beckerman, "Poetics of Place," 257.

101 Hester Blum, "The Prospect of Oceanic Studies," *PMLA* 125, no. 3 (2010): 670. Also cf. Serpil Oppermann, "Storied Seas and Living Metaphors in the Blue Humanities," *Configurations* 27, no. 4 (2019): 443–461.

102 George B. Handley, "Toward an Environmental Phenomenology of Diaspora," *MFS Modern Fiction Studies* 55, no. 3 (2009): 649–657. "If methodologies of the nation and the postnation have been landlocked, in other words, then an oceanic turn might allow us to derive new forms of relatedness from the necessarily unbounded examples provided in the maritime world." Blum, "The Prospect of Oceanic Studies," 671. This questioning of the primacy of continents in thinking

about America has recently become important in archipelagic American studies. Brian Russell Roberts and Michelle Ann Stephens, eds., *Archipelagic American Studies* (Durham, NC: Duke University Press, 2017). Even though my reading of *Panic in a Suitcase* does not and cannot focus on the island as a key topographical entity that leads to rethinking American empire, which the archipelagic perspective so expertly accomplishes, it is driven by a similar impulse to question the automatic assignment of meaning to topographies, here specifically in relation to migration and "Second Worlds."

103 The author's interview with Yelena Akhtiorskaya, May 16, 2021.

Chapter 2   Redefining Survival

1 David Bezmozgis, "An Animal to the Memory," in *Natasha and Other Stories* (New York: Farrar, Straus and Giroux, 2004), 65–78.

2 Bezmozgis, "An Animal to the Memory," 68, 69.

3 Gary Shteyngart, *A Russian Debutante's Handbook* (New York: Riverhead Books, 2002).

4 Shteyngart, *A Russian Debutante's Handbook*, 56.

5 Maria Kuznetsova, *Something Unbelievable* (New York: Random House, 2021).

6 David Bezmozgis, *The Free World* (London: Penguin Books, 2012); Boris Fishman, *A Replacement Life: A Novel* (New York: Harper, 2014); Julia Alekseyeva, *Soviet Daughter: A Graphic Revolution* (Portland, OR: Microcosm Publishing, 2017).

7 Tarik Amar, "A Disturbed Silence: Discourse on the Holocaust in the Soviet West as an Anti-Site of Memory," in *The Holocaust in the East: Local Perpetrators and Soviet Responses*, ed. Michael David-Fox, Peter Holquist, and Alexander M. Martin (Pittsburgh: University of Pittsburgh Press, 2014), 166.

8 Zvi Gitelman, "The Holocaust in the East: Participation and Presentation," in *The Holocaust in the East: Local Perpetrators and Soviet Responses*, ed. Michael David-Fox, Peter Holquist, and Alexander M. Martin (Pittsburgh: University of Pittsburgh Press, 2014), 190.

9 Gitelman, "The Holocaust in the East," 190.

10 Amar, "A Disturbed Silence," 166.

11 Harriet Murav, *Music from a Speeding Train: Jewish Literature in Post-Revolution Russia* (Stanford, CA: Stanford University Press, 2011), 194; Olga Gershenson, *The Phantom Holocaust: Soviet Cinema and Jewish Catastrophe* (New Brunswick, NJ: Rutgers University Press, 2013), 223–228.

12 Murav, *Music from a Speeding Train*; Gershenson, *The Phantom Holocaust*. These studies belong to a recent upsurge of scholarly works on film, photography, literature, and monuments in the USSR and post-Soviet Russia showing various manifestations of the memory of the Jewish genocide, confirming Mordechai Altshuler's thesis that the memory of the Holocaust had become a "unifying force" among Soviet Jewry just after World War II. See Mordechai Altshuler, "Jewish Holocaust Commemoration Activity in the USSR under Stalin," *Yad Vashem Studies* 30 (2002): 271. Cf. also Arkadi Zeltser, *Unwelcome Memory: Holocaust Monuments in the Soviet Union*, trans. A. S. Brown (Jerusalem: Yad Vashem, 2018); David Shneer, *Through Soviet Jewish Eyes: Photography, War, and the Holocaust* (New Brunswick, NJ: Rutgers University Press, 2011). While these grassroots activities may to some extent find their parallels in the postwar United

States within Jewish communities, as shown, for instance, by Hasia Diner, the mainstreaming of Holocaust memory that has taken place in the United States since the 1970s, and which peaked in the early 1990s, is without a counterpart in the Soviet Union and its successor states. See Hasia R. Diner, *We Remember with Reverence and Love: American Jews and the Myth of Silence after the Holocaust, 1945–1962* (New York: New York University Press, 2010).

13 Murav, *Music from a Speeding Train*, 152.

14 Murav, *Music from a Speeding Train*, 151.

15 Yitzhak Arad, *The Holocaust in the Soviet Union* (Lincoln: University of Nebraska Press, 2009), 87. Arad estimates the total Jewish population in these territories to be 4.28–4.32 million.

16 Cf. John Goldlust, "A Different Silence: The Survival of More than 200,000 Polish Jews in the Soviet Union during World War II as a Case Study in Cultural Amnesia," in *Shelter from the Holocaust: Rethinking Jewish Survival in the Soviet Union*, ed. Mark Edele, Sheila Fitzpatrick, and Atina Grossmann (Detroit: Wayne State University Press, 2017), 31.

17 Thomas Lacroix and Elena Fiddian-Qasmiyeh, "Refugee and Diaspora Memories: The Politics of Remembering and Forgetting," *Journal of Intercultural Studies* 34, no. 6 (2013): 689.

18 Cf. Michael Rothberg, *Multidirectional Memory: Remembering the Holocaust in the Age of Decolonization* (Stanford, CA: Stranford University Press, 2009), 20.

19 Max Silverman, *Palimpsestic Memory: The Holocaust and Colonialism in French and Francophone Fiction and Film* (New York: Berghahn Books, 2015), 3, emphasis added.

20 The recent collection *Growing in the Shadow of Antifascism* makes this point especially clear. While the introduction focuses mainly on the ways of recovering marginalized memorialization, it also criticizes (post–)Cold War historiography on its bias toward communist memorialization of the Holocaust, singling out Thomas C. Fox, Jeffrey Herfm, and Lucy Davidowicz; see Kata Bohus, Peter Hallama, and Stephan Stach, introduction to *Growing in the Shadow of Antifascism: Remembering the Holocaust in State-Socialist Eastern Europe,* ed. Kata Bohus, Peter Hallama, and Stephan Stach (Budapest: CEU Press, 2022), 13.

21 Julia Creet, "Introduction: The Migration of Memory and the Memories of Migration," in *Memory and Migration: Multidisciplinary Approaches to Memory Studies*, ed. Julia Creet and Andreas Kitzmann (Toronto: Toronto University Press, 2010), 10.

22 Astrid Erll, "Travelling Memory," *Parallax*, 17, no. 4 (2011), 15.

23 Erll, "Traveling Memory," 14.

24 Bezmozgis, *The Free World*.

25 Astrid Erll, *Memory in Culture*, trans. Sara B. Young (Basingstoke, UK: Palgrave Macmillan, 2011), 170.

26 Erll, *Memory in Culture*, 151.

27 Cf. Leah Garrett, *Young Lions: How Jewish Authors Reinvented the American War Novel* (Evanston, IL: Northwestern University Press, 2015).

28 Victoria Aarons and Alan L. Berger, *Third-Generation Holocaust Representation: Trauma, History, and Memory* (Evanston, IL: Northwestern University Press, 2017), 8.

29 Gennady Estraikh and Harriet Murav, preface to *Soviet Jews in World War II: Fighting, Witnessing, Remembering,* ed. Harriet Murav and Gennady Estraikh (Brighton: Academic Studies Press, 2014), 8.

Notes to Pages 41–43 • 143

30 Alina Bothe and Markus Nesselrodt, "Survivor: Towards a Conceptual History," *The Leo Baeck Institute Year Book* 61, no. 1 (November 2016): 74.

31 Raul Hilberg, *Perpetrators, Victims, Bystanders: The Jewish Catastrophe, 1933–1945* (New York: Aaron Asher Books, 1992), 187; see also Bothe and Nesselrodt, "Survivor," 72.

32 Irina Aleksander, "David Bezmozgis on *The Free World*," *Paris Review*, April 5, 2011, https://www.theparisreview.org/blog/2011/04/05/david-bezmozgis-on -%E2%80%98the-free-world%E2%80%99/.

33 The author's interview with David Bezmozgis, May 18, 2021.

34 The designation of Samuil as a true believer comes from an interview with David Bezmozgis: Penguin Books UK, "The Free World—Interview with David Bezmozgis," April 13, 2011, https://www.youtube.com/watch?v=gAGHcJWMHIQ.

35 Bezmozgis, *The Free World*, 76.

36 Bezmozgis, *The Free World*, 194.

37 Bezmozgis, *The Free World*, 194.

38 Bezmozgis, *The Free World*, 77.

39 Bezmozgis, *The Free World*, 76.

40 Bezmozgis, *The Free World*, 77.

41 Bezmozgis, *The Free World*, 77.

42 Bezmozgis, *The Free World*, 75.

43 Bezmozgis, *The Free World*, 243. Edele notes that medals guaranteed preferential treatment when entering university, but he talks about Soviet veterans generally. Cf. Mark Edele, *Soviet Veterans of World War II: A Popular Movement in an Authoritarian Society, 1941–1991* (Oxford: Oxford University Press, 2008),133.

44 Anna Shternshis, "Between the Red and Yellow Stars: Ethnic and Religious Identity of Soviet Jewish World War II Veterans in New York, Toronto, and Berlin," *Journal of Jewish Identities* 4, no. 1 (January 2011): 43–64; Sveta Roberman, "Commemorative Activities of the Great War and the Empowerment of Elderly Immigrant Soviet Jewish Veterans in Israel," *Anthropological Quarterly* 80, no. 4 (Fall 2007): 1035–1064; Joseph Cronin, *Russian-Speaking Jews in Germany's Jewish Communities, 1990–2005* (Cham, Switzerland: Palgrave Macmillan, 2019).

45 Mordechai Altshuler, "Jewish Combatants of the Red Army Confront the Holocaust," in *Soviet Jews in World War II: Fighting, Witnessing, Remembering*, ed. Harriet Murav and Gennady Estraikh (Brighton: Academic Studies Press, 2014), 16.

46 Shternshis, "Between the Red and Yellow Stars," 43. According to Sveta Roberman, there were 20,000 Jewish Soviet veterans in Israel in 2007. The calculations for other countries are based on the relative number of veterans to the number of immigrants from the former Soviet Union in Israel. See Sveta Roberman, "Fighting to Belong: Soviet WWII Veterans in Israel," *Ethos* 35 no. 4 (2007): 452. See also Shternshis, "Between the Red and Yellow Stars," 63. Five hundred thousand Jewish soldiers were enlisted in the Soviet army during the Great Patriotic War. Of them, between 140,000 and 180,000 were killed. See Zvi Gitelman, *A Century of Ambivalence: The Jews of Russia and the Soviet Union, 1881 to the Present*, 2nd ed. (Bloomington: Indiana University Press, 2001), 129.

47 Shternshis, "Between the Red and Yellow Stars," 43.

48 Shternshis, "Between the Red and Yellow Stars," 55.

49 Deborah Dash Moore, *GI Jews: How World War II Changed a Generation* (Cambridge, MA: Belknap Press, 2004), 9.

50 Moore, *GI Jews*, ix; Garrett, *Young Lions*, 122–132.

144 • Notes to Pages 43–48

51 Cf., e.g., Pew Research Center, *A Portrait of Jewish Americans*, October 1, 2013, https://www.pewforum.org/2013/10/01/jewish-american-beliefs-attitudes-culture-survey/.

52 Cf. Shneer, *Through Soviet Jewish Eyes*.

53 Cf. Edele, *Soviet Veterans*.

54 Cf. Ida Firer, "Ida Firer. Full, Unedited Interview," March 17, 2009, https://www.blavatnikarchive.org/item/24691.

55 Roberman refers to this as the "migrating past." See Roberman, "Commemorative Activities," 1038. Cf. also Shternshis, "Between the Red and Yellow Stars," 63.

56 Cf. Benjamin Mueller, "Medals and Memories for Jewish Veterans from Russia," *New York Times*, May 10, 2015, https://www.nytimes.com/2015/05/10/nyregion/medals-and-memories-for-jewish-world-war-ii-veterans-from-russia.html; Katie Zavadski and Konstantin Sergeyev, "Photos and War Stories From Brighton Beach's Victory Day Parade," *New York Magazine*, May 9, 2015, http://nymag.com/daily/intelligencer/2015/05.

57 Bezmozgis, *The Free World*, 142.

58 Bezmozgis, *The Free World*, 17.

59 Bezmozgis, *The Free World*, 18.

60 Anna Temkina and Elena Zdravomyslova, "The Crisis of Masculinity in Late Soviet Discourse," *Russian Studies in History* 51, no. 2 (2012): 13–34; Lilya Kaganovsky, *How the Soviet Man Was Unmade: Cultural Fantasy and Male Subjectivity under Stalin* (Pittsburgh: University of Pittsburgh Press, 2008).

61 Bezmozgis, *The Free World*, 106.

62 Bezmozgis, *The Free World*, 106.

63 Bezmozgis, *The Free World*, 106.

64 The author's interview with David Bezmozgis, May 18, 2021.

65 Estraikh and Murav, preface to *Soviet Jews in World War II*, 8.

66 Bezmozgis, *The Free World*, 107.

67 Bezmozgis, *The Free World*, 106; Transnational recirculation of the memory of Jewish life in Eastern Europe and leftist engagement before the Holocaust constitutes an important turn in recent historically informed texts, and this novel, as well as Alekseyeva's *Soviet Daughter* and Sana Krasikov's *Patriots*, discussed in chapter 3, can be read in this context. Cf. Ivan Jablonka, *A History of the Grandparents I Never Had*, trans. Jane Kuntz (Stanford, CA: Stanford University Press, 2016); David Slucki, *Sing This at My Funeral* (Detroit: Wayne State University Press, 2019); Sana Krasikov, *The Patriots: A Novel* (New York: Spiegel & Grau, 2017).

68 The author's interview with David Bezmozgis, May 18, 2021.

69 Estraikh and Murav, preface to *Soviet Jews in World War II*, 8.

70 Bezmozgis, *The Free World*, 196.

71 Bezmozgis, *The Free World*, 105.

72 Jeet Heer, "*The Free World* by David Bezmozgis," *Quill and Quire*, accessed September 1, 2020, https://quillandquire.com/review/the-free-world/.

73 Bezmozgis, *The Free World*, 195.

74 Bezmozgis, *The Free World*, 236.

75 The author's interview with David Bezmozgis, May 18, 2021.

76 The author's interview with David Bezmozgis, May 18, 2021.

77 David Breithaupt, "The Rumpus Interview with Boris Fishman," *The Rumpus*, October 30, 2014, https://therumpus.net/2014/10/the-rumpus-interview-with-boris-fishman/.

Notes to Pages 48–54 • 145

78 Breithaupt, "The Rumpus Interview with Boris Fishman."
79 The author's interview with Boris Fishman, September 13, 2020.
80 Aleida Assmann, "History, Memory, and the Genre of Testimony," *Poetics Today* 27, no. 2 (2006): 267.
81 Fishman, *A Replacement Life*, 203.
82 Cf. Gershenson, *The Phantom Holocaust*, 225.
83 Fishman, *A Replacement Life*, 4.
84 Fishman, *A Replacement Life*, 33.
85 Fishman, *A Replacement Life*, 26.
86 Sasha Senderovich, *How the Soviet Jew Was Made* (Cambridge, MA: Harvard University Press, 2022), 225.
87 Susan Slyomovics, *How to Accept German Reparations* (Philadelphia: University of Pennsylvania Press, 2015), 26.
88 In her prologue and chapter 1, "Financial Pain," Slyomovics analyzes her mother and grandmother as having extremely divergent attitudes toward compensation, with her mother's approach evolving after the grandmother's passing.
89 Natan Sznaider, "Pecunifying Respectability?: On the Impossibility of Honorable Restitution," in *Restitution and Memory: Material Restoration in Europe*, ed. Dan Diner and Gotthart Wunberg (New York: Berghahn Books, 2007), 61; cf. also pages 24–25.
90 Claims Conference, "Summary of Major Holocaust Compensation Programs," September 11, 2000, http://www.claimscon.org/forms/allocations/Summary%20 of%20Major%20Holocaust%20Compensation%20Programs.pdf.
91 Fishman, *A Replacement Life*, 35–36.
92 Fishman, *A Replacement Life*, 117.
93 Shoshana Felman, *The Juridical Unconscious: Trials and Traumas in the Twentieth Century* (Cambridge, MA: Harvard University Press, 2002), 4–5.
94 Bothe and Nesselrodt, "Survivor," 71; Samuel Totten, "First-Person Accounts," in *The Holocaust Encyclopedia*, ed. Walter Laquer and Judith Tydor Baumel (New Haven, CT: Yale University Press, 2001), 209.
95 Cf. Geoffrey Hartman, "Tele-Suffering and Testimony in the Dot Com Era," in *Visual Culture and the Holocaust*, ed. Barbie Zelizer (New Brunswick, NJ: Rutgers University Press, 2001), 111–124.
96 Fishman, *A Replacement Life*, 129.
97 Fishman, *A Replacement Life*, 130.
98 Fishman, *A Replacement Life*, 179.
99 Fishman, *A Replacement Life*, 194.
100 Fishman, *A Replacement Life*, 179.
101 Fishman, *A Replacement Life*, 305.
102 Fishman, *A Replacement Life*, 160–161.
103 Fishman, *A Replacement Life*, 6.
104 Fishman, *A Replacement Life*, 234.
105 Fishman, *A Replacement Life*, 118.
106 Fishman, *A Replacement Life*, 318.
107 Ernst van Alphen, "Second-Generation Testimony, Transmission of Trauma, and Postmemory," *Poetics Today* 27, no. 2 (2006): 474.
108 Slyomovics, *How to Accept German Reparations*, 48.
109 Alekseyeva, *Soviet Daughter*, 6.
110 Aarons and Berger, *Third-Generation Holocaust Representation*, 8ff.

Notes to Pages 54–58

111 Even though the graphic narrative is concerned with the relationship between a great-grandmother and great-granddaughter, we know from the story that Lola's daughter—Julia's grandmother—was born before the war and survived the war in the Soviet interior with her mother. I return to "third-generation" Holocaust fiction in the conclusion of this chapter, addressing there how generational thinking usually presents the generations of migrant memory and the generations of Holocaust/war memory on two different planes. Cf. Astrid Erll, "Generation in Literary History: Three Constellations of Generationality, Genealogy, and Memory," *New Literary History* 45, no. 3 (Summer 2014): 385–409.

112 Alekseyeva, *Soviet Daughter*, 20.

113 Alekseyeva, *Soviet Daughter*, 24.

114 Alekseyeva, *Soviet Daughter*, 37.

115 Alekseyeva, *Soviet Daughter*, 37.

116 Alekseyeva, *Soviet Daughter*, 37.

117 David Bezmozgis, "An Animal to the Memory," 65–78; Gary Shteyngart, *Little Failure: A Memoir* (New York: Random House, 2014).

118 Religiosity as an assimilation tool of Russian-speaking Jewish migrants, cf. Zvi Gitelman, *The New Jewish Diaspora: Russian-Speaking Immigrants in the United States, Israel, and Germany* (New Brunswick, NJ: Rutgers University Press, 2016), 213.

119 Maria Kuznetsova, *Oksana, Behave!* (New York: Random House, 2019).

120 Ralph Fisher, *Pattern for Soviet Youth: A Study of the Congresses of the Komsomol, 1918–1954* (New York, 1959), 67, quoted in Anne E. Gorsuch, "'A Woman is Not a Man': The Culture of Gender and Generation in Soviet Russia, 1921–1928," *Slavic Review* 55, no. 3 (1996): 636.

121 Alekseyeva, *Soviet Daughter*, 40.

122 Alekseyeva, *Soviet Daughter*, 55.

123 Alekseyeva, *Soviet Daughter*, 55.

124 Cf. Gitelman, *A Century of Ambivalence*, 93.

125 Alekseyeva, *Soviet Daughter*, 189.

126 Alekseyeva, *Soviet Daughter*, 191.

127 Jablonka, *A History of the Grandparents I Never Had.*

128 Slucki, *Sing this at My Funeral.*

129 Ann Rigney, "Remembering Hope: Transnational Activism beyond the Traumatic," *Memory Studies* 11, no. 3 (July 2018): 370.

130 Cf. Oren Baruch Stier, "Different Trains: Holocaust Artifacts and the Ideologies of Remembrance," *Holocaust and Genocide Studies* 19, no. 1 (2005): 81–106.

131 Alekseyeva, *Soviet Daughter*, 143.

132 Alekseyeva, *Soviet Daughter*, 156.

133 Alekseyeva, *Soviet Daughter*, 146–147.

134 Cf. Murav, *Music from a Speeding Train.*

135 "An Alternative Track" is a chapter in Gershenson's study. On Soviet Jewish soldiers as agents of creating Holocaust memory, see Murav, *Music from a Speeding Train*; Shneer, *Through Soviet Jewish Eyes.*

136 Alekseyeva, *Soviet Daughter*, 144.

137 Alekseyeva, *Soviet Daughter*, 160, 162.

138 For Alekseyeva's family photos and graphic novel panels side by side, see NPR Staff, "'Soviet Daughter': How A Great-Grandmother's Diary Became a Graphic Novel," January 22, 2017, https://www.npr.org/2017/01/22/509158334/soviet

Notes to Pages 58–62 • 147

-daughter-how-a-great-grandmothers-diary-became-a-graphic-novel?t
=1582062699458.

139 Emplotment is a term developed by Hayden White that Murav uses to talk about Soviet writing on the Holocaust; cf. Murav, *Music from a Speeding Train*, 194.

140 Zoë Vania Waxman, *Writing the Holocaust: Identity, Testimony, Representation* (Oxford: Oxford University Press, 2006), 89.

141 Rothberg, *Multidirectional Memory*, 152.

142 Waxman, *Writing the Holocaust*, 5.

143 See, e.g., Anna Hájková, "Between Love and Coercion: Queer Desire, Sexual Barter and the Holocaust," *German History* 39, no. 1 (2021): 112–133.

144 For a characteristic disclaimer, see Waxman, *Writing the Holocaust*, 3; Eliyana R. Adler and Kateřina Čapková, ed., *Jewish and Romani Families in the Holocaust and Its Aftermath* (Newark, NJ: Rutgers University Press, 2020); Celia Donert and Eve Rosenhaft, eds., *The Legacies of the Romani Genocide in Europe since 1945* (New York: Routledge, 2021).

145 Cf. respectively Aomar Boum and Sarah Abrevaya Stein, ed., *The Holocaust and North Africa* (Stanford, CA: Stanford University Press, 2018); Sarah Phillips Casteel, "Outside the Frame: The Josef Nassy Collection and the Boundaries of Holocaust Art," *Jewish Social Studies* 27, no. 1 (2022): 43–82.

146 Aarons and Berger, *Third-Generation Holocaust Representation*, 8.

147 Bezmozgis, *The Free World*, 340.

148 David G. Roskies and Naomi Diamant, *Holocaust Literature: A History and Guide* (Waltham, MA: Brandeis University Press, 2012), 157.

Chapter 3   Afterlives of Communism

1 Igor Derysh, "'Red Scare Tactics': GOP Senator Called Out for Questioning Whether Biden Pick is a Commie," *Salon*, November 19, 2021, https://www.salon .com/2021/11/19/red-scare-tactics-senator-called-out-for-questioning-whether -biden-pick-is-a-commie/; see also "Kennedy Questions Biden Nominee on Membership in Communist Organization," November 18, 2021, https://www .kennedy.senate.gov/public/2021/11/kennedy-questions-biden-nominee-on -membership-in-communist-organization.

2 Derysh, "'Red Scare Tactics.'"

3 Dan Mangan and Jacob Pramuk, "Biden Bank Regulator Pick Saule Omarova Withdraws after Senate Fight over Her Background," CNBC, December 7, 2021, https://www.cnbc.com/2021/12/07/biden-bank-regulator-pick-saule-omarova -withdraws-after-senate-fight-over-her-background.html.

4 Kate Weigand, *Red Feminism: American Communism and the Making of Women's Liberation* (Baltimore: Johns Hopkins University Press, 2002), 4.

5 Gary Shteyngart, *Little Failure: A Memoir* (New York: Random House, 2014), 145.

6 Shteyngart, *Little Failure*, 145

7 Shteyngart, *Little Failure*, 145.

8 Author's interview with Anya Ulinich, February 15, 2021. Private exchanges with Sasha Senderovich about the cover of his book *How the Soviet Jew was Made* (Cambridge, MA: Harvard University Press, 2022).

9 For Shteyngart as a satirist and a review of secondary literature on his work from this perspective, see Geoff Hamilton, *Understanding Gary Shteyngart* (Columbia: University of South Carolina Press, 2017), 24–25.

148 • Notes to Pages 62–69

10 Adam Rovner, "So Easily Assimilated: The New Immigrant Chic," *AJS Review* 30, no. 2 (2006): 317.

11 Rovner, "So Easily Assimilated," 317; for elaborate analysis of the Soviet Jew in these narratives, see Sasha Senderovich, "Scenes of Encounter: The 'Soviet Jew' in Fiction by Russian Jewish Writers in America," *Prooftexts* 35, no. 1 (2015): 98–132.

12 Tony Michels, *Jewish Radicals: A Documentary History* (New York: New York University Press, 2012), 5.

13 Michels, *Jewish Radicals*, 11.

14 Michels, *Jewish Radicals*, 12.

15 Michels, *Jewish Radicals*, 13.

16 Michels, *Jewish Radicals*, 15.

17 Susan A. Glenn, *The Jewish Cold War: Anxiety and Identity in the Aftermath of the Holocaust* (Ann Arbor: Michigan Publishing, University of Michigan Library, 2014), https://hdl.handle.net/2027/spo.13469761.0024.001.

18 Cf. the introduction to this book.

19 Author's interview with Sana Krasikov, April 2, 2023.

20 Konrad H. Jarausch, Christian F. Ostermann, and Andreas Etges, "Rethinking, Representing, and Remembering the Cold War: Some Cultural Perspectives," in *The Cold War*, ed. Konrad H. Jarausch, Christian F. Ostermann, and Andreas Etges (Oldenburg, Germany: De Gruyter, 2017), 13. See also: Muriel Blaive, "'The Cold War? I Have it at Home with my Family': Memories of the 1948–1989 Period Beyond the Iron Curtain," in *The Cold War*, 194–214.

21 Krasikov's omniscient narrator does include an early twentieth-century immigration story as background when introducing Florence's husband, Leo Brink, but it is very marginal.

22 Author's interview with Sana Krasikov, April 2, 2023.

23 Herbert Romerstein, "Disinformation as a KGB Weapon in the Cold War," *Journal of Intelligence History* 1, no. 1 (2001): 54. Even though there are newer definitions, especially after the uptick in research concerning "fake news" from the late 2010s, this definition from a Soviet handbook is most relevant in the context of the novel.

24 Sana Krasikov, *The Patriots: A Novel* (New York: Spiegel & Grau, 2017), xiii.

25 Krasikov, *The Patriots*, xiii.

26 Krasikov, *The Patriots*, 313.

27 Krasikov, *The Patriots*, 313.

28 Krasikov, *The Patriots*, 315, italics in original.

29 Krasikov, *The Patriots*, 315.

30 Author's interview with Sana Krasikov, April 2, 2023.

31 Author's interview with Sana Krasikov, April 2, 2023.

32 Krasikov has been praised for the historical background research she did for the novel: "*The Patriots* is hung, as a narrative, on a series of true-life events, the actual activities of real organizations, from the U.S.-Soviet trade deals of the late '20s, through the war, to Golda Meir's visit to Moscow in 1948, to the anti-Semitic purge of 1952 (the Doctors' Plot), and onward. Krasikov's research has an exemplary thoroughness, whether describing a Stalin rally, or a Thai sex parlour, or listing the parts of a jet fighter." Wynn Wheldon, "The Future Wasn't There: Review of 'The Patriots' by Sana Krasikov," *Commentary*, January 2017,

https://www.commentary.org/articles/wynn-wheldon/the-future-wasnt-there/. Krasikov herself lists historical monographs in the acknowledgments. See Joshua Rubenstein, *Stalin's Secret Pogrom: The Postwar Inquisition of the Jewish Anti-Fascist Committee* (New Haven, CT: Yale University Press, 2001).

33 Krasikov, *The Patriots*, 314; Florence's son, Julian, hears this about his name when he is denied his doctorate in 1977. On Jewishness and Judaism in the prewar Soviet Union, see Zvi Gitelman, "Jewish Nationality and Religion," in *Religion and Nationalism in Soviet and East European Politics,* ed. Pedro Ramet (Durham, NC: Duke University Press, 1989), 59–80. More generally about the function of "nationalities" in the Soviet Union, see Terry Dean Martin, *The Affirmative Action Empire: Nations and Nationalism in the Soviet Union, 1923–1939* (Ithaca, NY: Cornell University Press, 2001).

34 Krasikov, *The Patriots*, 422.

35 Krasikov, *The Patriots*, 421.

36 Krasikov, *The Patriots*, 421, emphasis added.

37 Krasikov, *The Patriots*, 421–422.

38 Krasikov, *The Patriots*, 437.

39 Krasikov, *The Patriots*, 437.

40 Krasikov, *The Patriots*, 437–438.

41 Krasikov, *The Patriots*, 452.

42 Krasikov, *The Patriots*, 452.

43 Krasikov, *The Patriots*, 448.

44 Krasikov, *The Patriots*, 424.

45 Ioana Luca, "Secret Police Files, Tangled Life Narratives: The 1.5 Generation of Communist Surveillance," *Biography* 38, no. 3 (2015): 370.

46 Luca, "Secret Police Files," 367.

47 Luca, "Secret Police Files," 365–366.

48 Cf. London Review Bookshop, "Keith Gessen and Vadim Nikitin on Russia, Socialism and the Soviet Inheritance," May 15, 2019, https://www.youtube.com/watch?v=dYTAyXXIr4s.

49 Keith Gessen, *A Terrible Country* (New York: Viking, 2018), 324.

50 Boris Fishman, "'A Terrible Country' That's Impossible Not to Love," *New York Times*, August 10, 2018, https://www.nytimes.com/2018/08/10/books/review/keith-gessen-terrible-country.html.

51 Gessen, *A Terrible Country*, 41.

52 Gessen, *A Terrible Country*, 6.

53 Gessen, *A Terrible Country*, 37.

54 Masha Gessen, *Ester and Ruzya: How My Grandmothers Survived Hitler's War and Stalin's Peace* (New York: Dial Press, 2004).

55 Gessen, *A Terrible Country*, 319.

56 Gessen, *A Terrible Country*, 15.

57 Gessen, *A Terrible Country*, 270.

58 Gessen, *A Terrible Country*, 290, emphasis in original.

59 Paul Connerton, *How Societies Remember* (Cambridge: Cambridge University Press, 1989), 39.

60 Gessen, *A Terrible Country*, 72.

61 Jarausch, Ostermann, and Etges, "Rethinking, Representing, and Remembering the Cold War," 5.

150 • Notes to Pages 75–79

62 Jarausch, Ostermann, and Etges, "Rethinking, Representing, and Remembering the Cold War," 5.

63 Gessen, *A Terrible Country*, 41.

64 Gessen, *A Terrible Country*, 132.

65 Cf., e.g., Kevin Platt, ed., *Global Russian Cultures* (Madison: University of Wisconsin Press, 2019); Monica Popescu, *At Penpoint: African Literatures, Postcolonial Studies, and the Cold War* (Durham, NC: Duke University Press, 2020).

66 Gayatri Chakravorty Spivak, "Are You Postcolonial? To the Teachers of Slavic and Eastern European Literatures," in "Are We Postcolonial? Post-Soviet Space," ed. Gayatri Chakravorty Spivak, Nancy Condee, Harsha Ram and Vitaly Chernetsky, *PMLA* 121, no. 3 (2006): 829.

67 Gessen, *A Terrible Country*, 22.

68 Gessen, *A Terrible Country*, 148.

69 Gessen, *A Terrible Country*, 150.

70 Gessen, *A Terrible Country*, 172.

71 Gessen, *A Terrible Country*, 182.

72 Gessen, *A Terrible Country*, 166.

73 Gessen, *A Terrible Country*, 159.

74 Carla Blumenkranz, Keith Gessen, Mark Greif, Sarah Leonard, and Sarah Resnick, *Occupy!: Scenes from Occupied America* (London: Verso, 2011).

75 Marijeta Bozovic and Rossen Djagalov, "Post-Soviet Aesthetics," in *After Marx: Literature, Theory, and Value in the Twenty-First Century*, ed. Coleen Lye and Christopher Nealon (Cambridge: Cambridge University Press, 2022), 144 and passim.

76 Sheila Fitzpatrick and Robert Gellately, "Introduction to the Practices of Denunciation in Modern European History," *The Journal of Modern History* 68, no. 4, 1789–1989 (1996): 756.

77 Fitzpatrick and Gellately, "Introduction," 756.

78 Gessen, *A Terrible Country*, 93.

79 My thinking about the afterlives of a repressive system as encompassing both structural/social and personal/individual aspects is inspired by Sadiya Hartman's prologue to *Lose Your Mother: A Journey along the Atlantic Slave Route* (New York: Macmillan, 2008). On afterlife in cultural memory, see also Marianne Hirsch and Leo Spitzer, *Ghosts of Home: The Afterlife of Czernowitz in Jewish Memory* (Berkeley: University of California Press, 2011). For narratives about state socialism, see Marci Shore, *A Taste of Ashes: The Afterlife of Totalitarianism in Eastern Europe* (New York: Crown Publishers, 2013).

80 Michels, *Jewish Radicals*; Paweł Śpiewak, *Żydokomuna: Interpretacje historyczne* (Warszawa: Wydawnictwo Czerwone i Czarne, 2012).

81 See Michael Rothberg, *The Implicated Subject: Beyond Victims and Perpetrators* (Stanford, CA: Stanford University Press, 2019).

82 See *Granta Magazine*, "Sana Krasikov and Viv Groskop in Conversation," March 16, 2017, https://www.youtube.com/watch?v=1XUvdiL-h1Y.

83 Paul Dawson, *The Return of the Omniscient Narrator: Authorship and Authority in Twenty-First Century Fiction* (Columbus: Ohio State University Press, 2013), 3

84 Dawson, *The Return of the Omniscient Narrator*, 3.

85 Serguei Alex Oushakine, "Introduction: Jokes of Repression," *East European Politics and Societies* 25, no. 4 (2011): 655.

Notes to Pages 80–82 • 151

Chapter 4 Soviet Intimacy

1 Lara Vapnyar, "Puffed Rice and Meatballs," in *Broccoli and Other Tales of Food and Love* (New York: Anchor Books, 2009), 51. In the story, Vapnyar talks about Katya's "lover." My phrase "American lover" alludes to Anzia Yerzierska's "American friend," a nonimmigrant figure that she addresses in her *Promised Land*—a passage from which Vapnyar discussed in her essay "The Writer as Tour Guide," in *The Writer Uprooted: Contemporary Jewish Exile Literature*, ed. Alvin H. Rosenfeld (Bloomington: Indiana University Press, 2009), 92–109.

2 Vapnyar, "Puffed Rice and Meatballs," 52.

3 Vapnyar, "The Writer as Tour Guide."

4 On *zagranitsa* (literally, "abroad") as the imaginary West, see Alexei Yurchak, *Everything Was Forever, Until It Was No More: The Last Soviet Generation* (Princeton, NJ: Princeton University Press, 2003), 158–162.

5 See Karolina Krasuska, "Post-Soviet Migrant Memory of the Holocaust," in *The Palgrave Handbook of Holocaust Literature and Culture*, ed. Victoria Aarons and Phyllis Lassner (Cham, Switzerland: Palgrave Macmillan, 2020), 251–265.

6 The author's interview with Lara Vapnyar, August 3, 2021.

7 The author's interview with Lara Vapnyar, August 3, 2021.

8 Ellen Litman, "Searching for My People," March 18, 2014, https://www.jewishbookcouncil.org/pb-daily/searching-for-my-people.

9 In the following, I will be referring to stories set in the 1980s that represent only the end phase of late socialism in the Soviet Union, which, as Alexei Yurchak has shown, share the characteristics of the late-Soviet period. Cf. Yurchak, *Everything Was Forever, Until It Was No More*. The asylum application narratives mentioned in the previous chapter in my reading of *The Free World* were based precisely on the contrast and conflict between the "First" and "Second Worlds." These narrative traits also shape the oral histories in the interviews conducted by HIAS. "MyStory: Gary Shteyngart," accessed November 8, 2021, https://www.youtube.com/watch?v=vWEHbzzbFKk&list=PLTOplRW33Yq_BwMG0G_YnjlWDC YfPGXSP.

10 Cf. Anna Shternshis, *Soviet and Kosher: Jewish Popular Culture in the Soviet Union, 1923–1939* (Bloomington: Indiana University Press, 2006); Anna Shternshis, *When Sonia Met Boris: An Oral History of Jewish Life Under Stalin* (Oxford: Oxford University Press, 2017); Sasha Senderovich, *How the Soviet Jew Was Made* (Cambridge, MA: Harvard University Press, 2022); and Marat Grinberg, *The Soviet Jewish Bookshelf: Jewish Culture and Identity Between the Lines* (Waltham, MA: Brandeis University Press, 2022).

11 For a classic take on articulation, see Stuart Hall, "On Postmodernism and Articulation: An Interview with Stuart Hall," in *Stuart Hall: Critical Dialogues in Cultural Studies*, ed. David Morley and Kuan-Hsing Chen (New York: Routledge, 1996), 141.

12 Senderovich, *How the Soviet Jew Was Made*, 6. No research yet explores what Soviet Jewishness meant in women's texts, nor what women figures they produced, a lacuna waiting to be filled. (See also Yelena Furman, "Somewhat Nebulous Contours: On Sasha Senderovich's 'How the Soviet Jew Was Made,'" *Los Angeles Review of Books*, January 15, 2023, https://lareviewofbooks.org/article/somewhat-nebulous-contours-on-sasha-senderovichs-how-the-soviet-jew-was-made/.) As Ann Pellegrini has demonstrated, a focus on racialized male figures currently

152 • Notes to Pages 83–85

dominates research and has tended to displace analysis of racialized sexual difference in the case of Jewish women; see Ann Pellegrini, *Performance Anxieties: Staging Psychoanalysis, Staging Race* (New York: Routledge, 2014).

13 Kristen Ghodsee, *Why Women Have Better Sex Under Socialism: And Other Arguments for Economic Independence* (New York: Nation Books, 2018), epub, 10.

14 Kristen Ghodsee, "Why Women Had Better Sex Under Socialism," *New York Times*, August 12, 2017, https://www.nytimes.com/2017/08/12/opinion/why-women-had-better-sex-under-socialism.html.

15 Francesca Stella, *Lesbian Lives in Soviet and Post-Soviet Russia.: Post/Socialism and Gender Sexualities* (Basingstoke, UK: Palgrave Macmillan, 2015), 26.

16 Cf. Eric Naiman, *Sex in Public: The Incarnation of Early Soviet Ideology* (Princeton, NJ: Princeton University Press, 2019); and Dan Healy, *Russian Homophobia from Stalin to Sochi* (New York: Bloomsbury Academic, 2017), xiii.

17 Rustam Alexander, "Sex Education and the Depiction of Homosexuality under Khrushchev," in *The Palgrave Handbook of Women and Gender in Twentieth-Century Russia and the Soviet Union*, ed. Melanie Ilic (London: Palgrave Macmillan, 2018), 351.

18 Alexander, "Sex Education," 352.

19 Jonathan Zimmerman, *Too Hot to Handle* (Princeton, NJ: Princeton University Press, 2015), 63. Makarenko established the educational system in communist council children's collectives.

20 Alexander, "Sex Education," 355.

21 Zimmerman, *Too Hot to Handle*, 63.

22 Stella, *Lesbian Lives*, 35.

23 Stella, *Lesbian Lives*, 32. See Elena Zdravomyslova, "The Café Saigon Tusovka: One Segment of the Informal-Public Sphere of Late-Soviet Society," in *Biographical Research in Eastern Europe: Altered Lives and Broken Biographies*, ed. Robert Miller and Rubin Humphrey (Aldershot, UK: Ashgate, 2003), 141–180.

24 Sarah D. Phillips, "'There Are No Invalids in the USSR!': A Missing Soviet Chapter in the New Disability History," *Disability Studies Quarterly* 29, no. 3 (2009), https://dsq-sds.org/article/view/936. For the quotation, Phillips cites V. Fefelov, *В СССР инвалидов нет!* (London: Overseas Publications Interchange, 1986).

25 Phillips, "'There Are No Invalids in the USSR!'"

26 Phillips compares this with some Western models: "The Soviet state's approach to disability was not really the 'individual, tragic' model found in the U.S., Great Britain, and elsewhere and so criticized by disability rights advocates beginning in the 1960s. Rather, the Soviet state employed a functional model of disability, based on a person's perceived 'usefulness for society.'" Phillips, "'There Are No Invalids in the USSR!'"

27 Phillips, "'There Are No Invalids in the USSR!'"

28 This statement was made in 1987 on a Russian American TV show called a tele-bridge, and though the broader context was somewhat different, since then it has become frequently quoted as typical of official Soviet government prudery. See Lynne Attwood, "Sex and the Cinema," in *Sex and Russian Society*, ed. Igor Kon and James Riodan (Bloomington: Indiana University Press, 1993), 64–85; and Lilya Kaganovsky, "The Cultural Logic of Late Socialism," *Studies in Russian and Soviet Cinema* 3, no. 2 (2009): 186.

29 The author's interview with Lara Vapnyar, August 3, 2021.

30 The author's interview with Lara Vapnyar, August 3, 2021.

Notes to Pages 85–88 • 153

31 Yurchak, *Everything Was Forever, Until It Was No More.*
32 Cf. Nadia Kalman, *The Cosmopolitans* (Livingston, AL: Livingston Press, 2010); Maria Kuznetsova, *Oksana, Behave!* (New York: Random House, 2019); Julia Alekseyeva, *Soviet Daughter: A Graphic Revolution* (Portland, OR: Microcosm Press, 2017); Sana Krasikov, *The Patriots: A Novel* (New York: Spiegel & Grau, 2017).
33 Cf. Karen Ryan, "Failures of Domesticity in Contemporary Russian-American Literature: Vapnyar, Krasikov, Ulinich, and Reyn," *TranscUlturAl* 1, no. 4 (2011): 63–75.
34 The author's interview with Lara Vapnyar, August 3, 2021.
35 Ellen Litman, *Mannequin Girl: A Novel* (New York: W. W. Norton & Company, 2014), 35.
36 Litman, *Mannequin Girl*, 36.
37 Litman, *Mannequin Girl*, 36.
38 Phillips, "'There Are No Invalids in the USSR!'"
39 Phillips, "'There Are No Invalids in the USSR!'"
40 Catriona Kelly, *Children's World: Growing Up in Russia, 1890–1991* (New Haven, CT: Yale University Press, 2007), 261.
41 Phillips, "'There Are No Invalids in the USSR!'"
42 Christie Davies, "Goffman's Concept of the Total Institution: Criticisms and Revisions," *Human Studies* 12, no. 1/2 (1989): 78.
43 Erving Goffman, *Asylums* (Harmondsworth, UK: Penguin, 1968), 11, quoted in Christie Davies, "Goffman's Concept of the Total Institution," 77–78.
44 Davies, "Goffman's Concept of the Total Institution," 79.
45 Davies, "Goffman's Concept of the Total Institution," 93.
46 Davies, "Goffman's Concept of the Total Institution," 82.
47 Litman, *Mannequin Girl*, 48.
48 Litman, *Mannequin Girl*, 43.
49 Litman, *Mannequin Girl*, 80.
50 Litman, *Mannequin Girl*, 37.
51 Litman, *Mannequin Girl*, 36.
52 Litman, *Mannequin Girl*, 81.
53 Litman, *Mannequin Girl*, 47.
54 Edit Zsadányi, "Voicing the Subaltern by Narrating the Communist Past through the Focalization of a Child in Gábor Németh's 'Are You a Jew?' and Endre Kukorelly's 'The Fairy Valley,'" in *Postcolonial Europe? Essays on Post-Communist Literatures and Cultures*, ed. Dobrota Pucherová and Róbert Gáfrik (Leiden, Netherlands: Brill, 2015), 180.
55 Zsadányi, "Voicing the Subaltern," 180. In an interview Ellen Litman talked about the novel as autobiographically informed and about her intimate knowledge of these institutions, see the author's interview with Ellen Litman, February 9, 2023.
56 Litman, *Mannequin Girl*, 148.
57 Litman, *Mannequin Girl*, 99.
58 Litman, *Mannequin Girl*, 99.
59 Yurchak, *Everything Was Forever, Until It Was No More.*
60 Davies, "Goffman's Concept of the Total Institution."
61 David Hoffmann and Annette Timm. "Utopian Biopolitics: Reproductive Policies, Gender Roles, and Sexuality in Nazi Germany and the Soviet Union," in *Beyond Totalitarianism: Stalinism and Nazism Compared*, ed. Michael Geyer and Sheila Fitzpatrick (Cambridge: Cambridge University Press, 2008), 102–103.

154 • Notes to Pages 88–94

62 Kelly, *Children's World*, 510–511.
63 Litman, *Mannequin Girl*, 46.
64 Litman, *Mannequin Girl*, 95–96.
65 Lara Vapnyar, "A Question for Vera," in *There Are Jews in My House* (New York: Anchor Books, 2004),83. Vapnyar includes her own experience of being interpellated into Jewishness as a six-year-old in her essay, "The Writer as Tour Guide."
66 Vapnyar, "A Question for Vera," 90.
67 Litman, *Mannequin Girl*, 128.
68 Litman, *Mannequin Girl*, 142.
69 Litman, *Mannequin Girl*, 252–253.
70 Litman, *Mannequin Girl*, 93.
71 Litman, *Mannequin Girl*, 95.
72 Litman, *Mannequin Girl*, 146.
73 Litman, *Mannequin Girl*, 289.
74 Litman, *Mannequin Girl*, 279.
75 Kelly, *Children's World*, 511.
76 Cf. Kirsty Liddiard, "Unpacking Intimate Citizenship: What Can We Learn from Disabled People?" *University of Leeds, Centre for Disability Studies* (blog), June 20, 2019, https://disability-studies.leeds.ac.uk/unpacking-intimate -citizenship-what-can-we-learn-from-disabled-people/.
77 Lara Vapnyar, "Love Lessons, Mondays, at 9 A.M.," *New Yorker*, June 16, 2003, https://www.newyorker.com/magazine/2003/06/16/love-lessons-mondays-9-am. Reprinted in Lara Vapnyar, "Love Lessons—Mondays, 9 A.M. in Lara Vapnyar, *There Are Jews in My House* (New York: Anchor Books: 2004), 120–149.
78 The author's interview with Lara Vapnyar, August 3, 2021.
79 Wellingon Square Bookshop, "The Avid Reader Interviews Lara Vapnyar Author of *Scent of Pine*," April 29, 2014, https://www.youtube.com/watch?v=x3MhIJ IIKac.
80 Lara Vapnyar, *The Scent of Pine: A Novel* (New York: Simon and Schuster, 2014), 17.
81 Larissa I. Remennick writes about "communist chastity" in "The 'Terra Incognita' of Russian Sex: Seven Decades of Socialism and the Morning After," *Journal of Sex Research* 33, no. 4 (1996): 383.
82 Vapnyar, *The Scent of Pine*, 2.
83 Vapnyar, *The Scent of Pine*, 1.
84 Vapnyar, *The Scent of Pine*, 1.
85 Igor Kon, *The Sexual Revolution in Russia: From the Age of the Czars to Today* (New York: Simon and Schuster, 1995).
86 Lynne Attwood and Olga Issoupova, "To Give Birth or Not to Give Birth? Having Children in Soviet and Post-Soviet Russia," in *The Palgrave Handbook of Women and Gender in Twentieth-Century Russia and the Soviet Union*, ed. Melanie Ilic (London: Palgrave Macmillan, 2018), 447.
87 Anya Ulinich, *Lena Finkle's Magic Barrel* (New York: Penguin, 2014), 21.
88 Ulinich, *Lena Finkle's Magic Barrel*, 27.
89 Ulinich, *Lena Finkle's Magic Barrel*, 28.
90 Ulinich, *Lena Finkle's Magic Barrel*, 28.
91 Ulinich, *Lena Finkle's Magic Barrel*, 29.
92 Ulinich, *Lena Finkle's Magic Barrel*, 29. Cf. Eliot Borenstein, *Overkill: Sex and Violence in Contemporary Russian Popular Culture* (Ithaca, NY: Cornell University Press, 2008).

Notes to Pages 94–97 • 155

93 Lara Vapnyar, "Soviet-Era Sex Ed," *New York Times*, March 1, 2014, https://www.nytimes.com/2014/03/02/opinion/sunday/soviet-era-sex-ed.html.

94 Vapnyar, "Soviet-Era Sex Ed."

95 Vapnyar, "Soviet-Era Sex Ed."

96 Vapnyar, *The Scent of Pine*, 13.

97 Vapnyar, *The Scent of Pine*, 16.

98 Britt P. Tevis, "Jews Not Admitted: Anti-Semitism, Civil Rights, and Public Accommodation Laws," *Journal of American History* 107, no. 4 (2021): 847. The Seligman affair was national news, connected with the refusal to allow Joseph Seligman, the son of a wealthy Jewish banker, entry to an exclusive Saratoga Springs hotel, where he had been staying with his family for a decade.

99 The author's interview with Lara Vapnyar, August 3, 2021.

100 Perhaps the absence or denial of Jewish concerns in Lena's memories of Russia in the 1980s comes from the author's struggles to present them in a clear format that American readers could comprehend.

101 The previously discussed graphic novel *Soviet Daughter* in chapter 2 includes traces of queerness, as does Nadia Kalman's *The Cosmopolitans*, discussed in chapter 5. Other examples of Soviet-born queer presences in fiction include David Bezmozgis's short story "Minyan," Yelena Moskovich's novels *The Natashas*, *Virtuoso*, and *A Door Behind A Door*, Olga Zilberbourg's short stories *Like Water and Other Stories*, and Ruth Madievsky's novel *All Night Pharmacy*.

102 Cheburashka Collective, https://twitter.com/the_cheburashki?lang=en.

103 Kolektiv Goluboy Vagon, accessed September 3, 2023, https://www.kolektivgoluboyvagon.com/.

104 The word "goluboy" was and still is associated with slang words for homosexual men, emerging from gay subcultures of the second half of the twentieth century. See Andrea Trovesi, "Warm, Blue and Bulgarian: The Development and Diffusion of Three Expressions to Denote a 'Male Homosexual' in Central and Eastern European Languages," in *Go East! LGBTQ+ Literature in Eastern Europe*, ed. Andrej Zavrl and Alojzija Zupan Sosič (Ljubljana, Slovenia: Ljubljana University Faculty of Arts Press, 2020), 121–128. Also used in Stella, *Lesbian Lives*.

105 Anna Fishzon, "How Brezhnev Era Animated Films Queered Stagnation," in *Russian Performances: Word, Object, Action*, ed. Julie Buckler, Julie Cassiday, and Boris Wolfson (Madison: University of Wisconsin Press, 2014), 201.

106 Fishzon, "How Brezhnev Era Animated Films Queered Stagnation."

107 Lara Vapnyar, "Lydia's Grove," in *There Are Jews in My House* (New York: Anchor, 2004), 73.

108 On stigmatizing "non-Russian" surnames in the USSR, cf., e.g., Masha Gessen, *The Future is History: How Totalitarianism Reclaimed Russia* (London: Granta Books, 2018), 12. This is particularly visible in the school context of *Mannequin Girl*, where Jewish girls are consistently grouped together for small group schoolwork. See Litman, *Mannequin Girl*, 46.

109 Eve Kosofsky Sedgwick, *Between Men: English Literature and Male Homosocial Desire* (New York: Columbia University Press, 1985), 2–3.

110 Vapnyar, "Lydia's Grove," 66.

111 Vapnyar, "Lydia's Grove," 67.

112 Vapnyar, "Lydia's Grove," 66.

113 Vapnyar, "Lydia's Grove," 69.

114 Stella, *Lesbian Lives*, 29.

156 • Notes to Pages 97–100

115 Gessen, *The Future is History*, 43.
116 Stella, *Lesbian Lives*, 32.
117 Stella, *Lesbian Lives*, 34.
118 Stella, *Lesbian Lives*, 35. Speech marks as per the original, thus noting the lack of universalism of specifically located nonnormative categories.
119 Stella, *Lesbian Lives*, 26.
120 Ken Plummer, *Telling Sexual Stories: Power, Change, and Social Worlds* (New York: Routledge, 1993), 151.
121 Plummer, *Telling Sexual Stories*, 151.
122 Plummer, *Telling Sexual Stories*, 151.
123 Plummer, *Telling Sexual Stories*, 151.
124 See Małgorzata Fidelis, *Gender, historia i komunizm*, in *Kobiety w Polsce 1945–1989: Nowoczesność, równouprawnienie, komunizm*, eds. Katarzyna Stańczak-Wiślicz, Piotr Perkowski, Małgorzata Fidelis, and Barbara Klich-Kluczewska (Kraków: Universitas, 2020), 32–33.
125 Cf. Sheila Fitzpatrick, *The Russian Revolution* (Oxford: Oxford University Press, 2008); Robert Stites, *The Women's Liberation Movement in Russia: Feminism, Nihilism, and Bolshevism, 1860–1930* (Princeton, NJ: Princeton University Press, 1978); Gail Lapidus, *Women in Soviet Society* (Los Angeles: University of California Press, 1980).
126 Fidelis, *Gender, historia i komunizm*, 35. Michael David-Fox states, "Debates in the field have from the start faced the same fundamental dilemma of grappling with Soviet novelty and uniqueness, on the one hand, and their opposites— historical continuity, universalistic processes, and international comparability— on the other." Michael David-Fox, *Crossing Borders: Modernity, Ideology, and Culture in Russia and the Soviet Union* (Pittsburgh: University of Pittsburgh Press, 2014), 2.
127 Matti Bunzl, "Jews, Queers, and Other Symptoms: Recent Work in Jewish Cultural Studies," *GLQ: A Journal of Lesbian and Gay Studies* 6, no. 2 (2000): 330.

Chapter 5   Keyword: Migration

1 Executive Order 13769 of January 27, 2017, "Protecting the Nation from Foreign Terrorist Entry into the United States," *Federal Register* (January 2, 2017), https://www.federalregister.gov/documents/2017/02/01/2017-02281/protecting -the-nation-from-foreign-terrorist-entry-into-the-united-states.
2 Anti-Trump Soviet Immigrants, Facebook Group, https://www.facebook.com /groups/362019824152220; "Soviet Jewish Refugee Solidarity Sign-On Letter," https://docs.google.com/forms/d/187JdJQSkBoFjpl4HdtfCkS5GomtdCU-Y13 -OhzP5Kjs/viewform?edit_requested=true. Cf. Gabe Cahn, "Soviet Jews Push Back on Trump's Executive Order," February 3, 2017, https://www.hias.org/blog /soviet-jews-push-back-trumps-executive-order.
3 Julia Ioffe, "This Is What It's Like to Come to the United States as a Refugee," *The Atlantic*, January 29, 2017, https://www.theatlantic.com/politics/archive/2017/01 /this-is-what-its-like-to-come-to-the-united-states-as-a-refugee/514850/.
4 These voices are not representative of Soviet-born Jews in the United States, and I am not reading them as such. Cf., for instance, Renee Gross, "Religion and Culture: Trump Travel Ban Dividing LA Jewish Community," February 24, 2017,

https://archive.kpcc.org/news/2017/02/24/69361/religion-and-culture-trump
-travel-ban-dividing-la/.

5 Caroline Rody, *The Interethnic Imagination: Roots and Passages in Contemporary Asian American Fiction* (Oxford: Oxford University Press, 2009).

6 Cf. respectively Cathy Schlund-Vials, *Modeling Citizenship: Jewish and Asian American Writing* (Philadelphia: Temple University Press, 2011); and Dean J. Franco, *Race, Rights, and Recognition: Jewish American Literature Since 1969* (Ithaca, NY: Cornell University Press, 2017).

7 Viet Thanh Nguyen, introduction to *The Displaced: Refugee Writers on Refugee Lives*, ed. Viet Thanh Nguyen (New York: Abrams Press, 2018), 11, quoted in Yogita Goyal, "'We Are All Migrants': The Refugee Novel and the Claims of Universalism," *MFS Modern Fiction Studies* 66, no. 2 (2020): 242.

8 Goyal, "'We Are All Migrants,'" 242.

9 Goyal, "'We Are All Migrants,'" 242.

10 Goyal, "'We Are All Migrants,'" 242.

11 Bharati Mukherjee, "Immigrant Writing: Changing the Contours of a National Literature," *American Literary History* 23, no. 3 (2011): 683. For linking Mukherjee to Soviet-born literature of immigration, see also Karolina Krasuska, "Narratives of Generationality in 21st-Century North American Jewish Literature: Krauss, Bezmozgis, Kalman," *East European Jewish Affairs* 46, no. 3 (2016): 285–310. Claudia Sadowski-Smith also uses Mukherjee in her literature chapter in *The New Immigrant Whiteness: Race, Neoliberalism, and Post-Soviet Migration to the United States* (New York: New York University Press, 2018).

12 Mukherjee, "Immigrant Writing," 695.

13 See Yến Lê Espiritu, "Toward a Critical Refugee Study: The Vietnamese Refugee Subject in US Scholarship," *Journal of Vietnamese Studies* 1, no. 1–2 (2006): 410–433.

14 Dalia Kandiyoti's work, especially *Migrant Sites: America, Place, and Diaspora Literatures* (Hanover, NH: University Press of New England, 2009), is a good example.

15 Cf. Jonathan Freedman, *Klezmer America: Jewishness, Ethnicity, Modernity* (New York: Columbia University Press, 2009); Schlund-Vials, *Modeling Citizenship*; Bryan Cheyette, *Diasporas of the Mind: Jewish and Postcolonial Writing and the Nightmare of History* (New Haven, CT: Yale University Press, 2013).

16 Nadia Kalman, *The Cosmopolitans* (Livingston, AL: Livingston Press, 2010).

17 Cynthia Ozick, "Sholem Aleichem's Revolution," *New Yorker*, March 20, 1988, https://www.newyorker.com/magazine/1988/03/28/sholem-aleichems-revolution.

18 Barbara Kirshenblatt-Gimblett, "Imagining Europe: The Popular Arts of American Jewish Ethnography," in *Divergent Centers: Shaping Jewish Cultures in Israel and America*, ed. Deborah Dash Moore and Ilan Troen (New Haven, CT: Yale University Press, 2001), 155–191.

19 Peter Novick, *The Holocaust in American Life* (Boston: Houghton-Mifflin, 1999), 7.

20 Benjamin Schreier, *The Rise and Fall of Jewish American Literature: Ethnic Studies and the Challenge of Identity* (Philadelphia: University of Pennsylvania Press, 2020), 72.

21 David Suchoff, "The Cold War Canon Debate, and Yiddish, 1954–1992," in *Living with America 1946–1996*, ed. Cristina Giorcelli and Rob Kroes (Amsterdam: VU University Press, 1997), 211–222, quoted in Schreier, *The Rise and Fall*, 83.

22 Kirshenblatt-Gimblett, "Imagining Europe," 155–191.

Notes to Pages 104–106

23 Schreier, *The Rise and Fall*, 79.

24 Kalman, *The Cosmopolitans*, 121–122.

25 For Orientalization of Jews in the German context, see Ritchie Robertson, *The "Jewish Question" in German Literature, 1749–1939: Emancipation and Its Discontents* (Oxford, UK: Clarendon Press, 1999); for the U.S. context, see Eric L. Goldstein, *The Price of Whiteness: Jews, Race, and American Identity* (Princeton, NJ: Princeton University Press, 2006); and Jonathan Freedman, "Transgressions of a Model Minority," *Shofar* 23, no. 4 (2005): 69–97.

26 Precisely because of its role as othering in the hegemonic American Jewish narrative, the shtetl with its non-normative temporality can be reclaimed by gender and queer scholars and artists. However, this is not the strategy here in the novel. For examples of this in relation to subversive masculinity in a scholarly text, see Daniel Boyarin, *Unheroic Conduct: The Rise of Heterosexuality and the Invention of the Jewish Man* (Berkeley: University of California Press, 1997). For an overview of its artistic uses, see Simi Horwitz, "Jewish Drag Kings Reclaim Male Roles for Women," *Forward*, May 8, 2014, http://forward.com/culture/197781/jewish-drag-kings-reclaim-male-roles-for-women/.

27 Kalman, *The Cosmopolitans*, 122.

28 Kalman, *The Cosmopolitans*, 62. The Strausses might have easily served as the target of a 1973 comic strip in *Mad* magazine critiquing upper-middle-class Jews in the United States who have become successful. As Kirshenblatt-Gimblett notes, the comic depicts such families as descendants of people from Anatevka; see Kirshenblatt-Gimblett, "The Imagining of Europe." This genealogical thinking adds important context to Jean's pronouncements in *The Cosmopolitans*.

29 A number of recent studies attempt such a decentering of Jewishness, both inter- and transethnically. Some question the tacitly assumed centrality of Ashkenazi culture in the United States by emphasizing Sephardic presences; see, e.g., Dalia Kandiyoti, "What Is the 'Jewish' in 'Jewish American Literature'?" *Studies in American Jewish Literature* 31, no. 1 (2012): 48–60. How this emphasis on Sephardism can be productively used for the comparative study of ethnicities has been demonstrated by, among others, Sarah Phillips Casteel, "Sephardism and Marranism in Native American Fiction of the Quincentenary," *MELUS* 37, no. 2 (Summer 2012): 59–81. On the other hand, some critics have decentered Jewishness by abandoning the concept of diaspora; see Caryn Aviv and David Shneer, *New Jews: The End of the Jewish Diaspora* (New York: New York University Press, 2005). Others consider various diasporas comparatively; see Cheyette, *Diasporas of the Mind*.

30 The Molochniks are the object of Orientalization, but they themselves are guilty of it too in relation to Pratik and his family. Examples of Orientalized discourse abound in the novel, especially in the chapters covering wedding preparations and the wedding itself of Pratik and Yana. Most of these Orientalizing traits come from the familiar occidental repertoire, and as such are not worth analyzing here in detail, beyond stating that they function as a tool to demystify the Molochniks.

31 Werner Sollors, *Beyond Ethnicity: Consent and Descent in American Culture* (Oxford: Oxford University Press, 1987), 234.

32 Kalman, *The Cosmopolitans*, 35.

33 Rebecca L. Walkowitz, *Cosmopolitan Style: Modernism beyond the Nation* (New York: Columbia University Press, 2006), 2.

34 Alan Barnard and Anthony Good, *Research Practices in the Study of Kinship* (London: Academic Press, 1984), quoted in Mary Bouquet, "Family Trees and

Their Affinities: The Visual Imperative of the Genealogical Diagram," *Journal of the Royal Anthropological Institute* 2, no. 1 (1996): 60–61.

35 Bouquet, "Family Trees and Their Affinities," 60.

36 Cf. Kalman, *The Cosmopolitans*, 23.

37 Kalman, *The Cosmopolitans*, 176.

38 Kalman, *The Cosmopolitans*, 92.

39 Author's interview with Nadia Kalman, December 30, 2021, and email exchange.

40 Bezmozgis's *Immigrant City and Other Stories* (2019) is his second volume of short stories, and it collects his stories published previously in the *New Yorker* and *Harper's Magazine* between 2005 and 2007, and in *Zoetrope: All Stories* and *Tablet* in 2016–2017, in addition to a story simultaneously published in the Toronto-based *The Walrus*. The earlier stories are closer to his 2003 collection, *Natasha and Other Stories*, including one, "Roman's Song," that shares a character with the older collection. Newer stories often feature an adult 1.5-generation immigrant, sometimes even his own children.

41 David Bezmozgis, *Immigrant City and Other Stories* (New York: HarperCollins, 2019), 5.

42 Bezmozgis, *Immigrant City*, 3.

43 Bezmozgis, *Immigrant City*, 6.

44 Bezmozgis, *Immigrant City*, 7.

45 Bezmozgis, *Immigrant City*, 12.

46 Bezmozgis, *Immigrant City*, 12.

47 Bezmozgis, *Immigrant City*, 8.

48 Bezmozgis, *Immigrant City*, 13. This thinking brings to mind Michael Rothberg's concept of multidirectional memory, especially in the context of migration; Michael Rothberg "Multidirectional Memory in Migratory Settings: The Case of Post-Holocaust Germany," *Transnational Memory: Circulation, Articulation, Scales* (2014): 123–145.

49 Yến Lê Espiritu, "Refugee," in *Keywords for Asian American Studies*, ed. Cathy J. Schlund-Vials, Linda Trinh Võ, and K. Scott Wong (New York: New York University Press, 2015), 208.

50 Bezmozgis, *Immigrant City*, 7.

51 Bezmozgis, *Immigrant City*, 7.

52 Bezmozgis, *Immigrant City*, 12.

53 See Schreier, *The Rise and Fall*, 11, 67.

54 Bezmozgis, *Immigrant City*, 6.

55 Joan Wallach Scott, *Parité!: Sexual Equality and the Crisis of French Universalism* (Chicago: University of Chicago Press, 2005). On Quebec's 2019 Laicity Act, see Darryl Hunter and Paul Clarke, "Quebec's Laicity Act, Teachers, and Dress Codes in Canadian Case Law: Introspection Before Legal Action." *Education & Law Journal* 31, no. 2 (2022): 169–199.

56 Joan Wallach Scott, "Gender: A Useful Category of Historical Analysis," *The American Historical Review* 91, no. 5 (1986): 1067.

57 Random House, "Be Recruited by Ben Stiller and Gary Shteyngart! Book Trailer for *Lake Success*," August 14, 2018, https://www.youtube.com/watch?v=uPwrEPvSjmo.

58 CNBC Television, "'Lake Success' and the Inner Life of Hedge Funders," September 20, 2018, https://www.youtube.com/watch?v=JXRQ4dFUsDQ.

59 Gary Shteyngart, *Lake Success: A Novel* (New York: Random House, 2018), 20.

60 Shteyngart, *Lake Success*, 19.

61 Shteyngart, *Lake Success*, 64.

62 Shteyngart, *Lake Success*, 30.

63 See the publisher's description of *Lake Success*, Penguin Random House, "Lake Success," accessed September 3, 2023, https://www.penguinrandomhouse.com/books/246822/lake-success-by-gary-shteyngart/.

64 Michael Salter, "The Problem with a Fight Against Toxic Masculinity," *The Atlantic*, February 27, 2019, https://www.theatlantic.com/health/archive/2019/02/toxic-masculinity-history/583411/. The popular term points toward very real problems of male violence and sexism. But it risks misrepresenting what actually causes them.

65 Cf. "Ratings & Reviews for *Lake Success*," GoodReads, accessed November 20, 2021, https://www.goodreads.com/book/show/36739942/reviews?reviewFilters={%22workId%22:%22kca://work/amzn1.gr.work.v1.oJnMqoRmfB86-DzKT7BFag%22,%22after%22:%22MTAxNCwxNTQwNjU1MjgwMDAz%22}.

66 Ron Charles, "Gary Shteyngart Takes Aim at White Male Privilege," *Washington Post*, August 28, 2018, https://www.washingtonpost.com/entertainment/books/gary-shteyngart-takes-aim-at-white-male-privilege/2018/08/28/319f2028-aa61-11e8-b1da-ff7faa680710_story.html.

67 CUSchooloftheArts, "Complex Issues: Gary Shteyngart's 'Lake Success,'" May 28, 2020, https://www.youtube.com/watch?v=g4CvYN4Cugw.

68 Julie Bosman, "New Novel from Shteyngart Will Be an 'International Thriller,'" *New York Times*, March 25, 2014, https://www.nytimes.com/2014/03/26/business/media/new-novel-from-shteyngart-will-be-an-international-thriller.html.

69 CUSchooloftheArts, "Complex Issues."

70 Gary Shteyngart, *Our Country Friends: A Novel* (New York: Random House, 2021). See also Gary Shteyngart, June 28, 2023, Centrum Kultury Jidysz/Center for Yiddish Culture, Book Launch of the Polish translation *Our Country Friends*: Gary Shteyngart in conversation with Karolina Krasuska, https://www.facebook.com/centrumkulturyjidysz/videos/284000507504794.

71 Geoff Hamilton, *Understanding Gary Shteyngart* (Columbia: University of South Carolina Press, 2017), 45.

72 Cf. David Brauner, "The Sons of Phil: Rothian Self-Satire and Self-Incrimination in Shalom Auslander *Foreskin's Lament* and Gary Shteyngart's *Little Failure*," *Open Library of Humanities* 3, no. 2 (2017): 15; for "vivid sexual content," see Hamilton, *Understanding Gary Shteyngart*, 15.

73 Cf. Brauner, "The Sons of Phil."

74 David Gooblar, "Introduction: Roth and Women," *Philip Roth Studies* 8, no. 1 (2012): 7–15; Debra Shostak, "Roth and Gender," in *The Cambridge Companion to Philip Roth*, ed. Timoth Parrish (Cambridge: Cambridge University Press, 2007).

75 For the metaphorical use of accent as a migrant trait, see Masha Rumer, *Parenting with an Accent: How Immigrants Honor Their Heritage, Navigate Setbacks, and Chart New Paths for Their Children* (Boston: Beacon Press, 2021).

76 Shteyngart, *Lake Success*, 55.

77 Shteyngart, *Lake Success*, 36. "Good immigrant" resonates with the formulation in the 1970s Naturalization Act, requiring "good character"; see Schlund-Vials, *Modeling Citizenship*, 4.

78 Schlund-Vials, *Modeling Citizenship*, 1.

79 Shteyngart, *Lake Success*, 37.

80 Shteyngart, *Lake Success*, 39.

Notes to Pages 115–119 • 161

81 Shteyngart, *Lake Success*, 39.
82 Schlund-Vials, *Modeling Citizenship*.
83 Shteyngart, *Lake Success*, 37.
84 Adrian Wanner, "Russian Jews as American Writers: A New Paradigm for Jewish Multiculturalism?" *MELUS* 37, no. 2 (June 2012): 157–176.
85 Shteyngart, *Lake Success*, 18.
86 CUSchooloftheArts, "Complex Issues."
87 Mark McGurl calls the Amazon logo "the cheerfully phallic" logo; see Mark McGurl, *Everything and Less: Novel in the Age of Amazon* (London: Verso, 2021), 155.
88 Mark McGurl, *The Program Era: Postwar Fiction and the Rise of Creative Writing* (Cambridge, MA: Harvard University Press, 2009).
89 Shteyngart, *Lake Success*, 27.
90 McGurl, *Everything and Less*, 237. For "high cultural pluralism," see McGurl, *The Program Era*, 41.
91 McGurl, *Everything and Less*, 237.
92 Shteyngart, *Lake Success*, 19.
93 McGurl, *Everything and Less*, 230; Shteyngart, *Lake Success*, 62. This is another perspective from which we can approach Anya Ulinich's imaginary dialogue with Philip Roth that I recounted in the introduction to this book. For McGurl, Roth is emblematic for "high cultural pluralism" and (Jewish) voice-centered literary style. What Lena Finkle finds affinity with is the style; Roth, on the other hand, moves this affinity to the identity level and erases it by contrasting his nonimmigrant Jewish masculinity with immigrant Jewish femininity.
94 Shteyngart, *Lake Success*, 22.
95 Shteyngart, *Lake Success*, 22.
96 Shteyngart, *Lake Success*, 22. Shteyngart illustrates the entanglement between literature and business even further: Luis plans his next project to center on hedge-fund managers or the "overlords" (26). Barry on his journey phantasizes about becoming a writer and decides "to take note of things, just like a real writer would" (67).
97 Caren Irr, *Toward the Geopolitical Novel: U.S. Fiction in the Twenty-First Century* (New York: Columbia University Press, 2013), 28.
98 Irr, *Toward the Geopolitical Novel*, 26.
99 David Bezmozgis, "The End of Jewish American Literature, Again," *Tablet*, September 17, 2014, http://www.tabletmag.com/jewish-arts-and-culture/books/184354/bezmozgis-american-jewish-literature.
100 Sigrid Weigel, "'Generation' as a Symbolic Form: On the Genealogical Discourse of Memory since 1945," *Germanic Review: Literature, Culture, Theory* 77, no. 4 (2002): 265.
101 Weigel, "'Generation' as a Symbolic Form."
102 Judith Roof, "Generational Difficulties; or, The Fear of a Barren History," in *Generations: Academic Feminists in Dialogue*, ed. Devoney Looser and E. Ann Kaplan (Minneapolis: Minnesota University Press, 1997), 73.
103 Schreier, *The Rise and Fall*, 67.
104 Kalman, *The Cosmopolitans*, 62
105 A parallel formulation in queer studies on "generational narrative" and community building may be found in Lauren Berlant and Michael Warner's text: "Community

162 • Notes to Pages 119–123

is imagined through scenes of intimacy, coupling, and kinship; a historical relation to futurity is restricted to generational narrative and reproduction." Lauren Berlant and Michael Warner, "Sex in Public," *Critical Inquiry* 24, no. 2 (Winter 1998): 554. This formulation of a specifically diachronic "generational narrative" to talk about "co-articulated" "heteronormativity and 'Holocaust' normativity" is used in Jordana Silverstein, "'If Our Grandchildren Are Jewish': Heteronormativity, Holocaust Postmemory and the Reproduction of Melbourne Jewish Families," *History Australia* 10, no. 1 (2013): 167.

106 Rody, *The Interethnic Imagination*, 5.

107 Sollors, *Beyond Ethnicity*.

108 The author's interview with Lara Vapnyar, August 3, 2021; the author's interview with Anya Ulinich, February 15, 2021; the author's interview with David Bezmozgis, May 18, 2021; the author's interview with Boris Fishman, September 13, 2020.

109 Jonathan Freedman, "Do American and Ethnic American Studies Have a Jewish Problem; or, When Is an Ethnic not an Ethnic, and What Should We Do about It?" *MELUS* 37, no. 2 (2012): 36.

Conclusion

1 For the construct of the "Soviet Jew," see Sasha Senderovich, "Scenes of Encounter: The 'Soviet Jew' in Fiction by Russian Jewish Writers in America," *Prooftexts* 35, no. 1 (2015): 98–132 and Benjamin Schreier, *The Rise and Fall of Jewish American Literature: Ethnic Studies and the Challenge of Identity* (Philadelphia: University of Pennsylvania Press, 2020).

2 Roxanne Dunbar-Ortiz, *Not "A Nation of Immigrants": Settler Colonialism, White Supremacy, and a History of Erasure and Exclusion* (Boston: Beacon Press, 2021).

3 Victoria Aarons, Avinoam J. Patt, and Mark Schechner, eds., *The New Diaspora: The Changing Landscape of American Jewish Fiction* (Detroit: Wayne State University Press, 2015).

4 Claudia Sadowski-Smith, *The New Immigrant Whiteness: Race, Neoliberalism, and Post-Soviet Migration to the United States* (New York: New York University Press, 2018).

5 These possible engagements and stakes are also the criteria for selecting the literary texts to discuss here. While my readings cover a broad range of texts, I focus on those that make such dialogues possible.

6 Judith Butler, "What is Critique? An Essay on Foucault's Virtue," in *The Political*, ed. David Ingram (Oxford, UK: Blackwell, 2002), 215.

7 Butler, "What is Critique?" 215.

8 Andrew Furman, *Contemporary Jewish American Writers and the Multicultural Dilemma: The Return of the Exiled* (Syracuse, NY: Syracuse University Press, 2000), 5.

9 Furman, *Contemporary Jewish American Writers*, 4–5, emphasis added.

10 Furman, *Contemporary Jewish American Writers*, 10, emphasis added.

11 Even before the year 2000, Asian American studies scholars criticized the underlying premise of his argument, multicultural inclusivity, as illusory; it is rather an inclusive veneer aestheticizing the difference without in fact admitting the subjects into the realm of citizenry. In fact, the economic realm, caring only about market value and producing capital, featured there as a democratizing factor, with little reflection in citizenry. Simultaneously, scholars challenged

Notes to Pages 123–126 • 163

umbrella terms such as "multicultural mix" as problematic because of the diverse histories of US imperialisms vis-à-vis various national/racialized groups and their resulting position within the American polity. Also, ideas about a "distinct voice" "peculiar to . . . [the] sociocultural experience" (Furman, *Contemporary Jewish American Writers*, 10) of any identity-based group came under productive scrutiny from various feminist perspectives. An intersectional approach pointed to multiple positions that a subject may take or be put into, depending on context, drawing attention to the aporias within a homogenous group identity and the rhetoric of a "distinct voice." Thinking along these lines, the contested question of contemporary "white mainstream" is fundamentally not relevant because the category excludes Jews of color, a segment that is on the rise, as the 2020 Pew Research Center survey indicated "Jewish Americans in 2020." As a result, the debate on the "white mainstream" and its historical relevance for the Jewish experience in the Americas, which renders different results when approached from the perspective of American and European history, may be based on faulty binary thinking, as recent studies have convincingly demonstrated. Yet from another angle, identity as a concept came under attack, notably with queer feminism, pointing to the misnomer of identity as an expression of the self, stable, eternal, inborn, and independent from one's actions. It was only recently that scholars formulated an argument about Jewish American literature along these lines and questioning the idea of this literature as a predetermined *expression* of the inner truth of a demographic. For a characteristic formulation at the turn of the millennium criticizing multiculturalism, see Lisa Lowe, *Immigrant Acts: On Asian American Cultural Politics* (Durham, NC: Duke University Press, 1996). The discourse has dramatically shifted since then, and a point of reference for dialogues today could be, e.g., Yên Lê Espiritu, Lan Duong, Ma Vang, Victor Bascara, Khatharya Um, Lila Sharif, and Nigel Hatton, *Departures: An Introduction to Critical Refugee Studies* (Berkeley: University of California Press, 2022).

12 Cf. Serhii Plokhy, *The Russo-Ukrainian War: The Return of History* (New York: W. W. Norton, 2023).

13 On gendered Orthodoxy, cf. Ayala Fader, *Mitzvah Girls* (Princeton, NJ: Princeton University Press, 2009). See also Jessica Roda, *For Women and Girls Only: Reshaping Jewish Orthodoxy through the Arts* (New York: New York University Press, 2024).

14 Cf. Lila Corwin Berman, Kate Rosenblatt, and Ronit Y. Stahl, "Continuity Crisis: The History and Sexual Politics of an American Jewish Communal Project," *American Jewish History* 104, no. 2 (2020): 167–194.

15 Author's interview with Boris Fishman, September 13, 2020.

16 Lori Harrison-Kahan and Josh Lambert, "Guest Editors' Introduction Finding Home: The Future of Jewish American Literary Studies," *MELUS* 37, no. 2 (2012): 11. Critically on the canonized stories of Soviet-born Jews in North America and the need for new narratives, see Julia Alekseyeva, Tova Benjamin, Oksana Mironova, and Sasha Senderovich, "We Need New Stories of Post-Soviet Jews: A Letter from the Issue Committee," *Jewish Currents*, March 28, 2022, https://jewishcurrents.org/we-need-new-stories-of-post-soviet-jews. My work hopes to contribute to this endeavor.

17 On the situatedness of the field, see the special section "The American Literary History Forum," with articles by Benjamin Schreier, Sarah Philips Casteel, and Dean Franco and the introduction to the forum: Dara E. Goldman and Brett

164 • Notes to Page 126

Ashley Kaplan, "Twenty-First-Century Jewish Writing and the World," *American Literary History* 33, no. 4 (2021): 703–708. For literary Jewish studies engagement with Zionism as a paradigm, see Benjamin Schreier, "Slouching Toward Bethlehem: A Critique of Jewish American Literary-Historical Zionism," *Cultural Critique* 119 (2023): 44–81. Since the beginning of 2023, a series of privately organized Zoom seminars under the rubric of "Decolonizing U.S. Jewish Literatures" have been taking place, testifying to the critical impetus of the field.

18 This trend is visible in Association for Jewish Studies conferences and (as already discussed in the introduction) publications, but also in funding, with larger projects focusing on Jews of color really taking off; cf. "Jews of Color: Histories and Futures" initiative, from University in Colorado in Boulder under Samira Mehta.

19 Roundtable "Queering Jewish Studies," 2023 Association for Jewish Studies, December 18, 2022, organized by Anna Hájková and Karolina Krasuska. A forum based on the roundtable is forthcoming in the journal *Jewish Social Studies*.

Bibliography

Author interviews

Yelena Akhtiorskaya, May 16, 2021.
David Bezmozgis, May 18, 2021.
Boris Fishman, September 13, 2020.
Nadia Kalman, December 30, 2021.
Sana Krasikov, April 2, 2023.
Ellen Litman, February 9, 2023.
Gary Shteyngart, June 28, 2023 (Centrum Kultury Jidysz/Center for Yiddish Culture, Book Launch of the Polish translation *Our Country Friends*: Gary Shteyngart in conversation with Karolina Krasuska, https://www.facebook.com/centrum kulturyjidysz/videos/284000507504794).
Anya Ulinich, February 15, 2021.
Lara Vapnyar, August 3, 2021.

Sources

Aarons, Victoria. "Reinventing Philip Roth in the Fiction of Others." *Revue Française d'Études Américaines* 1 (2021): 62–74.

Aarons, Victoria, and Alan L. Berger. *Third-Generation Holocaust Representation: Trauma, History, and Memory*. Evanston, IL: Northwestern University Press, 2017.

Aarons, Victoria, Avinoam J. Patt, and Mark Schechner, eds. *The New Diaspora: The Changing Landscape of American Jewish Fiction*. Detroit: Wayne State University Press, 2015.

Adler, Eliyana R., and Kateřina Čapková, eds. *Jewish and Romani Families in the Holocaust and Its Aftermath*. Newark, NJ: Rutgers University Press, 2020.

Aleksander, Irina. "David Bezmozgis on *The Free World*." *Paris Review*. April 5, 2011. https://www.theparisreview.org/blog/2011/04/05/david-bezmozgis-on -%E2%80%98the-free-world%E2%80%99/.

Alexander, Rustam. "Sex Education and the Depiction of Homosexuality under Khrushchev." In *The Palgrave Handbook of Women and Gender in*

Twentieth-Century Russia and the Soviet Union, edited by Melanie Ilic, 349–364. London: Palgrave Macmillan, 2018.

Akhtiorskaya, Yelena. *Panic in a Suitcase*. New York: Riverhead Books, 2014.

Akhtiorskaya, Yelena, and Alexey Yurenev. "Welcome to Брайтон Бич, Brooklyn." *New York Times*. December 14, 2018. https://www.nytimes.com/2018/12/14/nyregion/brighton-beach-photo-essay.html.

Alekseyeva, Julia. *Soviet Daughter: A Graphic Revolution*. Portland, OR: Microcosm Publishing, 2017.

Alekseyeva, Julia, Tova Benjamin, Oksana Mironova, and Sasha Senderovich. "We Need New Stories of Post-Soviet Jews: A Letter from the Issue Committee." *Jewish Currents*. March 28, 2022. https://jewishcurrents.org/we-need-new-stories-of-post-soviet-jews.

Alter, Alexandra, and Rachel Abrams. "Sexual Assault Allegations against Biographer Halt Shipping of His Roth Book." *New York Times*. May 17, 2021. https://www.nytimes.com/2021/04/21/books/philip-roth-blake-bailey.html.

Altshuler, Mordechai. "Jewish Combatants of the Red Army Confront the Holocaust." In *Soviet Jews in World War II: Fighting, Witnessing, Remembering*, edited by Harriet Murav and Gennady Estraikh, 16–35. Boston Academic Studies Press, 2014.

———. "Jewish Holocaust Commemoration Activity in the USSR under Stalin." *Yad Vashem Studies* 30 (2002): 271–295.

Amar, Tarik. "A Disturbed Silence: Discourse on the Holocaust in the Soviet West as an Anti-Site of Memory." In *The Holocaust in the East: Local Perpetrators and Soviet Responses*, edited by Michael David-Fox, Peter Holquist, and Alexander M. Martin, 158–184. Pittsburgh: University of Pittsburgh Press, 2014.

Anti-Trump Soviet Immigrants, Facebook Group, https://www.facebook.com/groups/362019824152220.

Antopol, Molly. *The UnAmericans*. W. W. Norton & Company, 2014.

Arad, Yitzhak. *The Holocaust in the Soviet Union*. Lincoln: University of Nebraska Press, 2009.

Assmann, Aleida. "History, Memory, and the Genre of Testimony." *Poetics Today* 27, no. 2 (2006): 261–273.

Attwood, Lynne. "Sex and the Cinema." In *Sex and Russian Society*, edited by Igor Kon and James Riodan, 64–85. Bloomington: Indiana University Press, 1993.

Attwood, Lynne, and Olga Isupova. "To Give Birth or Not to Give Birth? Having Children in Soviet and Post-Soviet Russia." In *The Palgrave Handbook of Women and Gender in Twentieth-Century Russia and the Soviet Union*, edited by Melanie Ilic, 447–461. London: Palgrave Macmillan, 2018.

Aviv, Caryn, and David Shneer. *New Jews: The End of the Jewish Diaspora*. New York: New York University Press, 2005.

Barnard, Alan, and Anthony Good. *Research Practices in the Study of Kinship*. London: Academic Press, 1984.

Bassin, Mark. "Inventing Siberia: Visions of the Russian East in the Early Nineteenth Century." *American Historical Review* 96, no. 3 (1991): 763–794.

Beckerman, Baruch. "Poetics of Place and the Transformation of the Russian Jewish American Self in Lara Vapnyar's *The Scent of Pine* and Yelena Akhtiorskaya's *Panic in a Suitcase*." *East European Jewish Affairs* 46, no. 3 (2016): 245–262.

Beckerman, Gal. *When They Come for Us, We'll Be Gone: The Epic Struggle to Save Soviet Jewry*. Boston: Houghton Mifflin Harcourt, 2010.

Benjamin, Tova. "Introduction: The Soviet Jewry Movement, Revisited." *Jewish Currents*. May 23, 2022. https://jewishcurrents.org/introduction-the-soviet-jewry-movement-revisited.

Berlant, Lauren, and Michael Warner. "Sex in Public." *Critical Inquiry* 24, no. 2 (Winter 1998): 547–566.

Bezmozgis, David. "An Animal to the Memory." In *Natasha and Other Stories*. New York: Farrar, Straus and Giroux, 2004.

———. "The End of Jewish American Literature, Again." *Tablet*. September 17, 2014. https://www.tabletmag.com/sections/arts-letters/articles/bezmozgis-american-jewish-literature.

———. *The Free World*. 2nd ed. London: Penguin Books, 2012.

———. *Immigrant City and Other Stories*. New York: HarperCollins, 2019.

Bilocerkowycz, Jaro. "A New Cold War Emerging as Russia Launches Full-Scale Invasion of Ukraine." *The Conversation*. February 25, 2022. https://theconversation.com/a-new-cold-war-emerging-as-russia-launches-full-scale-invasion-of-ukraine-175872.

Blum, Hester. "The Prospect of Oceanic Studies." *PMLA* 125, no. 3 (2010): 670–677.

Blumenkranz, Carla, Keith Gessen, Mark Greif, Sarah Leonard, and Sarah Resnick. *Occupy!: Scenes from Occupied America*. London: Verso, 2011.

Bohus, Kata, Peter Hallama, and Stephan Stach. Introduction to *Growing in the Shadow of Antifascism: Remembering the Holocaust in State-Socialist Eastern Europe*, edited by Kata Bohus, Peter Hallama, and Stephan Stach, 1–18. Budapest: CEU Press, 2022.

Borenstein, Eliot. *Overkill: Sex and Violence in Contemporary Russian Popular Culture*. Ithaca, NY: Cornell University Press, 2008.

Bosman, Julie. "New Novel from Shteyngart Will Be an 'International Thriller.'" *New York Times*. March 25, 2014. https://www.nytimes.com/2014/03/26/business/media/new-novel-from-shteyngart-will-be-an-international-thriller.html.

Bothe, Alina, and Markus Nesselrodt. "Survivor: Towards a Conceptual History." *The Leo Baeck Institute Year Book* 61, no. 1 (November 2016): 57–82.

Boum, Aomar, and Sarah Abrevaya Stein, eds. *The Holocaust and North Africa*. Stanford, CA: Stanford University Press, 2018.

Bouquet, Mary. "Family Trees and Their Affinities: The Visual Imperative of the Genealogical Diagram." *Journal of the Royal Anthropological Institute* 2, no. 1 (1996): 43–66.

Boyarin, Daniel. *Unheroic Conduct: The Rise of Heterosexuality and the Invention of the Jewish Man*. Berkeley: University of California Press, 1997.

Bozovic, Marijeta, and Rossen Djagalov. "Post-Soviet Aesthetics." In *After Marx: Literature, Theory, and Value in the Twenty-First Century*, edited by Coleen Lye and Christopher Nealon. Cambridge: Cambridge University Press, 2022.

Bramen, Carrie Tirado. *The Uses of Variety: Modern Americanism and the Quest for National Distinctiveness*. Cambridge, MA: Harvard University Press, 2001.

Brauner, David. "The Sons of Phil: Rothian Self-Satire and Self-Incrimination in Shalom Auslander *Foreskin's Lament* and Gary Shteyngart's *Little Failure*." *Open Library of Humanities* 3, no. 2 (2017): 15.

Breithaupt, David. "The Rumpus Interview with Boris Fishman." *The Rumpus*. October 30, 2014. https://therumpus.net/2014/10/the-rumpus-interview-with-boris-fishman/.

Bremmer, Ian. "The New Cold War Could Soon Heat Up: Why Russia and the West Might Escalate the Fight Over Ukraine." *Foreign Affairs*. May 5, 2022.

https://www.foreignaffairs.com/articles/russia-fsu/2022-05-05/new-cold-war-could-soon-heat.

Brodkin Sacks, Karen. *How Jews Became White Folks and What That Says about Race in America*. New Brunswick, NJ: Rutgers University Press, 1998.

Bunzl, Matti. "Jews, Queers, and Other Symptoms: Recent Work in Jewish Cultural Studies." *GLQ: A Journal of Lesbian and Gay Studies* 6, no. 2 (2000): 321–341.

Butler, Judith. "What is Critique? An Essay on Foucault's Virtue." In *The Political*, edited by David Ingram, 212–226. Oxford: Blackwell, 2002.

Cahn, Gabe. "Soviet Jews Push Back on Trump's Executive Order." February 3, 2017. https://www.hias.org/blog/soviet-jews-push-back-trumps-executive-order.

Casteel, Sarah Phillips. "Landscapes: American and the Americas." In *The Cambridge History of Jewish American Literature*, edited by Hana Wirth-Nesher, 413–421. Cambridge: Cambridge University Press, 2016.

———. "Outside the Frame: The Josef Nassy Collection and the Boundaries of Holocaust Art." *Jewish Social Studies* 27, no. 1 (2022): 43–82.

———. "Sephardism and Marranism in Native American Fiction of the Quincentenary." *MELUS* 37, no. 2 (Summer 2012): 59–81.

Charles, Ron. "Gary Shteyngart Takes Aim at White Male Privilege." *Washington Post*. August 28, 2018. https://www.washingtonpost.com/entertainment/books/gary-shteyngart-takes-aim-at-white-male-privilege/2018/08/28/319f2028-aa61-11e8-b1da-ff7faa680710_story.html.

Cheburashka Collective, https://twitter.com/the_cheburashki?lang=en.

Cheyette, Bryan. *Diasporas of the Mind: Jewish and Postcolonial Writing and the Nightmare of History*. New Haven, CT: Yale University Press, 2013.

Claims Conference. "Summary of Major Holocaust Compensation Programs." September 11, 2000. http://www.claimscon.org/forms/allocations/Summary%20of%20Major%20Holocaust%20Compensation%20Programs.pdf.

CNBC Television. "'Lake Success' and the Inner Life of Hedge Funders." September 20, 2018. https://www.youtube.com/watch?v=JXRQ4dFUsDQ.

Comer, Krista. *Landscapes of the New West: Gender and Geography in Contemporary Women's Writing*. Chapel Hill, NC: University of North Carolina Press, 1999.

Connerton, Paul. *How Societies Remember*. Cambridge: Cambridge University Press, 1989.

Corwin Berman, Lila, Kate Rosenblatt, and Ronit Y. Stahl. "Continuity Crisis: The History and Sexual Politics of an American Jewish Communal Project." *American Jewish History* 104, no. 2 (2020): 167–194.

Creese, Jennifer. "Negotiating and Performing 'Jewish Australian' Identity in South-East Queensland's Jewish Community: Creolization, National Identity and Power." *Journal of International Migration and Integration* 21, no. 4 (2020): 1279–1294.

Creet, Julia. "Introduction: The Migration of Memory and the Memories of Migration." In *Memory and Migration: Multidisciplinary Approaches to Memory Studies*, edited by Julia Creet and Andreas Kitzmann, 1–29. Toronto: Toronto University Press, 2010.

Cronin, Joseph. *Russian-Speaking Jews in Germany's Jewish Communities, 1990–2005*. Cham, Switzerland: Palgrave Macmillan, 2019.

CUSchooloftheArts. "Complex Issues: Gary Shteyngart's 'Lake Success.'" October 25, 2018, YouTube video, 1:11:51, https://www.youtube.com/watch?v=g4CvYN4Cugw.

David-Fox, Michael. *Crossing Borders: Modernity, Ideology, and Culture in Russia and the Soviet Union*. Pittsburg: University of Pittsburgh Press, 2014.

Davies, Christie. "Goffman's Concept of the Total Institution: Criticisms and Revisions." *Human Studies* 12, no. 1/2 (1989): 77–95.

Dawson, Paul. *The Return of the Omniscient Narrator: Authorship and Authority in Twenty-First Century Fiction*. Columbus: Ohio State University Press, 2013.

DeLoughrey, Elizabeth. "Heavy Waters: Waste and Atlantic Modernity." *PMLA* 125, no. 3 (2010): 703–712.

Derysh, Igor. "'Red Scare Tactics': GOP Senator Called Out for Questioning Whether Biden Pick Is a Commie." *Salon*. November 19, 2021. https://www.salon.com/2021/11/19/red-scare-tactics-senator-called-out-for-questioning-whether-biden-pick-is-a-commie/.

Diamant, Jeff. "How Younger U.S. Jews Are Similar to—and Different from—Older U.S. Jews." June 8, 2021. https://www.pewresearch.org/fact-tank/2021/06/08/how-younger-u-s-jews-are-similar-to-and-different-from-older-u-s-jews/.

Diner, Hasia R. *We Remember with Reverence and Love: American Jews and the Myth of Silence after the Holocaust, 1945–1962*. New York: New York University Press, 2010.

Dunbar-Ortiz, Roxanne. *Not "A Nation of Immigrants": Settler Colonialism, White Supremacy, and a History of Erasure and Exclusion*. Boston: Beacon Press, 2021.

Donert, Celia, and Eve Rosenhaft, eds. *The Legacies of the Romani Genocide in Europe since 1945*. New York: Routledge, 2021.

Edele, Mark. *Soviet Veterans of World War II: A Popular Movement in an Authoritarian Society, 1941–1991*. Oxford: Oxford University Press, 2008.

The Editors. "20 under 40." *New Yorker*. June 9, 2010. https://www.newyorker.com/magazine/2010/06/14/20-under-40.

Erll, Astrid. "Generation in Literary History: Three Constellations of Generationality, Genealogy, and Memory." *New Literary History* 45, no. 3 (Summer 2014): 385–409.

———. *Memory in Culture*. Translated by Sara B. Young. Basingstoke, UK: Palgrave Macmillan, 2011.

———. "Travelling Memory." *Parallax* 17, no. 4 (2011): 4–18.

Espiritu, Yến Lê. "Refugee." In *Keywords for Asian American Studies*, edited by Cathy J. Schlund-Vials, Linda Trinh Võ, and K. Scott Wong, 208. New York: New York University Press, 2015.

———. "Toward a Critical Refugee Study: The Vietnamese Refugee Subject in U.S. Scholarship." *Journal of Vietnamese Studies* 1, no. 1–2 (2006): 410–433.

Espiritu, Yến Lê, Lan Duong, Ma Vang, Victor Bascara, Khatharya Um, Lila Sharif, and Nigel Hatton. *Departures: An Introduction to Critical Refugee Studies*. Berkeley: University of California Press, 2022.

Estraikh, Gennady, and Harriet Murav. Preface to *Soviet Jews in World War II: Fighting, Witnessing, Remembering*, edited by Harriet Murav and Gennady Estraikh, 7–14. Boston: Academic Studies Press, 2014.

Etkind, Aleksander. *Warped Mourning: Stories of the Undead in the Land of the Unburied*. Stanford, CA: Stanford University Press, 2013.

Executive Order 13769 of January 27, 2017. "Protecting the Nation from Foreign Terrorist Entry into the United States." *Federal Register*. January 2, 2017. https://www.federalregister.gov/documents/2017/02/01/2017-02281/protecting-the-nation-from-foreign-terrorist-entry-into-the-united-states.

Fader, Ayala. *Mitzvah Girls*. Princeton, NJ: Princeton University Press, 2009.

Fefelov, V. *В СССР инвалидов нет!* London: Overseas Publications Interchange, 1986.

Felman, Shoshana. *The Juridical Unconscious: Trials and Traumas in the Twentieth Century.* Cambridge, MA: Harvard University Press, 2002.

Fidelis, Małgorzata. *Gender, historia i komunizm.* In *Kobiety w Polsce 1945–1989: Nowoczesność, równouprawnienie, komunizm,* with individual chapters by Katarzyna Stańczak-Wiślicz, Piotr Perkowski, Małgorzata Fidelis, and Barbara Klich-Kluczewska, 25–44. Kraków: Universitas, 2020.

Firer, Ida. "Ida Firer. Full, Unedited Interview." March 17, 2009. https://www.blavatnikarchive.org/item/24691.

Fisher, Ralph. *Pattern for Soviet Youth: A Study of the Congresses of the Komsomol, 1918–1954.* New York, 1959.

Fishman, Boris. *A Replacement Life: A Novel.* 2nd ed. New York: Harper, 2014.

———. "'A Terrible Country' That's Impossible Not to Love." *New York Times.* August 10, 2018. https://www.nytimes.com/2018/08/10/books/review/keith-gessen-terrible-country.html.

Fishzon, Anna. "How Brezhnev Era Animated Films Queered Stagnation." In *Russian Performances: Word, Object, Action,* edited by Julie Buckler, Julie Cassiday, and Boris Wolfson, 200–208. Madison: University of Wisconsin Press, 2014.

Fitzpatrick, Sheila. *The Russian Revolution.* Oxford: Oxford University Press, 2008.

Fitzpatrick, Sheila, and Robert Gellately. "Introduction to the Practices of Denunciation in Modern European History." *Journal of Modern History* 68, no. 4, 1789–1989 (1996): 747–767.

Franco, Dean J. *The Border and the Line: Race and Literature in Los Angeles.* Stanford, CA: Stanford University Press, 2019.

———. *Race, Rights, and Recognition: Jewish American Literature Since 1969.* Ithaca, NY: Cornell University Press, 2017.

Freedman, Jonathan L. "Do American and Ethnic American Studies Have a Jewish Problem; or, When Is an Ethnic Not an Ethnic, and What Should We Do about It?" *MELUS* 37, no. 2 (2012): 19–40.

———. *Klezmer America: Jewishness, Ethnicity, Modernity.* New York: Columbia University Press, 2009.

———. "Transgressions of a Model Minority." *Shofar* 23, no. 4 (2005): 69–97.

From Selfie to Groupie. Accessed March 7, 2021. https://web.archive.org/web/20220502114230/http://www.selfietogroupie.com/.

Frye Jacobson, Matthew. *Special Sorrows: The Diasporic Imagination of Irish, Polish, and Jewish Immigrants in the United States.* Cambridge, MA: Harvard University Press, 1995.

Furman, Andrew. *Contemporary Jewish American Writers and the Multicultural Dilemma: Return of the Exiled.* Syracuse, NY: Syracuse University Press, 2000.

Furman, Yelena. "Hybridizing the Canon: Russian-American Writers in Dialogue with Russian Literature." *Canadian Slavonic Papers* 58, no. 3 (2016): 205–228.

———. "Somewhat Nebulous Contours: On Sasha Senderovich's 'How the Soviet Jew Was Made.'" *Los Angeles Review of Books.* January 15, 2023. https://lareviewofbooks.org/article/somewhat-nebulous-contours-on-sasha-senderovichs-how-the-soviet-jew-was-made/.

———. "Telling Their Hybrid Stories: Three Recent Works of Russian-American Fiction." *The Slavic and East European Journal* 59, no. 1 (Spring 2015): 116–124.

Garrett, Leah. *Young Lions: How Jewish Authors Reinvented the American War Novel.* Evanston, IL: Northwestern University Press, 2015.

Gershenson, Olga. *The Phantom Holocaust: Soviet Cinema and Jewish Catastrophe.* New Brunswick, NJ: Rutgers University Press, 2013.

Gessen, Keith. *A Terrible Country.* New York: Viking, 2018.

Gessen, Masha. *Ester and Ruzya: How My Grandmothers Survived Hitler's War and Stalin's Peace.* New York: Dial Press, 2004.

———. *The Future Is History: How Totalitarianism Reclaimed Russia.* London: Granta Books: 2018.

Ghodsee, Kristen. *Second World, Second Sex: Socialist Women's Activism and Global Solidarity during the Cold War.* Durham, NC: Duke University Press, 2019.

———. "Why Women Had Better Sex Under Socialism." *New York Times.* August 12, 2017. https://www.nytimes.com/2017/08/12/opinion/why-women-had-better-sex-under-socialism.html.

———. *Why Women Have Better Sex Under Socialism: And Other Arguments for Economic Independence.* New York: Nation Books, 2018.

Gitelman, Zvi. *A Century of Ambivalence: The Jews of Russia and the Soviet Union, 1881 to the Present.* 2nd ed. Bloomington: Indiana University Press, 2001.

———. "Exiting from the Soviet Union: Emigrés or Refugees?" *Michigan Journal of International Law* 43 (1982): 43–61.

———. "The Holocaust in the East: Participation and Presentation." In *The Holocaust in the East: Local Perpetrators and Soviet Responses*, edited by Michael David-Fox, Peter Holquist, and Alexander M. Martin, 185–192. Pittsburgh: University of Pittsburgh Press, 2014.

———. "Jewish Nationality and Religion." In *Religion and Nationalism in Soviet and East European Politics*, edited by Pedro Ramet, 59–80. Durham, NC: Duke University Press, 1989.

———, ed. *The New Jewish Diaspora: Russian-Speaking Immigrants in the United States, Israel, and Germany.* New Brunswick, NJ: Rutgers University Press, 2016.

Glenn, Susan A. *The Jewish Cold War: Anxiety and Identity in the Aftermath of the Holocaust.* Ann Arbor: Michigan Publishing, University of Michigan Library, 2014. https://hdl.handle.net/2027/spo.13469761.0024.001.

Goffman, Erving. *Asylums.* Harmondsworth, UK: Penguin, 1968.

Goldlust, John. "A Different Silence: The Survival of More than 200,000 Polish Jews in the Soviet Union during World War II as a Case Study in Cultural Amnesia." In *Shelter from the Holocaust: Rethinking Jewish Survival in the Soviet Union*, edited by Mark Edele, Sheila Fitzpatrick, and Atina Grossmann, 29–94. Detroit: Wayne State University Press, 2017.

Goldman, Dara E., and Brett Ashley Kaplan. "Twenty-First-Century Jewish Writing and the World." *American Literary History* 33, no. 4 (2021): 703–708.

Goldstein, Eric L. *The Price of Whiteness: Jews, Race, and American Identity.* Princeton, NJ: Princeton University Press, 2006.

Gonzalez, David. "In Brighton Beach, a Bittersweet Place." *Lens* (blog). November 23, 2012. https://lens.blogs.nytimes.com/2012/11/23/brighton-beach-bittersweet/.

Gooblar, David. "Introduction: Roth and Women." *Philip Roth Studies* 8, no. 1 (2012): 7–15.

Goodman, Brian. "American Jewish Writers and the Cold War: The Dissident Generation." In *The Bloomsbury Handbook to Cold War Literary Cultures*, edited by Greg Barnhisel, 113–130. London: Bloomsbury, 2022.

———. "Philip Roth's Other Europe: Counter-Realism and the Late Cold War." *American Literary History* 27, no. 4 (2015): 717–740.

Gorsuch, Anne E. "'A Woman is Not a Man': The Culture of Gender and Generation in Soviet Russia, 1921–1928." *Slavic Review* 55, no. 3 (1996): 636–660.

Gosk, Hanna. "Tożsamościotwórcze aspekty polonistycznych studiów postzależnościowych." *Teksty Drugie: teoria literatury, krytyka, interpretacja*, no. 3 (2012): 51–62.

Goyal, Yogita. "'We Are All Migrants': The Refugee Novel and the Claims of Universalism." *MFS Modern Fiction Studies* 66, no. 2 (2020): 239–259.

Grabowska, Magdalena. "Revolution(s), Socialist Legacies, and Transnational Silences in the Trajectories of Polish Feminism." *Signs* 37, no. 2 (January 2012): 385–411.

Granta Magazine. "Sana Krasikov and Viv Groskop in Conversation." March 16, 2017. https://www.youtube.com/watch?v=1XUvdiL-h1Y.

Grinberg, Marat. *The Soviet Jewish Bookshelf: Jewish Culture and Identity Between the Lines*. Waltham, MA: Brandeis University Press, 2022.

Gross, Renee. "Religion and Culture: Trump Travel Ban Dividing LA Jewish Community." February 24, 2017. Accessed November 12, 2021. https://www.kpcc.org/news/2017/02/24/69361/religion-and-culture-trump-travel-ban-dividing-la/ (site discontinued).

Gurbych, Sergii. *Mother Tongue, Other Tongue: Soviet-Born Jewish Writers in Their New Language Environment*. Heidelberg, Germany: Winter Verlag, 2021.

Hájková, Anna. "Between Love and Coercion: Queer Desire, Sexual Barter and the Holocaust." *German History* 39, no. 1 (2021): 112–133.

Hall, Stuart. "On Postmodernism and Articulation: An Interview with Stuart Hall." In *Stuart Hall: Critical Dialogues in Cultural Studies*, edited by David Morley and Kuan-Hsing, Chen, 131–150. New York: Routledge, 1996.

Hamilton, Geoff. *Understanding Gary Shteyngart*. Columbia: University of South Carolina Press, 2017.

Handley, George B. "Toward an Environmental Phenomenology of Diaspora." *MFS Modern Fiction Studies* 55, no. 3 (2009): 649–657.

Harrison-Kahan, Lori, and Josh Lambert. "Guest Editors' Introduction Finding Home: The Future of Jewish American Literary Studies." *MELUS* 37, no. 2 (2012): 5–18.

Hartman, Geoffrey. "Tele-Suffering and Testimony in the Dot Com Era." In *Visual Culture and the Holocaust*, edited by Barbie Zelizer, 111–124. New Brunswick, NJ: Rutgers University, 2001.

Hartman, Sadiya. Prologue to *Lose Your Mother: A Journey along the Atlantic Slave Route*. New York: Macmillan, 2008.

Healy, Dan. *Russian Homophobia from Stalin to Sochi*. New York: Bloomsbury Academic, 2017.

Heer, Jeet. "*The Free World* by David Bezmozgis." *Quill and Quire*. Accessed September 1, 2020. https://quillandquire.com/review/the-free-world/.

HIAS. "MyStory: Gary Shteyngart." Accessed November 8, 2021. https://www.youtube.com/watch?v=vWEHbzzbFKk&list=PLTOplRW33Yq_BwMG0G_YnjlWDCYfPGXSP.

Hilberg, Raul. *Perpetrators, Victims, Bystanders: The Jewish Catastrophe, 1933–1945*. New York: Aaron Asher Books, 1992.

Himka, John-Paul, and Joanna Beata Michlic, eds. *Bringing the Dark Past to Light: The Reception of the Holocaust in Postcommunist Europe*. Lincoln: University of Nebraska Press, 2013.

Hirsch, Marianne. *The Generation of Postmemory: Writing and Visual Culture after the Holocaust*. New York: Columbia University Press, 2012.

Hirsch, Marianne, and Leo Spitzer. *Ghosts of Home: The Afterlife of Czernowitz in Jewish Memory*. Berkeley: University of California Press, 2011.

———. "Incongruous Images: 'Before, During and After': The Holocaust." *History and Theory* 48, no. 4 (2009): 9–25.

Hoberman, Michael. *A Hundred Acres of America: The Geography of Jewish Literary History*. New Brunswick, NJ: Rutgers, 2018.

Hoffmann, David, and Annette Timm. "Utopian Biopolitics: Reproductive Policies, Gender Roles, and Sexuality in Nazi Germany and the Soviet Union." In *Beyond Totalitarianism: Stalinism and Nazism Compared*, edited by Michael Geyer and Sheila Fitzpatrick, 87–129. Cambridge: Cambridge University Press, 2008.

Horwitz, Simi. "Jewish Drag Kings Reclaim Male Roles for Women." *Forward*. May 8, 2014. https://forward.com/culture/197781/jewish-drag-kings-reclaim-male-roles-for-women/.

Howe, Irving. Introduction to *Jewish American Stories*, edited by Irving Howe, 1–17. New York: Penguin, 1997.

Hunter, Darryl, and Paul Clarke. "Quebec's Laicity Act, Teachers, and Dress Codes in Canadian Case Law: Introspection Before Legal Action." *Education & Law Journal* 31, no. 2 (2022): 169–199.

Idov, Michael. *Ground Up*. New York: Farrar, Straus and Giroux, 2008.

Ioffe, Julia. "This Is What It's Like to Come to the United States as a Refugee." *The Atlantic*. January 29, 2017. https://www.theatlantic.com/politics/archive/2017/01/this-is-what-its-like-to-come-to-the-united-states-as-a-refugee/514850/.

Irr, Caren. *Toward the Geopolitical Novel: U.S. Fiction in the Twenty-First Century*. New York: Columbia University Press, 2013.

Jablonka, Ivan. *A History of the Grandparents I Never Had*. Translated by Jane Kuntz. Stanford, CA: Stanford University Press, 2016.

Jameson, Elizabeth. "Bringing It All Back Home: Rethinking the History of Women and the Nineteenth-Century West." In *A Companion to the American West*, edited by William Daverell, 179–200. Oxford, UK: Blackwell, 2004.

Jarausch, Konrad H., Christian F. Ostermann, and Andreas Etges. "Rethinking, Representing, and Remembering the Cold War: Some Cultural Perspectives." In *The Cold War*, edited by Konrad H. Jarausch, Christian F. Ostermann, and Andreas Etges. Oldenburg, Germany: De Gruyter, 2017.

Kaganovsky, Lilya. "The Cultural Logic of Late Socialism." *Studies in Russian and Soviet Cinema* 3, no. 2 (2009): 185–199.

———. *How the Soviet Man Was Unmade: Cultural Fantasy and Male Subjectivity under Stalin*. Pittsburgh: University of Pittsburgh Press, 2008.

Kalman, Nadia. *The Cosmopolitans*. Livingston, AL: Livingston Press, 2010.

Kandiyoti, Dalia. *Migrant Sites: America, Place, and Diaspora Literatures*. Hanover, NH: University Press of New England, 2009.

———. "What Is the 'Jewish' in 'Jewish American Literature'?" *Studies in American Jewish Literature* 31, no. 1 (2012): 48–60.

Katsnelson, Anna. "Introduction to the New Wave of Russian Jewish American Culture." *East European Jewish Affairs* 46, no. 3 (2016): 241–244.

———. "Transnationalism in Contemporary Post-Soviet North American Literature." *Twentieth Century Literature* 65, no. 1–2 (2019): 145–166.

Katz, Jonathan. "Learning to Undo Ashke-normativity: A Jew in the Motherland." *New Voices*. October 22, 2014. https://newvoices.org/2014/10/22/learning-to-undo-ashke-normativity-a-jew-in-the-motherland/.

174 • Bibliography

Kelly, Catriona. *Children's World: Growing Up in Russia, 1890–1991*. New Haven, CT: Yale University Press, 2007.

Kelner, Shaul. "Where Is the Next Soviet Jewry Movement? How Identity Education Forgot the Lessons that Jewish Activism Taught." In *Beyond Jewish Identity: Rethinking Concepts and Imagining Alternatives*, edited by Jon A. Levisohn and Ari Y. Kelman, 193–215. Brookline, MA: Academic Studies Press, 2019.

"Kennedy Questions Biden Nominee on Membership in Communist Organization." November 18, 2021. https://www.kennedy.senate.gov/public/2021/11/kennedy-questions-biden-nominee-on-membership-in-communist-organization.

Khanin, Vladimir (Ze'ev). "The Diaspora of Russian-Speaking Jews: Political Attitudes and Political Influence." *Osteuropa* 9–11 (2019): 107–115.

Kielar, Diana. "'We Need New Names': Conditions of Belonging in the Contemporary US Immigrant Novel." PhD diss., Brandeis University, 2021.

Kirshenblatt-Gimblett, Barbara. "Imagining Europe: The Popular Arts of American Jewish Ethnography." In *Divergent Centers: Shaping Jewish Cultures in Israel and America*, edited by Deborah Dash Moore and Ilan Troen, 155–191. New Haven, CT: Yale University Press, 2001.

Klots, Yasha. "The Ultimate City: New York in Russian Immigrant Narratives." *Slavic and East European Journal* 55, no. 1 (2011): 38–57.

Kolektiv Goluboy Vagon. Accessed September 3, 2023. https://www.kolektivgoluboyvagon.com/.

Kon, Igor. *The Sexual Revolution in Russia: From the Age of the Czars to Today*. New York: Simon and Schuster, 1995.

Kramer, Michael P. "Acts of Assimilation: The Invention of Jewish American Literary History." *Jewish Quarterly Review* 103, no. 4 (2013): 556–579.

Krasikov, Sana. "The Muddle." *New Yorker*, August 15, 2022, https://www.newyorker.com/magazine/2022/08/15/the-muddle.

———. *The Patriots: A Novel*. New York: Spiegel & Grau, 2017.

Krasuska, Karolina. "Narratives of Generationality in 21st-Century North American Jewish Literature: Krauss, Bezmozgis, Kalman." *Eastern European Jewish Affairs* 46, no. 3 (2016): 285–310.

———. "Post-Soviet Migrant Memory of the Holocaust." In *The Palgrave Handbook of Holocaust Literature and Culture*, edited by Victoria Aarons and Phyllis Lassner, 251–265. Cham, Switzerland: Palgrave Macmillan, 2020.

Krauss, Nicole. *The History of Love: A Novel*. 2nd ed. New York: W. W. Norton & Company, 2006.

Kucia, Marek. "The Europeanization of Holocaust Memory and Eastern Europe." *East European Politics & Societies* 30, no. 1 (2016): 97–119.

Kuznetsova, Maria. *Something Unbelievable*. New York: Random House, 2021.

———. *Oksana, Behave!* New York: Random House, 2019.

Lacroix, Thomas, and Elena Fiddian-Qasmiyeh. "Refugee and Diaspora Memories: The Politics of Remembering and Forgetting." *Journal of Intercultural Studies* 34, no. 6 (2013): 684–696.

Lambert, Josh. *The Literary Mafia: Jews, Publishing, and Postwar American Literature*. New Haven, CT: Yale University Press, 2022.

———. "Since 2000." In *The Cambridge History of Jewish American Literature*, edited by Hana Wirth-Nasher, 624–641. Cambridge: Cambridge University Press, 2015.

Lapidus, Gail. *Women in Soviet Society*. Los Angeles: University of California Press, 1980.

Levantovskaya, Margarita. "Homes without a Homeland: Finding Diasporic Intimacy in Contemporary Russian-Jewish-American Fiction." *Comparative Literature* 69, no. 4 (2017): 394–412.

Lewis, Martin W., and Kären E. Wigen. *The Myth of Continents: A Critique of Metageography*. Los Angeles: University of California Press, 1997.

Liddiard, Kirsty. "Unpacking Intimate Citizenship: What Can We Learn from Disabled People?" *University of Leeds, Centre for Disability Studies* (blog). June 20, 2019. https://disability-studies.leeds.ac.uk/unpacking-intimate-citizenship-what-can-we-learn-from-disabled-people/.

Litman, Ellen. *Mannequin Girl: A Novel*. New York: W. W. Norton & Company, 2014.

———. "Searching for My People." March 18, 2014. https://www.jewishbookcouncil.org/pb-daily/searching-for-my-people.

London Review Bookshop. "Keith Gessen and Vadim Nikitin on Russia, Socialism and the Soviet Inheritance." May 15, 2019. https://www.youtube.com/watch?v=dYTAyXXIr4s.

Lowe, Lisa. *Immigrant Acts: On Asian American Cultural Politics*. Durham, NC: Duke University Press, 1996.

Luca, Ioana. "Secret Police Files, Tangled Life Narratives: The 1.5 Generation of Communist Surveillance." *Biography* 38, no. 3 (2015): 363–394.

Madievsky, Ruth. *All-Night Pharmacy*. New York: Catapult, 2023.

Mangan, Dan, and Jacob Pramuk. "Biden Bank Regulator Pick Saule Omarova Withdraws after Senate Fight over Her Background." CNBC. December 7, 2021. https://www.cnbc.com/2021/12/07/biden-bank-regulator-pick-saule-omarova-withdraws-after-senate-fight-over-her-background.html.

Marsh, Laura. "Philip Roth's Revenge Fantasy." *New Republic*. March 22, 2021. https://newrepublic.com/article/161640/philip-roths-revenge-fantasy-review-blake-bailey.

Martin, Terry Dean. *The Affirmative Action Empire: Nations and Nationalism in the Soviet Union, 1923–1939*. Ithaca, NY: Cornell University Press, 2001.

McGurl, Mark. *Everything and Less: Novel in the Age of Amazon*. London: Verso, 2021.

———. *The Program Era: Postwar Fiction and the Rise of Creative Writing*. Cambridge, MA: Harvard University Press, 2009.

Michels, Tony. *Jewish Radicals*. New York: New York University Press, 2012.

Migration Policy Institute. "U.S. Immigration Trends." Accessed September 3, 2023. https://www.migrationpolicy.org/programs/data-hub/us-immigration-trends#source.

Moore, David Chioni. "Is the Post- in Postcolonial the Post- in Post-Soviet? Toward a Global Postcolonial Critique." *PMLA* 116, no. 1 (2001): 111–128.

Moore, Deborah Dash. *GI Jews: How World War II Changed a Generation*. Cambridge, MA: Belknap Press, 2004.

Moses, Michael Valdez. "Magical Realism at World's End." *Literary Imagination: The Review of the Association of Literary Scholars and Critics* 3, no. 1 (2001): 105–133.

Mueller, Benjamin. "Medals and Memories for Jewish Veterans from Russia." *New York Times*. May 10, 2015. https://www.nytimes.com/2015/05/10/nyregion/medals-and-memories-for-jewish-world-war-ii-veterans-from-russia.html.

Mukherjee, Bharati. "Immigrant Writing: Changing the Contours of a National Literature." *American Literary History* 23, no. 3 (2011): 680–696.

Müller, Martin. "In Search of the Global East: Thinking Between North and South." *Geopolitics* 25, no. 3 (2020): 734–755.

Murav, Harriet. *Music from a Speeding Train: Jewish Literature in Post-Revolution Russia*. Stanford, CA: Stanford University Press, 2011.

Naiman, Eric. *Sex in Public: The Incarnation of Early Soviet Ideology*. Princeton, NJ: Princeton University Press, 2019.

Nguyen, Viet Thanh. Introduction to *The Displaced: Refugee Writers on Refugee Lives*, edited by Viet Thanh Nguyen. New York: Abrams Press, 2018.

Novick, Peter. *The Holocaust in American Life*. Boston: Houghton-Mifflin, 1999.

NPR Staff. "'Soviet Daughter': How a Great-Grandmother's Diary Became a Graphic Novel." January 22, 2017. https://www.npr.org/2017/01/22/509158334/soviet -daughter-how-a-great-grandmothers-diary-became-a-graphic-novel?t =1582062699458.

Oppenheim, Jay (Koby). "Group Distinctiveness and Ethnic Identity among 1.5 and Second-Generation Russian-Speaking Jewish Immigrants in Germany and the U.S." PhD diss., City University of New York, 2016.

Oppermann, Serpil. "Storied Seas and Living Metaphors in the Blue Humanities." *Configurations* 27, no. 4 (2019): 443–461.

Orleck, Annelise. *The Soviet Jewish Americans*. The New Americans Series. Westport, CT: Greenwood Publishing Group, 1999.

Oskman, Tahneer. *How Come the Boys Got to Keep Their Noses: Women and Jewish American Identity in Contemporary Graphic Memoirs*. New York: Columbia University Press, 2016.

Oushakine, Serguei Alex. "Introduction: Jokes of Repression." *East European Politics and Societies* 25, no. 4 (2011): 655–657.

Ozick, Cynthia. "Sholem Aleichem's Revolution." *New Yorker*. March 20, 1988. https://www.newyorker.com/magazine/1988/03/28/sholem-aleichems-revolution.

"Panic in a Suitcase." GoodReads. Accessed March 8, 2021. https://www.goodreads .com/book/show/18693848-panic-in-a-suitcase.

Pellegrini, Ann. *Performance Anxieties: Staging Psychoanalysis, Staging Race*. New York: Routledge, 2014.

Penguin Books UK. "The Free World—Interview with David Bezmozgis." April 13, 2011, https://www.youtube.com/watch?v=gAGHcJWMHIQ.

Penguin Random House. "Lake Success." Accessed September 3, 2023. https://www .penguinrandomhouse.com/books/246822/lake-success-by-gary-shteyngart/.

Penzin, Alexei. "Post-Soviet Singularity and Codes of Cultural Translation." June 17, 2009. http://monumenttotransformation.org/atlas-of-transformation/html/s /singularity/post-soviet-singularity-and-codes-of-cultural-translation-alexei-penzin .html

Pew Research Center. *Jewish Americans in 2020*. May 11, 2021. https://www .pewresearch.org/religion/wp-content/uploads/sites/7/2021/05/PF_05.11.21 _Jewish.Americans.pdf.

Pew Research Center. *A Portrait of Jewish Americans*. October 1, 2013. https://www .pewforum.org/2013/10/01/jewish-american-beliefs-attitudes-culture-survey/.

Phillips, Sarah D. "'There Are No Invalids in the USSR!': A Missing Soviet Chapter in the New Disability History." *Disability Studies Quarterly* 29, no. 3 (2009). https:// dsq-sds.org/article/view/936.

Platt, Kevin, ed. *Global Russian Cultures*. Madison: University of Wisconsin Press, 2019.

Plokhy, Serhii. *The Russo-Ukrainian War: The Return of History*. New York: W. W. Norton, 2023.

Plummer, Ken. *Telling Sexual Stories: Power, Change, and Social Worlds*. New York: Routledge, 1993.

Pocket Samovar. Accessed September 3, 2023. https://www.pocketsamovar.com/.

Popescu, Monica. *At Penpoint: African Literatures, Postcolonial Studies, and the Cold War*. Durham, NC: Duke University Press, 2020.

Punctured Lines: Post-Soviet Literature in and outside the Former Soviet Union. Accessed September 3, 2023. https://puncturedlines.wordpress.com/.

Random House. "Be Recruited by Ben Stiller and Gary Shteyngart! Book Trailer for *Lake Success*." August 14, 2018. https://www.youtube.com/watch?v=uPwrEPvSjmo.

"Ratings & Reviews for *Lake Success*." GoodReads. Accessed November 20, 2021. https://www.goodreads.com/book/show/36739942/reviews?reviewFilters ={%22workId%22:%22kca://work/amzn1.gr.work.v1.oJnMqoRmfB86-DzKT7BFa g%22,%22after%22:%22MTAxNCwxNTQwNjU1MjgwMDAz%22}.

Remennick, Larissa I. *Russian Jews on Three Continents: Identity, Integration, and Conflict*. London: Routledge, 2012.

———. "The 'Terra Incognita' of Russian Sex: Seven Decades of Socialism and the Morning After." *Journal of Sex Research* 33, no. 4 (1996): 383–387.

Reyn, Irina. *Mother Country*. New York: Thomas Dunne Books, 2019.

Rigney, Ann. "Remembering Hope: Transnational Activism beyond the Traumatic." *Memory Studies* 11, no. 3 (July 2018): 368–380.

Roberman, Sveta. "Commemorative Activities of the Great War and the Empowerment of Elderly Immigrant Soviet Jewish Veterans in Israel." *Anthropological Quarterly* 80, no. 4 (Fall 2007): 1035–1064.

———. "Fighting to Belong: Soviet WWII Veterans in Israel." *Ethos* 35, no. 4 (2007): 447–477.

Roberts, Brian Russell, and Michelle Ann Stephens, eds. *Archipelagic American Studies*. Durham, NC: Duke University Press, 2017.

Robertson, Richie. *The "Jewish Question" in German Literature, 1749–1939: Emancipation and Its Discontents*. Oxford, UK: Clarendon Press, 1999.

Roda, Jessica. *For Women and Girls Only: Reshaping Jewish Orthodoxy through the Arts*. New York: New York University Press, 2024.

Rody, Caroline. *The Interethnic Imagination: Roots and Passages in Contemporary Asian American Fiction*. Oxford: Oxford University Press, 2009.

Romerstein, Herbert. "Disinformation as a KGB Weapon in the Cold War." *Journal of Intelligence History* 1, no. 1 (2001): 54–67.

Roof, Judith. "Generational Difficulties; or, The Fear of a Barren History." In *Generations: Academic Feminists in Dialogue*, edited by Devoney Looser and E. Ann Kaplan. Minneapolis: Minnesota University Press, 1997.

Roskies, David G., and Naomi Diamant. *Holocaust Literature: A History and Guide*. Waltham, MA: Brandeis University Press, 2012.

Rothberg, Michael. *The Implicated Subject: Beyond Victims and Perpetrators*. Stanford, CA: Stanford University Press, 2019.

———. *Multidirectional Memory: Remembering the Holocaust in the Age of Decolonization*. Stanford, CA: Stranford University Press, 2009.

———. "Multidirectional Memory in Migratory Settings: The Case of Post-Holocaust Germany." *Transnational Memory: Circulation, Articulation, Scales* (2014): 123–145.

Rovner, Adam. "So Easily Assimilated: The New Immigrant Chic." *AJS Review* 30, no. 2 (2006): 313–324.

178 • Bibliography

Rubenstein, Joshua. *Stalin's Secret Pogrom: The Postwar Inquisition of the Jewish Anti-Fascist Committee*. New Haven, CT: Yale University Press, 2001.

Rumer, Masha. *Parenting with an Accent: How Immigrants Honor Their Heritage, Navigate Setbacks, and Chart New Paths for Their Children*. Boston: Beacon Press, 2021.

Ryan, Karen. "Failures of Domesticity in Contemporary Russian-American Literature: Vapnyar, Krasikov, Ulinich, and Reyn," *TranscUlturAl: A Journal of Translation and Cultural Studies* 1, no. 4 (2011): 63–75.

Sabatos, Charles. "Panic in a Suitcase." *East European Jewish Affairs* 46, no. 3 (2016): 369–370.

Sadowski-Smith, Claudia. *The New Immigrant Whiteness: Race, Neoliberalism, and Post-Soviet Migration to the United States*. New York: New York University Press, 2018.

Sadowski-Smith, Claudia, and Ioana Luca. "Introduction: Postsocialist Literatures in the United States." *Twentieth Century Literature* 65, no. 1–2 (2019): 1–22.

Salter, Michael. "The Problem with a Fight against Toxic Masculinity." *The Atlantic*. February 27, 2019. https://www.theatlantic.com/health/archive/2019/02/toxic -masculinity-history/583411/.

Sarna, Jonathan. "Toward a Comprehensive Policy Planning for Russian-Speaking Jews in North America." 2013. http://www.brandeis.edu/hornstein/sarna /contemporaryjewishlife/russian-speakingjewscomeofage-jppi.pdf.

Saunders, Robert. *Popular Geopolitics and Nation Branding in the Post-Soviet Realm*. New York: Routledge, 2016.

Sax, David. "Rise of the New Yiddishists." *Vanity Fair*. April 8, 2009. https://www .vanityfair.com/culture/2009/04/yiddishists200904.

Schachter, Allison. *Women Writing Jewish Modernity, 1919–1939*. Evanston, IL: Northwestern University Press, 2021.

Schlund-Vials, Cathy. *Modeling Citizenship. Jewish and Asian American Writing*. Philadelphia: Temple University Press, 2011.

———. "The Subjects of 1975: Delineating the Necessity of Critical Refugee Studies." *MELUS: Multi-Ethnic Literature of the United States* 41, no. 3 (2016): 199–203.

Schreier, Benjamin. *The Impossible Jew: Identity and the Reconstruction of Jewish American Literary History*. New York: New York University Press, 2015.

———. *The Rise and Fall of Jewish American Literature: Ethnic Studies and the Challenge of Identity*. Philadelphia: University of Pennsylvania Press, 2020.

———. "Slouching toward Bethlehem: A Critique of Jewish American Literary-Historical Zionism." *Cultural Critique* 119 (2023): 44–81.

Scott, Joan Wallach. "Gender: A Useful Category of Historical Analysis." *The American Historical Review* 91, no. 5 (1986): 1053–1075.

———. *Parite!: Sexual Equality and the Crisis of French Universalism*. Chicago: University of Chicago Press, 2005.

Sedgwick, Eve Kosofsky. *Between Men: English Literature and Male Homosocial Desire*. New York: Columbia University Press, 1985.

Senderovich, Sasha. *How the Soviet Jew Was Made*. Cambridge, MA: Harvard University Press, 2022.

———. "Russian Jewish American Lit Goes Boom!" *Tablet*. June 17, 2014. https:// www.tabletmag.com/sections/arts-letters/articles/russian-jewish-am-lit.

———. "Scenes of Encounter: The 'Soviet Jew' in Fiction by Russian Jewish Writers in America." *Prooftexts* 35, no. 1 (2015): 98–132.

Shandler, Jeffrey. *Shtetl: A Vernacular Intellectual History.* Vol. 5. Rutgers University Press, 2014.

Shneer, David. *Through Soviet Jewish Eyes: Photography, War, and the Holocaust.* New Brunswick, NJ: Rutgers University Press, 2011.

Shore, Marci. *A Taste of Ashes: The Afterlife of Totalitarianism in Eastern Europe.* New York: Crown Publishers, 2013.

Shostak, Debra. "Return to the Breast: The Body, the Masculine Subject, and Philip Roth." *Twentieth Century Literature* 45, no. 3 (Autumn 1999).

———. "Roth and Gender." In *The Cambridge Companion to Philip Roth*, edited by Timothy Parrish. Cambridge: Cambridge University Press, 2007.

Shternshis, Anna. "Between the Red and Yellow Stars: Ethnic and Religious Identity of Soviet Jewish World War II Veterans in New York, Toronto, and Berlin." *Journal of Jewish Identities* 4, no. 1 (January 2011): 43–64.

———. *Soviet and Kosher: Jewish Popular Culture in the Soviet Union, 1923–1939.* Bloomington: Indiana University Press, 2006.

———. *When Sonia Met Boris: An Oral History of Jewish Life Under Stalin.* Oxford: Oxford University Press, 2017.

Shteyngart, Gary. *Lake Success: A Novel.* New York: Random House, 2018.

———. *Little Failure: A Memoir.* New York: Random House, 2014.

———. *Our Country Friends: A Novel.* New York: Random House, 2021.

———. *A Russian Debutante's Handbook.* New York: Riverhead Books, 2002.

Sicher, Efraim. "Odessa Time, Odessa Space: Rethinking Cultural Space in a Cosmopolitan City." *Jewish Culture and History* 16, no. 3 (2015): 221–241.

Silverman, Max. *Palimpsestic Memory: The Holocaust and Colonialism in French and Francophone Fiction and Film.* New York: Berghahn Books, 2015.

Silverstein, Jordana. "'If Our Grandchildren Are Jewish': Heteronormativity, Holocaust Postmemory, and the Reproduction of Melbourne Jewish Families." *History Australia* 10, no. 1 (2013): 167–186.

Slucki, David. *Sing This at My Funeral.* Detroit: Wayne State University Press, 2019.

Slyomovics, Susan. *How to Accept German Reparations.* Philadelphia: University of Pennsylvania Press, 2015.

Sollors, Werner. *Beyond Ethnicity: Consent and Descent in American Culture.* Oxford: Oxford University Press, 1987.

Song, Min Hyoung. *The Children of 1965: On Writing, and Not Writing, as an Asian American.* Durham, NC: Duke University Press, 2013.

The Soviet Issue. *Jewish Currents.* Accessed September 3, 2023. https://jewishcurrents .org/issue/winter-spring-2022.

"Soviet Jewish Refugee Solidarity Sign-On Letter," https://docs.google.com/forms/d /187JdJQSkBoFjpl4HdtfCkS5GomtdCU-Y13-OhzP5Kjs/viewform?edit _requested=true.

Soyer, Daniel. "Back to the Future: American Jews Visit the Soviet Union in the 1920s and 1930s." *Jewish Social Studies* 6, no. 3 (Spring–Summer 2000): 124–159.

Śpiewak, Paweł. *Żydokomuna: Interpretacje historyczne.* Warszawa: Wydawnictwo Czerwone i Czarne, 2012.

Spivak, Gayatri Chakravorty. "Are You Postcolonial? To the Teachers of Slavic and Eastern European Literatures.", *PMLA* 121, no. 3 (2006): 828–836.

———. "Subaltern Studies: Deconstructing Historiography." In *The Spivak Reader*, edited by Donna Landry and Gerald McLean, 203–236. London: Routledge, 1996.

Stella, Francesca. *Lesbian Lives in Soviet and Post-Soviet Russia: Post/Socialism and Gender Sexualities.* Basingstoke, UK: Palgrave Macmillan, 2015.

180 • Bibliography

Steven, Mark. *Red Modernism: American Poetry and the Spirit of Communism*. Johns Hopkins University Press, 2017.

Stier, Oren Brauch. *Committed to Memory: Cultural Mediations of the Holocaust*. Amherst: University of Massachusetts Press, 2003.

———. "Different Trains: Holocaust Artifacts and the Ideologies of Remembrance." *Holocaust and Genocide Studies* 19, no. 1 (2005): 81–106.

Stites, Robert. *The Women's Liberation Movement in Russia: Feminism, Nihilism, and Bolshevism, 1860–1930*. Princeton, NJ: Princeton University Press, 1978.

Stolberg, Eva-Maria. "The Siberian Frontier Between 'White Mission' and 'Yellow Peril,' 1890s–1920s." *Nationalities Papers* 32, no. 1 (2004): 165–181.

Stryker, Susan, "Transgender Studies: Queer Theory's Evil Twin." *GLQ: A Journal of Lesbian and Gay Studies* 10, no. 2 (2004): 212–215.

Suchland, Jennifer. "Is Postsocialism Transnational?" *Signs: Journal of Women in Culture and Society* 26, no. 4 (2011): 837–862.

Suchoff, David. "The Cold War Canon Debate, and Yiddish, 1954–1992." In *Living with America 1946–1996*, edited by Cristina Giorcelli and Rob Kroes, 211–222. Amsterdam: VU University Press, 1997.

———. "New Historicism and Containment: Toward a Post-Cold War Cultural Theory." *Arizona Quarterly: A Journal of American Literature, Culture, and Theory* 48, no. 1 (Spring 1992): 139–142.

Sznaider, Natan. "Pecunifying Respectability?: On the Impossibility of Honorable Restitution." In *Restitution and Memory: Material Restoration in Europe*, edited by Dan Diner and Gotthart Wunberg, 51–64. New York: Berghahn Books, 2007.

Tadevosyan, Margarit, and Maxim Shrayer. "Russian American Literature." In *Greenwood Encyclopedia of Multiethnic American Literature*, edited by Emmanuel S. Nelson, 1940–1951. Westport, CT: Greenwood Publishing Group, 2005.

Tatum, Stephen. "Postfrontier Horizons." *MFS Modern Fiction Studies* 50, no. 2 (2004): 460–468.

Temkina, Anna, and Elena Zdravomyslova. "The Crisis of Masculinity in Late Soviet Discourse." *Russian Studies in History* 51, no. 2 (2012): 13–34.

Tevis, Britt P. "Jews Not Admitted: Anti-Semitism, Civil Rights, and Public Accommodation Laws." *Journal of American History* 107, no. 4 (2021): 847–870.

Tlostanova, Madina. "Can the Post-Soviet Think? On Coloniality of Knowledge, External Imperial and Double Colonial Difference." *Intersections. East European Journal of Society and Politics* 1, no. 2 (2015): 38–58.

———. "Postcolonial Theory, the Decolonial Option, and Post-Socialist Writing." In *Postcolonial Europe? Essays on Post-Communist Literatures and Cultures*, edited by Dobrota Pucherová, and Róbert Gáfrik, 25–45. Leiden, Netherlands: Brill, 2015.

———. "Why the Post-Socialist Cannot Speak." In *Postcoloniality-Decoloniality-Black Critique: Joints and Fissures*, edited by Sabine Broeck and Carsten Junker, 165–178. Frankfurt, Germany: Campus Verlag, 2014.

Todorova, Maria. *Imagining the Balkans*. Updated edition. Oxford: Oxford University Press, 2009.

Tolts, Mark. "Demography of the Contemporary Russian-Speaking Jewish Diaspora." In *The New Jewish Diaspora*, edited by Zvi Gitelman, 23–40. New Brunswick, NJ: Rutgers University Press, 2016.

Totten, Samuel. "First-Person Accounts." In *The Holocaust Encyclopedia*, edited by Walter Laquer and Judith Tydor Baumel, 206–210. New Haven, CT: Yale University Press, 2001.

Trinity College English Department. "Yelena Akhtiorskaya at Trinity College." May 22, 2017. https://www.youtube.com/watch?v=RuUlM9hMGuk.

Trovesi, Andrea. "Warm, Blue and Bulgarian: The Development and Diffusion of Three Expressions to Denote a 'Male Homosexual' in Central and Eastern European Languages." In *Go East! LGBTQ+ Literature in Eastern Europe*, edited by Andrej Zavrland Alojzija Zupan Sosič, 121–128. Ljubljana, Slovenia: Ljubljana University Faculty of Arts Press, 2020.

Ulinich, Anya. *Lena Finkle's Magic Barrel: A Graphic Novel*. New York: Penguin, 2014.

———. "The Nurse and the Novelist." September 8, 2008. https://pen.org/fiction-short-story/nurse-and-novelist.

———. *Petropolis*. London: Penguin Books, 2008.

van Alphen, Ernst. "Second-Generation Testimony, Transmission of Trauma, and Postmemory." *Poetics Today* 27, no. 2 (2006): 473–488.

Vapnyar, Lara. "Love Lessons, Mondays, 9 A.M." *New Yorker*. June 16, 2003. https://www.newyorker.com/magazine/2003/06/16/love-lessons-mondays-9-am.

———. "Love Lessons—Mondays, 9 A.M." In *There Are Jews in My House*. 2nd ed. New York: Anchor Books, 2004.

———. "Lydia's Grove." In *There Are Jews in My House*. 2nd ed. New York: Anchor, 2004.

———. "Puffed Rice and Meatballs." In *Broccoli and Other Tales of Food and Love*. New York: Anchor Books, 2009.

———. "A Question for Vera." In *There Are Jews in My House*. 2nd ed. New York: Anchor, 2004.

———. *The Scent of Pine: A Novel*. New York: Simon and Schuster, 2014.

———. "Soviet-Era Sex Ed." *New York Times*. March 1, 2014. https://www.nytimes.com/2014/03/02/opinion/sunday/soviet-era-sex-ed.html.

———. "The Writer as Tour Guide." In *The Writer Uprooted: Contemporary Jewish Exile Literature*, edited by Alvin H. Rosenfeld, 92–109. Bloomington: Indiana University Press, 2008.

Von Eschen, Penny. *Paradoxes of Nostalgia: Cold War Triumphalism and Global Disorder since 1989*. Durham, NC: Duke University Press, 2022.

Wald, Alan M. *Exiles from a Future Time: The Forging of the Mid-Twentieth-Century Literary Left*. Chapel Hill: University of North Carolina Press, 2002.

———. *The New York Intellectuals: The Rise and Decline of the Anti-Stalinist Left from the 1930s to the 1980s*. Chapel Hill: University of North Carolina Press, 1987.

Walkowitz, Rebecca L. *Cosmopolitan Style: Modernism beyond the Nation*. New York: Columbia University Press, 2006.

Wanner, Adrian. "Moving beyond the Russian-American Ghetto: The Fiction of Keith Gessen and Michael Idov." *Russian Review* 73 (2014): 281–296.

———. *Out of Russia: Fictions of a New Translingual Diaspora*. Evanston, IL: Northwestern University Press, 2011.

———. "Russian Jews as American Writers: A New Paradigm for Jewish Multiculturalism?" *MELUS* 37, no. 2 (June 2012): 157–176.

———. "'There Is No Such City': The Myth of Odessa in Post-Soviet Immigrant Literature." *Twentieth Century Literature* 65, no. 1–2 (2019): 121–144.

Waxman, Zoë Vania. *Writing the Holocaust: Identity, Testimony, Representation*. Oxford: Oxford University Press, 2006.

Weigand, Kate. *Red Feminism: American Communism and the Making of Women's Liberation*. Baltimore: Johns Hopkins University Press, 2002.

Weigel, Sigrid. "'Generation' as a Symbolic Form: On the Genealogical Discourse of Memory since 1945." *The Germanic Review: Literature, Culture, Theory* 77, no. 4 (2002): 264–277.

Weiman-Kelman, Zohar. *Queer Expectations: A Genealogy of Jewish Women's Poetry.* Albany, NY: SUNY Press, 2018.

Wellington Square Bookshop. "The Avid Reader Interviews Lara Vapnyar Author of *Scent of Pine*." April 29, 2014. https://www.youtube.com/watch?v=x3MhIJIIKac.

Wheldon, Wynn. "The Future Wasn't There: Review of 'The Patriots' by Sana Krasikov." *Commentary*. January 2017. https://www.commentary.org/articles/wynn-wheldon/the-future-wasnt-there/.

White, Hayden. *Metahistory: The Historical Imagination in Nineteenth-Century Europe.* Baltimore: Johns Hopkins University Press, 2014.

Wirth-Nasher, Hana, ed. *The Cambridge History of Jewish American Literature.* Cambridge: Cambridge University Press, 2015.

Wisse, Ruth R. "Jewish American Renaissance." In *The Cambridge Companion of Jewish American Literature*, edited by Michael P. Kramer and Hana Wirth-Nasher, 190–211. New York: Cambridge University Press, 2006.

Wolff, Larry. *Inventing Eastern Europe: The Map of Civilization on the Mind of the Enlightenment.* Stanford, CA: Stanford University Press, 1994.

Wood, Alan. *Frozen Frontier: A History of Siberia.* London: Bloomsbury Academic, 2010.

Yurchak, Alexei. *Everything Was Forever, Until It Was No More: The Last Soviet Generation.* Princeton, NJ: Princeton University Press, 2003.

Zavadski, Katie, and Konstantin Sergeyev. "Photos and War Stories from Brighton Beach's Victory Day Parade." *New York Magazine.* May 9, 2015. https://nymag.com/intelligencer/2015/05/photos-brighton-beachs-victory-day-parade.html

Zdravomyslova, Elena. "The Café Saigon Tusovka: One Segment of the Informal-Public Sphere of Late-Soviet Society." In *Biographical Research in Eastern Europe: Altered Lives and Broken Biographies*, edited by Robert Miller and Rubin Humphrey, 141–180. Aldershot, UK: Ashgate, 2003.

Zeltser, Arkadi. *Unwelcome Memory: Holocaust Monuments in the Soviet Union.* Translated by A. S. Brown. Jerusalem: Yad Vashem, 2018.

Zimmerman, Jonathan. *Too Hot to Handle.* Princeton, NJ: Princeton University Press, 2015.

Zipperstein, Steven J. *Imagining Russian Jewry: Memory, History, Identity.* Seattle: University of Washington Press, 1999.

Zsadányi, Edit. "Voicing the Subaltern by Narrating the Communist Past through the Focalization of a Child in Gábor Németh's 'Are You a Jew?' and Endre Kukorelly's 'The Fairy Valley.'" In *Postcolonial Europe? Essays on Post-Communist Literatures and Cultures*, edited by Dobrota Pucherová and Robert Gáfrik, 175–193. Leiden, Netherlands: Brill, 2015.

Index

Aarons, Victoria, 40, 122
absence, and significance of Jewishness, 82
Absurdistan (Shteyngart), 62–63, 136n30
Afro-Russians, 20–25, 27
afterlife of communism. *See* communist postmemory
Akhtiorskaya, Yelena, 12, 19–20, 25–31, 32–34, 140n93, 140n102
Aleichem, Sholem, 103–104, 124
Alekseyeva, Julia, 40–41, 53–58, 60, 73
Althusser, Louis, 85
Altshuler, Mordechai, 141n12
Amar, Tarik, 37
"Animal to the Memory, An" (Bezmozgis), 35–36
anti-communist sentiment, 61–63
antisemitism: in *The Cosmopolitans*, 105–106; in "Immigrant City," 111; in *Mannequin Girl*, 88–89; in *The Patriots*, 66, 78; in *The Scent of Pine*, 95; in *Soviet Daughter*, 55; in *A Terrible Country*, 74, 78
anti-Soviet sentiment, 61–62
archipelagic American studies, 140n102
area studies, 74–75, 76, 77
Ashkenormativity, 2, 5, 105, 124, 158n29
assemblage memory, 58–60
assimilation narrative of migration, 114
Assman, Aleida, 48
"At the top of my voice" (Mayakovsky), 56

Babi Yar massacre, 57
Bassin, Mark, 21, 138n39

Beckerman, Baruch, 140n100
Benjamin, Walter, 7
Berger, Alan, 40
Berlant, Lauren, 161n105
Betrayers, The (Bezmozgis), 136n30
Bezmozgis, David: "An Animal to the Memory," 35–36; *The Betrayers*, 136n30; "The End of Jewish American Literature, Again," 118; *The Free World*, 36, 39, 41–47, 58, 60, 110, 119; "Immigrant City," 109–112; *Immigrant City and Other Stories*, 159n40; Vapnyar on, 85; on writing, 119–120, 121
Blaive, Muriel, 64
Blum, Hester, 140n102
boarding schools, 86–90
body: and articulation of otherness, 82–83; regulation of, in *Mannequin Girl*, 87–88
borderland, and *Petropolis*, 20–25, 32
Bouquet, Mary, 106
Bramen, Carrie Tirado, 138n51
Brighton Beach, New York, 25–27, 31, 32, 34, 140n93
Broad City (television series), 124
Broccoli and Other Tales of Food and Love (Vapnyar), 81
Brooklyn, New York, 25–27, 31
Bunzl, Matti, 99
Butler, Judith, 122

Casteel, Sarah Phillips, 17, 128n9
Cheburashka Collective, 95–96, 130n23

183

184 • Index

"Children of Loneliness" (Yezierska), 28
citizenship: intimate, 98–99; and model
immigrant, 114; sexual, 98
"coastal peoples," regional affinities of, in
Panic in a Suitcase, 32–33
Cold War: afterlives, 9–11; anti-communist
sentiment during, 62, 63; and area
studies, 74–75; belief in communist
ideals and system during, 44–45; and
frozenness of Eastern Europe/Soviet
space, 18; and Holocaust memory, 37;
immigrant metageography, 26; Jewish
Cold War, 18, 63–64; "new" Cold War,
8, 132n44; and presentation of Soviet
history, 99; shift to post-Soviet
experience from, 5; transnational
relation of stories of, 91–92
collectives, 95–96, 130n23
communism: de-mythologization of, 64; in
The Free World, 44–45; gender and
sexuality under, 83; and intimacy in
Vapnyar's works, 80–81; Jewish
involvement in, 63–64; and prejudice
against Soviet-born people, 61–62; in *A
Replacement Life*, 54, 55; in *The Scent of
Pine*, 91–92; use of term, 134n61. *See also*
communist postmemory
communist postmemory, 11, 13, 61–64,
78–79, 124; and *The Patriots*, 64–72; and
A Terrible Country, 72–78
community building, 105, 161n105
comparative literacy, 5–6, 14, 123, 124,
131n28
compensation, in *A Replacement Life*,
47–53
connectedness, through ocean in *Panic in a
Suitcase*, 33–34
contingent Jewishness, 27
cosmopolitanism, 105–106
Cosmopolitans, The (Kalman), 103–109, 119
Creet, Julia, 39
critique, Jewish American literature as site
of, 121–126

Dasbach, Julia Kolchinsky, 130n23
David-Fox, Michael, 156n126
Dawson, Paul, 79
denunciation, in *A Terrible Country*,
72–79

diaspora, 15–20; and *The Free World*,
41–47; and *Panic in a Suitcase*, 25–31;
and *Petropolis*, 20–25; post-Soviet
connections, 31–34; and *A Replacement
Life*, 47–53; and *Soviet Daughter*, 53–58.
See also displacement; migration
disabilities, 84, 86–90, 152n26
Disability Studies, 126
disinformation, and *The Patriots*, 64–72,
78–79
displacement, and Holocaust literature,
39–40. *See also* diaspora
distinct voice, 115–117, 123, 162n11
"DIY Jewishness," 6, 131n32

Eastern Europe: as decontextualized space,
16–17; as existing on temporal axis, 17; in
Jewish American literature, 12; Orientalization of, 12, 27, 104; and reframing of
space, 17–18; Ulinich's criticism of mode
of representation of, 15–16
"End of Jewish American Literature,
Again, The" (Bezmozgis), 118
erasure: of communist memory, 44–45,
46–47; of Holocaust in Soviet memory,
36–37, 44
Erll, Astrid, 6, 39, 60
ethnicity/ethnic identity: in *The Cosmopolitans*, 105–106, 112; interethnic imagination, 100–101, 102; and Jewish
involvement in labor movement, 63; in
Lake Success, 114, 115, 118; migration
literature and critical approach to, 103; as
mode of thinking, 119. *See also* Jewishness; Russianness
Everything Is Illuminated (Foer), 16, 17
"ex-second world," 18

family attachments, 13, 64, 78–79
Felman, Shoshana, 51
feminist theory, 82, 85
Fiddian-Qasmiyeh, Elena, 38
Fiddler on the Roof, 103–104, 105
Fidelis, Małgorzata, 99
Fishman, Boris, 39, 47–53, 58, 60, 119–120,
125
Fishzon, Anna, 96
Foer, Jonathan Safran, 15, 16, 17, 124, 134n5
Franco, Dean J., 22–23, 128n9

Freedman, Jonathan, 120, 128n9
Free World, The (Bezmozgis), 36, 39, 41–47, 58, 60, 110, 119
Furman, Andrew, 123
Furman, Yelena, 131n34, 137n32, 151n12

gender: and articulation of otherness, 82–83; and body regulation in *Mannequin Girl*, 87–88; commodification and regulation of, 83; and division in *Lake Success*, 112–113; and Jewish American literature, 4, 5, 6–7; in migration narratives, 102–103; in *Petropolis*, 24; and refugee solidarity myth, 109, 111–112
Gender and Sexuality Division of the Association for Jewish Studies, 126
genealogy: as mode of thinking, 118–119; queering and displacement of, in *The Cosmopolitans*, 106–109
geographical meaning. *See* metageography
Gershenson, Olga, 57
Gessen, Keith, 13, 63, 72–79, 137n31
Gessen, Masha, 73
Ghodsee, Kristen, 5, 83
Gitelman, Zvi, 36
Glenn, Susan, 18, 63–64
Goffman, Erving, 87
"good immigrants," 114, 160n77
Goyal, Yogita, 101, 102
Great Patriotic War, 41–42, 43, 70, 143n46
gulag postmemory, 64, 70, 71, 124. See also *Patriots, The* (Krasikov)

Harrison-Kahan, Lori, 2, 125–126
Hirsch, Marianne, 11
Hoberman, Michael, 15
Holocaust memory, 12–13, 58–60, 123–124; and displacement, 39–40; erasure of, 36–37; and *Fiddler on the Roof*, 104; in *The Free World*, 41–47; in Jewish American literature, 12–13; mainstreaming of, 141n12; and memory of migration, 40; post-Soviet migrant, 13, 36; and redefining of survival, 40–41, 42; in *A Replacement Life*, 39, 47–53; and Russianness in Bezmozgis's works, 35–36; in *Soviet Daughter*, 53–58; third-generation Holocaust writers, 40, 54, 73; and Ulinich's criticism of mode of

representation of Eastern Europe, 16; as unifying force among Soviet Jewry, 141n12
home, image of, in *A Terrible Country*, 75–76
homosexuality. *See* queerness
Howe, Irving, 17, 118
humor, in *The Free World*, 45–46

identity: in *Lake Success*, 115, 118; and multiculturalism, 162n11; in *Panic in a Suitcase*, 27; in *Petropolis*, 22–24. *See also* Jewishness; Russianness
Idov, Michael, 2, 137n32
"Immigrant City" (Bezmozgis), 109–112
Immigrant City and Other Stories (Bezmozgis), 159n40
immigrant(s): "good," 114, 160n77; versus refugee, 101–102
inclusion, 123
interethnic imagination, 100–101, 102
intermigrant solidarities, 14, 109–112. *See also* intra-Jewish hierarchies
intimacy: and articulation of otherness, 82–83; and communism in Vapnyar's works, 80–81; and community building, 161n105; in Vapnyar, Litman, and Ulinich's works, 85. *See also* sex and sexuality
intimate citizenship, 98–99
intra-Jewish hierarchies, 124; in *The Cosmopolitans*, 103–109; in "Immigrant City," 109–112; in *Lake Success*, 112–118. *See also* intermigrant solidarities
Ioffe, Julia, 100, 101, 111
Irr, Caren, 117

Jablonka, Ivan, 56
"Jewish American," in *The Patriots*, 69
Jewish American literature: and Cold War afterlives, 9–11; critique of, 6–9; Eastern Europe in, 12; Holocaust in, 12–13; and multiculturalism, 162n11; new direction of, 118–120; origin story of, 1; as site of critique, 121–126; Soviet-born writing and mainstream framing of, 2–4, 9; Soviet-born writing and rethinking categories of, 11–14; Soviet-born writing as challenge to gendered and nativist modes of, 4; spatial blind spot of, 17

186 • Index

Jewish Cold War, 18, 63–64
Jewishness: absence and significance of, 82; alternatives to expand category of, 125–126; camaraderie and, in *Mannequin Girl*, 88–89; contingent, 27; in *The Cosmopolitans*, 104–105; "DIY Jewishness," 6, 131n32; and forgetting in *A Terrible Country*, 74; Holocaust memory and American, 43; Litman on, 82; in "Lydia's Grove," 96; as organizing category, 121; and pan-ethnicity in *Lake Success*, 115, 118; in *The Patriots*, 66, 69, 70; in *A Replacement Life*, 54–55; Soviet-born, as seemingly un-American, 6; in Soviet-born writing, 125; and Vapnyar's works, 81–82. *See also* antisemitism; Ashkenormativity; Jewish American literature

Kalman, Nadia, 103–109, 119
Kaminsky, Ilya, 130n23
Kandiyoti, Dalia, 2, 128n9
Katsnelson, Anna, 127n4, 131n34
Kazin, Alfred, 7
Kelner, Shaul, 10
Kennedy, John, 61
Kirshenblatt-Gimblett, Barbara, 104, 158n28
Kolektiv Goluboy Vagon, 95–96
Komsomol, 61
Kon, Igor, 92
Krasikov, Sana, 13, 63, 64–72, 78–79, 137n31, 148n21, 148n32
Krauss, Nicole, 16
Kuznetsova, Maria, 36, 55

labor movement, Jewish involvement in American, 63
Lacroix, Thomas, 38
Lake Success (Shteyngart), 112–118, 119
Lambert, Josh, 2, 125–126
language games, in *The Patriots*, 70
leftism, 13, 63
Lena Finkle's Magic Barrel (Ulinich), 2–4, 92–94
Lewis, Martin, 16
Litman, Ellen, 13–14, 82, 85–90, 98, 153n55
Little Failure (Shteyngart), 55, 62, 86
"Love Lessons, Monday, 9 A.M." (Vapnyar), 90–91

Luca, Ioana, 10
"Lydia's Grove" (Vapnyar), 13–14, 95–98

Madievsky, Ruth, 127n5, 130n23
Magic Barrel (Malamud), 124, 128n13
magical realism, 15, 16, 17, 135n10
Makarenko, Anton Semyonovich, 83
Malamud, Bernard, 124, 128n13
Mannequin Girl (Litman), 13–14, 86–90
masculinity, 4, 112, 113, 161n93
Mayakovsky, Vladimir, 56
McCarthyism, 61, 62
McGurl, Mark, 115, 161n93
medals, in *The Free World*, 42–43
memory: assemblage, 58–60; codified, 50; erasure of communist, 44–45, 46–47; in *The Free World*, 41–42; Holocaust and, of migration, 40; inherited, 11; migration's impact on, 39–40, 44–47; multidirectional, 5, 117, 124, 159n48; palimpsestic, 38; in *A Replacement Life*, 47–53; in *Soviet Daughter*, 53–58; and Soviet Jewish veterans, 43–44; and Soviet perception of Holocaust, 43; traveling, 39; and Ulinich's criticism of mode of representation of Eastern Europe, 16. *See also* communist postmemory; Holocaust memory
metageography, 16, 18, 19, 21, 26, 32, 33, 135n10
Michels, Tony, 63
migration, 100–103, 118–120; assimilation narrative of, 114; in Bezmozgis works, 159n40; in *The Cosmopolitans*, 103–109; from former Soviet countries, 129n17; and *The Free World*, 41–47; and Holocaust remembrance, 40, 59; in "Immigrant City," 109–112; impact on memory, 39–40, 44–47; intertwining of tourism and, in Akhtiorskaya's texts, 30; in Jewish American literature, 122; in *Lake Success*, 112–118; post-Soviet, versus other ethnic groups, 133n46; in *A Replacement Life*, 47–53; in Soviet-born Jewish writing, 60; of Soviet-born Jews, 129n18; in *Soviet Daughter*, 53–58. *See also* diaspora; post-immigrant tourism
mishpokhe, 70
model immigrant, 114, 160n77

Index • 187

modernist impersonality, 79
Moore, Deborah Dash, 43
Moses, Michael Valdez, 135n10
Moskovich, Yelena, 2
motherhood, under Soviet regime, 97
Mukherjee, Bharati, 101, 102
multiculturalism, 123, 162n11
multidirectional memory, 5, 117, 124,
 159n48
Muradyan, Luisa, 130n23
Murav, Harriet, 37

narration: in *The Patriots*, 79, 148n21; in
 The Patriots and *A Terrible Country*, 79
"new" Cold War, 8, 132n44
"New Jewish Diaspora," 122
Nguyen, Viet Thanh, 101, 102, 114
Novick, Peter, 104
"Nurse and the Novelist, The" (Ulinich),
 15–16, 17

ocean: Akhtiorskaya on centrality of, 26;
 relatedness through, in *Panic in a
 Suitcase*, 33–34
Odessa, Ukraine, 25–27, 28–29, 31
Oksana, Behave! (Kuznetsova), 55
Omarova, Saule, 61
omniscient narration, 79, 148n21
Orientalization, 10, 12, 18, 24, 27, 104, 106,
 158n30
otherness, 12, 19–20, 75, 82–83, 96, 99, 111
Our Country Friends (Shteyngart), 113
Oushakine, Sergei, 79

palimpsestic memory, 38
Panic in a Suitcase (Akhtiorskaya), 12,
 19–20, 25–31, 32–34, 140n93, 140n102
Patriots, The (Krasikov), 13, 63, 64–72,
 78–79, 137n31, 148n21, 148n32
Petropolis (Ulinich), 12, 19–25, 32, 55
Phillips, Sarah D., 84, 152n26
place: defamiliarization of, of migrant
 Soviet arrival in U.S., 24–25; and
 post-Soviet diasporic connections, 31–34.
 See also space
Plummer, Ken, 98–99
post-immigrant tourism, 12, 19, 25–31, 33
postmemory, 11. *See also* communist
 postmemory

"post-Soviet," 18, 132n42
prejudice, against Soviet-born people,
 61–62
progressivism, American, as bound to
 Soviet and post-Soviet Russia, 64
"Puffed Rice and Meatballs" (Vapnyar),
 80–81, 84

queerness, 6–7, 83, 95–98, 108–109, 124,
 155n104. *See also* sex and sexuality
"Question for Vera, A" (Vapnyar), 89

race, in *Petropolis*, 22–24
racialization, 23, 59, 61, 90, 99, 109, 111, 112,
 119, 122, 151n12, 162n11
rediscovery, 26
refugees: in *The Free World*, 41–47;
 immigrants versus, 101–102; as part of
 global logic, 102; refugee crisis, 100;
 unqualified solidarity with, in "Immigrant City," 109–112
regional affinities, of "coastal peoples" in
 Panic in a Suitcase, 32–33
religion, in *The Free World*, 45–46
reparations, in *A Replacement Life*, 47–53
Replacement Life, A (Fishman), 39, 47–53,
 58, 60
restitution, in *A Replacement Life*, 47–53
Reyn, Irina, 2, 137n32
Roberman, Sveta, 143n46
Rody, Caroline, 100–101, 119
Roth, Philip, 2–4, 9, 113, 124, 129n20,
 161n93
Rothberg, Michael, 78, 159n48
router, as figure of transnational writing,
 117
Rumer, Masha, 160n75
"Russian" adjective, 36
Russian Debutante's Handbook, A
 (Shteyngart), 36, 62–63
Russianness, 6, 35–36
Russo-Ukrainian War, 123
Ryan, Karen, 85

Sadowski-Smith, Claudia, 10, 102
Saratoga Springs, New York, 94–95
Scent of Pine, The (Vapnyar), 13–14, 81,
 90–95, 137n31
Schachter, Allison, 7

188 • Index

Schostak, Debra, 129n20
Schreier, Benjamin, 9
Scott, Joan Wallach, 111–112
"Second World," 12, 19–20, 25, 26, 28, 31, 34, 77, 95. *See also* "ex-second world"
Sedgwick, Eve Kosofsky, 96
Seligman, Joseph, 155n98
Senderovich, Sasha, 10
settings, of Soviet-born Jewish writers, 31–34
sex and sexuality: commodification and regulation of, 83, 85; and Jewish American literature, 4, 5; in migration narratives, 102–103; Vapnyar on, 84. *See also* intimacy; queerness
sexual citizenship, 98
sexual education: in *Lena Finkle's Magic Barrel*, 92–94; in *Mannequin Girl*, 90; in *The Scent of Pine*, 90–95
sexual revolution, 92, 94
Shternshis, Anna, 43
shtetl, 15, 17, 56, 104, 105, 109, 158n26
Shteyngart, Gary, 36, 62–63, 85, 112–118, 119, 136n30; *Little Failure*, 55, 62, 86; *Our Country Friends*, 113
Siberia, 21, 22, 138n39
Silverman, Max, 38
Slucki, David, 56
Slyomovics, Susan, 49, 52–53, 145n88
socialism: Jewish involvement in American, 63; use of term, 134n61
solidarity, unqualified, with refugees in "Immigrant City," 109–112
Sollors, Werner, 105, 119
Something Unbelievable (Kuznetsova), 36
"Soviet-born" adjective, 7–8, 14
Soviet Daughter (Alekseyeva), 40–41, 53–58, 60, 73
"Soviet Jew," 10
Soviet Jewish veterans, 41–47, 143n46
Soviet Jewry movement, 4, 9–10, 82
Soviet Victory Day (May 9), 43–44
Soyer, Daniel, 18–19
space: Eastern Europe as decontextualized, 16–17; frozenness of Eastern Europe/ Soviet, and Cold War discourse, 18–19; function of post-Soviet, and relation to American settings, 19–20; negotiation of spatial networks, 137n32; and *Panic in a*

Suitcase, 25–31; and *Petropolis*, 20–25; post-Soviet, 32; reframing of, 17–18; travel and assigning meaning to, 28–29. *See also* place
Stella, Francesca, 83, 98
stereotypes, 45, 46, 97, 105
suffering, in *A Replacement Life*, 47–53
summer camps, in *The Scent of Pine*, 91, 92, 94–95
survival: in *The Free World*, 41–47; as personal experience, 59; redefinition of, 40–41, 42, 47, 59–60, 123–124; in *A Replacement Life*, 47–53; in *Soviet Daughter*, 53–58
Sznaider, Natan, 49

Tatum, Stephen, 20
Terrible Country, A (Gessen), 13, 63, 72–79, 137n31
testimony, 51
There Are Jews in My House (Vapnyar), 81, 96. *See also* "Lydia's Grove" (Vapnyar)
third-generation Holocaust literature, 40, 54, 60, 73
Tlostanova, Madina, 18
total institutions, 87, 88, 90
tourism, post-immigrant, 12, 19, 25–31, 33
traditions, in *The Cosmopolitans*, 103, 108, 109
transgenerational affinities, in *Soviet Daughter*, 53–58
travel, and ascribing meaning to space, 28–29. *See also* migration; post-immigrant tourism
traveling memory, 39
Trump travel ban, 100

Ulinich, Anya: and intimate citizenship, 98; *Lena Finkle's Magic Barrel*, 2–4, 92–94; "The Nurse and the Novelist," 15–16, 17; perspective in works of, 85–86; *Petropolis*, 12, 19–25, 32, 55; Roth in works of, 2–4, 129n20, 161n93; on writing, 120

Vapnyar, Lara: *Broccoli and Other Tales of Food and Love*, 81; and intimate citizenship, 98; Jewishness of, 81–82; "Lydia's Grove," 13–14, 95–98;

perspective in works of, 85–86; "Puffed Rice and Meatballs," 80–81, 84; "A Question for Vera," 89; Russian identity of, 85; *The Scent of Pine*, 13–14, 81, 90–95, 137n31; *There Are Jews in My House*, 81; on writing, 119–120

veterans, Soviet Jewish, 41–47, 143n46

voice, distinct, 115–117, 123, 162n11

Von Eschen, Penny, 10

Walkowitz, Rebecca, 106

Wanner, Adrian, 131n34, 137n34, 140n100, 161n84

Warner, Michael, 161n105

Waxman, Zoë, 59

Weigel, Sigrid, 118

whiteness, 4, 101, 114, 117, 121, 122, 133n46

Wigen, Kären, 16

working mothers, 97

World War II, 41–42, 43, 70, 143n46

Yezierska, Anzia, 28

Young Communist League. *See* Komsomol

Yurchak, Alexei, 85

Zilberbourg, Olga, 2, 130n23

About the Author

KAROLINA KRASUSKA is an associate professor at the American Studies Center (ASC) at the University of Warsaw and a founding member of the Gender/Sexuality Research Group at the ASC. She is a coeditor of *Women and the Holocaust: New Perspectives and Challenges* (with Andrea Pető and Louise Hecht) and the Polish translator of Judith Butler's *Gender Trouble*.